AT THE VERY EDGE OF THE FOREST

D0528817

ED

Other titles in the Cassell Education series:

At the Very Edge of the Forest

The Influence of Literature on Storytelling by Children

Carol Fox

CASSELL

To Robert, Jimmy, Justine, Sundari and Josh;
and their parents

Cassell
Villiers House
41/47 Strand
London WC2N 5JE

387 Park Avenue South
New York
NY 10016–8810

First published 1993

British Library Cataloguing-in-Publication Data
A catalogue record for this book is available from the British Library.

ISBN 0-304-32695-X (hardback)
      0-304-32697-6 (paperback)

Typeset by Colset Private Limited, Singapore
Printed and bound in Great Britain by
Redwood Books, Trowbridge, Wiltshire

Contents

Foreword

How well I remember the first time I listened to Josh talking like a book. The clear ring of his five-year-old voice turned me from an interested tutor, whose care it was to encourage students to gather evidence of children's language, into an *audience*, compelled by the teller's bard-like confidence to listen to his tale. Now, many years later, as I read this book, I still hear his strong narrative intent, the full-sized passion, the need to tell, all of which characterize the stories that are the evidence and theme of this important study.

It is not difficult to believe that children who are read to are likely to incorporate written language into their speech. But after the publication of Carol Fox's first analysis of spontaneous narratives in *Opening Moves* in 1983 it became clear that these oral compositions were not part of existing evidence of children's early language, nor of their pre-school literacy. Now we know that, for all their apparent informality, the stories have complex formal structures. They are layered, polysemic texts, the sources of which lie in a wide range of children's literature and with the 'sounded writing' of radio and television broadcasts. The novelty of their production depended on the presence of the tape recorder, which acted not simply as a collecting device, but also as a means of letting the children take the storytelling initiative which calls up the listeners.

Parents who are also teachers are perhaps more inclined than others to present evidence of their children's precocity in language learning. This does not always win for them favourable consideration from those who see in this the excesses of parental pride. Distinctively, Carol Fox was able to encourage a number of parents to listen to their children's stories. The result is not only a rich granary of pre-school narratives of different kinds from different sources. It is also a convincing demonstration that these children have a productive capacity which is imbued with the kind of confidence which comes from adult support. Since I first heard Josh and saw how his mother performed the astonishing balancing act of analysing the stories in depth, and, at the same time, letting her son know that they were undoubtedly his, I have been persuaded that the new knowledge that she has now made available is impressive in both its depth and detail.

Three things emerge as being of particular importance. First, the relation of this kind of storytelling to children's symbolic play, especially in its carnivalistic aspects, the 'over-the-topness' of it all. Play with words is specially clear. Enjoy Sundari as she explores the internal force of words as *poetic*, things to make things with. Think, then, of the long years of schooling ahead, and ask, will this enjoyment and the skill that it produces survive the years of school reading and writing?

Next, it is now fashionable to challenge the primacy of narrative in children's learning to read. The claim is that the reading of 'non-narrative' texts for the 'retrieval of information' is being neglected. This book makes it clear, beyond all doubt, that children use storying to sort out their own knowledge and ideas until they learn the contexts, as well as the forms, of non-narrative genres. Even more importantly, because they have short memories and restricted actual experiences, children explore the possibilities offered by the world-making of storytelling so as to enter into dialogue, not with the past, as adults do, but with their futures. Moreover, narratives are not a single genre. They are, as Carol Fox says, 'complex, abstract and independent of immediate contexts. In reading they offer a wider variety of discourse kinds than any other writing, and demand thinking and deep reasoning as well as imaginative empathy and feeling.'

Then, in every transcription I see quite clearly how children are free to invent stories because narrative fiction offers them 'an opportunity to escape from the intrusive gaze of others on their actual lives, while at the same time giving them the scope to talk about what is deeply meaningful to them in disguised metaphoric form'. The most dramatic evidence is that, in storying, children understand the potentiality of the complexity of language long before they have a fully conscious grasp of its nature.

Not all children tell stories in the same way, nor to the same extent. But we are bound to ask, what would we find if many more children than now do could have the experience of hearing books and stories read to them in infancy and discovered the enjoyment and the power of telling them? This is surely what most readers will consider after their encounters with this book. Although the evidence is linked with a wide range of academic studies, none of the analytic techniques is used simply to measure the children's abilities or to reduce their stories to the constituent parts. Instead, we see how the stories *invite* the commentaries of experts across a range of understanding and still remain the purposeful tellings of a group of pre-school children who have enjoyed being read to. We are bound to be impressed by Carol Fox's skill and scholarship, which show us the extent of the children's success with language, as yet unschooled. If, after the details have been thus laid out for our inspection, we say that we have always known children could tell stories, we are bound to admit that we have never known it in this way before.

Margaret Meek

Preface

In the last thirty years early language development has received so much more attention than the later stages of children's speech that we may well ask what else there is to know about it. This book is intended to show that there is indeed more to learn and to continue to learn. What we still know so little about, for both younger and older children, is how they enter the discourses of the adult cultures that surround them. Here the discourse under scrutiny is narrative discourse of a particular kind. The stories reported and analysed in this book are not narratives of personal experience. They are imaginative fantasy stories which make maximal use of written stories that the children had heard read aloud from books, before they could read and write themselves. The transcripts reveal young children playing themselves into the discourses of literature and literacy.

We already have very detailed accounts of the 'natural' language uttered by young children in the relaxed, everyday situations of their homes and communities. Gordon Wells and Michael Halliday, for example, have shown us how parents and children interact together to reconstruct a linguistic universe with a place in it for the child. In this study we must take for granted the existence of normal conversational experience between parents and children, for parents have very little part in the story transcripts. The children themselves are in control and usually construct the story without adult help or advice. Parents did play a part, in setting up the tape recorder and offering the child the opportunity to narrate, but otherwise they were passive listeners, accepting whatever it was that the child construed as a storytelling. In this sense the present study follows the tradition of most other studies of child language, collecting the data in the safety and security of home and familiar adults. It departs from other studies, however, in its focus on the language of imaginative play, and the connection between that language and the specific cultural practice of reading children's literature aloud during the pre-school years. This particular practice brings about in the children who experience it a very deep internalization of literacy and the languages associated with it. The very special uses of language that the reader will encounter in the children's stories mirror simultaneously several aspects of their being in the early years – their deepest affects, their most advanced cognitive competences, their aesthetic sense, and their linguistic creativity. In the past, studies of children's stories have tended to look at the structure of plots – beginnings, middles and ends – and also at story themes. Though both are important here too, this book starts from the premise that the most important thing about a story is the manner of its telling.

The book is organized as a progressive series of analyses, starting with surface features like obvious intertextualities that lead us back to written sources for the stories. It then moves on to look at the children's distinctive use of words, phrases and sentences. After that the analyses move from the parts to the whole, using first Labov's criteria for narrative structure and then the literary categories of Genette and Barthes. Each chosen system gives different insights into the children's narrative discourse, and each analysis, in contrast to the others, also shows us the strengths and limitations of particular ways of studying story.

There are two chapters which are exclusively concerned with theoretical issues, Chapters 3 and 6. In these I briefly outline the type of theory I believe necessary to deal with this kind of linguistic material. I argue that our ways of looking at child language in the past have too often omitted the affective and aesthetic dimensions which lie at the heart of imaginative uses of language. In my discussion of language acquisition in Chapter 3 and of narrative competences in Chapter 6, I propose that for the study of both language and story we need to develop accounts that include metaphorical thinking.

The language I am writing about, then, is that of pretend play, story, role-play, poetry and song. It is important not to marginalize the language of children's play. The stories transcribed in this book certainly show that the five storytellers possessed competences which were unexpectedly advanced for their ages, pulling them, as Vygotsky claimed for pretend play, well beyond their performance in everyday contexts. The stories show what language in the making looks like and give us glimpses of the children's linguistic future.

The children's stories themselves are spread throughout the text, as many as possible given in full and many more quoted from. Other stories are to be found in the appendices. The transcriptions are as exact as possible in terms of the words which were uttered. Unfortunately it was beyond my scope as a single researcher to add a phonological analysis to the other analyses in these pages. I am well aware that a focus on the children's patterns of stress and intonation would greatly enrich this study, and I apologize for the omission. I can only invite any other researcher interested in these aspects of the children's language to obtain copies of the tapes from me.

Carol Fox
University of Brighton
April 1993

Acknowledgements

First, I am indebted to the five children whose stories are the subject of this book, and to their parents who were so helpful to me in collecting the tape-recordings and checking my transcriptions. Margaret Meek has been my inspiration and mentor throughout the years of this study; Shirley Pybus and the late Dr Ken Yerrill were also major sources of help and advice during my time at the (then) Polytechnic of Newcastle-upon-Tyne. My gratitude also to the many friends and colleagues who have encouraged and supported my work over the years, particularly my colleagues at the University of Brighton, Henrietta Dombey, Heather Mines, Carole King, Trevor Harvey, Muriel Robinson and the late Maggie Squires. Joan Goody's support and patient listening have been invaluable. I also received invaluable help in transcribing, typing and word processing the material from Elizabeth Rowntree in Newcastle and Nicky Arnold in Sussex. My thanks also to my own parents, who first taught me to read and write and to love books.

Transcription Conventions

1. Everything the children uttered has been transcribed as faithfully as possible. Where one or more words was inaudible the transcript is marked *unclear*.

2. For each child the stories are numbered in the chronological order of their telling.

3. At the foot of the transcript the child's name, the story number and the child's age in years and months is given thus: *Josh   story 2   5:0*.

4. Punctuation is limited to question marks and quotation marks in dialogue sections.

5. Where a comma or full stop would be appropriate in writing, a space appears in the transcript. This represents the child's showing, either by intonation or by a short pause, that the end of a 'sense unit' had been reached. It is intended to make reading the transcripts easier.

6. From time to time the letter P appears in parentheses (P). This signals a pause of 3 seconds or more. Pauses in Sundari's stories can be as long as 16 seconds. (PP) signals a very long pause.

7. All hesitation phenomena ('um', 'er', etc.), false starts and syntactic garbles are included in the transcripts in brackets.

8. Conversations with an adult that occur during a storytelling are marked as in a play [*Adult: Child:*].

9. This is the language of very young children. It does not always use conventional adult grammar and some of it will seem strange or bizarre.

Chapter 1

Collecting the Stories

> one sunny morning little Joshua was awake   he found in his bedroom
> marvellous presents   he put them by his side and showed them to his
> mother   'Oh' he cried 'It's Christmas' and he got his stockings   (he w-) he
> went to his mummy and his daddy   and his (mummy) daddy said 'Oooh we'll
> like those   have you got a torch?   Oh here it is   we'll have that'   and that's
> the end   *(Josh   story 2   5:0)*

The research which is the subject-matter of this book started quite by accident. In
September 1980 I moved, with my 5-year-old son Josh, from London to Newcastle-
upon-Tyne to take up a research post in the Faculty of Education at Newcastle
Polytechnic. Josh quickly found a 5-year-old friend to play with and, to my amaze-
ment, could be heard trying to copy David's Geordie speech within a few days of our
arrival. I was so impressed by the speed of these early accent changes that I was deter-
mined somehow to tape-record them. Accordingly I suggested quite casually that the
two boys might like to play at telling one another stories on the tape-recorder. They
loved this new game. Taking turns they told six stories apiece, always listening to
themselves as soon as they had finished a story. Increasingly the game became daring,
rude and hilarious. Naughty words, slapstick violence and a great deal of giggling are
all on that first tape, initiating what would eventually become a collection of over 200
recorded stories.

   Much later I listened to the stories, eagerly anticipating the first signs of dialect
change in my son. There was indeed a change, for I instantly knew that the language
register Josh was using for his stories was quite different from the one used in everyday
conversations. The simple story above, recorded on that first occasion, exemplifies
what struck me so forcibly. The opening 'one sunny morning' is formal and conventional, and I was not used to Josh fictionalizing himself as 'little Joshua'. In his second
sentence Josh reverses the usual order of the two noun phrases, giving the words a
literary ring. The colloquial version would be 'he found some marvellous presents in
his bedroom'. The two clauses of the third sentence echo the rhythm of the second.
' "Oh" he cried "It's Christmas" ' is an entirely literary way of reporting speech; even

the choice of the verb 'cried' is resonant of the language of children's books. Though this story is a fictionalized version of a real event (Josh had just had his fifth birthday), Josh actually refers to a book near the end of his story. The torch had been a real birthday present and it had reminded Josh of Bill in the Ahlbergs' *Burglar Bill*. When Bill steals something he always says 'I'll have that!', and here Josh has put Bill's words into the father's mouth, transforming the original book material to his own story and characters. Put simply, then, what I heard Josh speaking on that tape was a written language. Although he was unable to read and write independently at that time, his whole idea of what a story was seemed to be bound up with books.

That this should be so ought not to have surprised me, for I had read many hundreds of stories aloud to Josh from the first year of his life. Later I calculated that he must have heard *thousands* of story readings in the years before starting school. As part of an earlier study in the late 1970s (Fox, 1979) I had observed the reading behaviour of 3- and 4-year-old children in a London nursery school, and found that the children who read early practised their reading on stories they already knew. When these children read the text of a familiar tale they were not so much reading the text word by word as reading the *story*. Knowing how the story went made predicting and guessing much easier. It seemed that a well-loved narrative, held in the mind, offered these children an untroubled passage to the printed page. However, I never asked those young readers to make up a story and tell it to me, and so it was not until that evening in 1980 that I realized that some children internalize the patterns and structures of written language well before the acquisition of independent literacy.

Between September and December of that year Josh recorded 39 stories. There was no formal procedure for recording, nothing that one could call a 'methodology'. Sometimes when we were alone together in the evening I would invite him to tell me a story and if he wanted to he did, otherwise he would do something else. We would both sit on the floor with the small cassette recorder in front of us; the built-in microphone ensured that he did not spoil the recordings by playing with the mike. *We never discussed the story to be told*. If Josh wanted to record, I soon learned, he usually had some inkling of what he wanted to say. He hugely enjoyed storytelling and would even use story sessions to delay bedtime. He always wanted to listen to himself after each story, becoming the audience for his own narrations. As Josh told stories I would transcribe them very soon afterwards so that I had a good chance of remembering anything that sounded unclear on the tape. At that time Josh's speech was not very clear, though after an ear/nose/throat operation in November his articulation improved enormously.

When I played some of the tapes to teachers' groups and tutors at the polytechnic I found that the literary flavour of the narrating and the intertextualities of the stories – that is, where the storyteller makes use of a motif, or theme, or language from a familiar book text – were striking to all who heard them. I decided to try to find out whether other young children who had a similar background of rich story-book experience would tell stories in the same literary manner. Early in 1981 I approached several families, most of whom I knew well, asking if the parents and younger children would like to participate in a storytelling study. The criteria for choosing the children were very simple:

- The child should have had the experience of hearing books and stories read aloud from early infancy.
- The child would need to enjoy telling stories.
- The child should not yet be an independent reader. A child who was already reading silently, I felt, would have much greater access to written story material which would not necessarily be traceable by parents. What I wanted to be able to show was the absorption of written material in the *pre-reading* period.
- The above criteria were all more important than the child's age, though I generally expected the children to be 5 or younger.

From the families I contacted four young storytellers emerged, in addition to Josh, who continued to record stories. I shall briefly introduce each child with a little background information. Beside each child's name I have given his or her age at the start of the series of recordings.

ROBERT (3:7)

Robert was the grandson of a colleague at Newcastle Polytechnic. He lived with his parents and 6½-year-old sister in Rochdale. Neither of his parents was professionally involved in education, but his grandfather was an English specialist. Robert's grandfather described him as an active, lively child who would often prefer to be 'doing' rather than reading. However, he had had books read to him from an early age. Robert's father and grandfather collected stories from him. His older sister also tape-recorded stories, and some of her narratives influenced Robert's. He was the youngest child in the study, and he told 26 stories in all, ending his storytelling when he was 4:1.

JUSTINE (4:1)

Justine's father was a lecturer in English in Education at Newcastle Polytechnic, and her mother was a secondary school teacher. Both parents had read to Justine from a very early age. She lived in a village in Wearside and was an only child. Her father conducted the storytelling sessions. Justine told 30 stories over a period of about a year, finishing her series of stories when she was 5:2.

JIMMY (4:9)

Jimmy's mother, a secondary school teacher of mathematics, was an old friend, and I had known Jimmy since he was born. He lived in London with his 6½-year-old brother and his mother. At the time of recording the stories, Jimmy and his brother were producing numerous drawings and paintings every day. They had a good collection of books and were read to regularly. They were very lively boys who greatly enjoyed superheroes, starwars toys and cartoon characters. There is a lot of laughter on Jimmy's tapes. He recorded 20 stories over a period of three weeks.

SUNDARI (5:4)

Sundari was the granddaughter of a friend and English teaching colleague. Sundari lived with her 7-year-old sister and her mother in a town in Norfolk. Both children had a very extensive experience of reading from an early age, but little exposure to TV. Sundari told 19 stories over a period of 3 months. As she was over 5 at the time of the recordings she was attending her infant school during this period.

JOSH (5:0)

Josh lived in London with his mother until his fifth birthday, then in Newcastle. He had been read to from the first year of his life, and had a particularly rich experience of invented oral storytelling from his father. He was an only child. Though his mother felt there was no cause for concern about his language/speech, in the reception class at school, which he attended during the storytelling period, he was judged to be a child who had little language. Josh told 86 stories over a period of 13 months, and was 6: 1 at the end of the story collection.

The social class background of the children is middle-class in terms of the educational attainment/professional status of their parents. Four of the five had parents or grandparents who were specialist English teachers. The families belonged to public libraries and the children possessed many books of their own. The books the children owned tended to be like those in the book corners of nursery and infant school classes, that is, good picture story-books by well-known children's authors, modern children's classics, traditional folk- and fairy-tales, and non-fiction information books. Though they might be regarded as privileged children in terms of their early literary experiences, they were not necessarily privileged in other ways. Two of them lived in small inner-city flats with no gardens, and three lived with their mothers but not their fathers. They were all happy children who mixed well with other children and whose parents provided an array of interesting activities for them. They were well-developed talkers and none of them was particularly shy. All the children except Sundari saw some television on most days, though at this stage none of them had unlimited access to TV. Josh was also used to hearing radio news programmes in the mornings and evenings, an experience which turned out to be influential on his storytelling.

Perhaps the most important background factor for this study was the liberality and relaxed attitudes towards the storytelling of the children's parents. They were supportive of their children's efforts, patient, uncensorious and never pressurizing the children to conform to their own idea of what a story was. If stories became silly or rude the parents accepted them and supported the spirit of what the children offered. I asked the parents to try not to intervene during a storytelling unless the children themselves asked questions or sought some help, and all the tapes I received showed how unintrusive the parents were. I also encouraged the parents to accept anything that was offered as a story, even if it turned out to be a poem or a song or another form usually regarded as non-narrative by adults. When I listen to the story-tapes I can often hear a sense of boundless freedom in the children, an enormous pleasure in the power of being able to say whatever they liked and being uninterrupted while they did it. I believe this is very important in revealing the true competences of the children, and I sometimes wonder if school can ever provide such relaxed conditions, or, indeed, if children can ever feel quite so confident in producing such meaningful, experimental, even excessive, material for their teachers.

The reader by now will have perceived that there was very little formal methodology in the data collection. Flexibility was the rule in everything. Since Josh's early stories provided me with a model of story collection, I felt it was important that the other children told their stories to their own parents rather than to me. Therefore whatever suited the parent and child was permissible, including the setting for storytelling, the person who took the role of story collector, the inclusion of brothers or sisters in storytelling sessions, the number of stories to be recorded on each occasion, the length and content of stories, and the duration of the whole storytelling period.

There were some disadvantages of this rather relaxed and unrestricted method of data collection. At the beginning I had no way of knowing whether any of the parents would be able to elicit enough material from the children to reflect the influence of books on their narratives, nor did I know whether other children would include the intertextualities that seemed to come so naturally to Josh. What made the crucial difference, I believe, was that the parents and the children construed the task as part of play, so that it was usually fun to do. Though very often it is obvious from listening to the tapes that the children had a story to tell and wanted to tell it 'for real' to the very best of their ability, it is also true that sometimes they were playing at being the storyteller. Robert tells 'tiny' stories and Justine tells stories 'for babies', Sundari announces that one story is 'a rubbish story' and tells another with nonsense words (based on Edward Lear), while Josh includes pretend newsreadings and weather forecasts in his story sessions. During the analysis of the tapes I found that play stories gave me some interesting insights into the children's categories and concepts of story.

In many ways my final data collection is rather 'untidy'. Jimmy took only three weeks to tell all his stories, whereas Justine and Josh told theirs over a period of a year. I also collected more material from Josh, which made the data unbalanced. However, I knew of no research which had collected such large quantities of tape-recorded story material from young children at home, and I felt justified in collecting stories from Josh whenever he wanted to tell them. This was not intended to be a quantitative study operating with a limited number of variables. Only one variable was really crucial – the children's early experience of hearing stories read aloud. This was essentially a study of children's spontaneous oral language production for which any restrictive methodology would have been inappropriate. Storytelling had to compete as a play activity with everything else these children normally did in their daily lives, and it was most important that they were not coerced or persuaded into telling stories when they didn't want to do it.

By the summer of 1981 I had received approximately 20 stories each from Sundari and Jimmy. The tapes from Justine and Robert were sent to me during the following year. I made the initial transcript of the tapes myself, and then they were checked by Miss Elizabeth Rowntree, an assistant recruited to the Language in the Nursery School Project in the Faculty of Education at Newcastle Polytechnic. When Elizabeth and I felt we had an accurate transcript we returned the tapes and transcripts to the parents for clarification of unclear passages, apparent nonsense or non-words, and questions to be answered about the story material. All the parents co-operated with this so that passages marked [unclear] on the transcripts were kept to a minimum. An important finding for me was that parents almost always know what their children are saying, even if to the researcher the words make no sense at all. There were joke words, made-up names, and references which were only meaningful in the context of the culture of the family. Parents understood them, but outsiders or teachers would not necessarily be able to make sense of them. The transcripts were numbered and dated in chronological order, so that there was a reference system for what turned out to be more than 46,000 words of child language.

Handing over the story collection to parents meant that I was not present during the storytelling of four of the children. Parents gave me valuable contextual notes, and other aspects of the setting become clear from the tapes themselves. The setting was certainly different for each child, and some of those differences may be of interest to other story collectors. Robert told stories in the family group, usually with both parents and his sister present. He was very young and needed more support in his telling than the other children. Sometimes he retold stories he knew well for his grandfather. Then he would hold the book and turn the pages as he told. He was not reading the words but telling the stories in as much of their original language as he could remember. He took turns at telling with his older sister and sometimes used some of her stories as a starting point for himself. Jimmy, too, told stories with his mother and his older brother present, and storytelling was a funny and sociable family game. Jimmy always drew his stories before he told them, and then he would tell the story of his drawing, a factor which had quite an effect on the structure of some of his narratives. Justine told her stories to her father, usually at bedtime. She sometimes refers to me on her tapes, showing that she knew I wanted the stories and that I would eventually listen to them. Sundari sometimes told stories to her mother and older sister, and sometimes she was quite alone – the only child who was quite happy to forego a physically present audience. Sometimes her sister told stories too, but these did not affect Sundari's narrations. Josh usually told his stories at bedtime, and always needed me to be there. He would think for a minute or two before we started recording, and once he told me that he waited 'for a picture in my head' to get his ideas for stories. For all the children the setting for storytelling was intimate with only close members of the family as the audience. I think this is a very different matter from telling stories in groups in school, as the children in Brian Sutton-Smith's major (1979) study did.[1] At home children know that their story material draws on culturally shared events – everyday incidents, books read together, games, even special words and names. They can trust that those present are clued into what they are talking about. The same applies in school, of course, but what is culturally shared in school will be different, and children are more likely to have an effect on one another's narrations. This is probably the reason why Sutton-Smith and his team found that the children in their study drew so extensively on TV material for the content of their stories. Though there must have been many kindergarten children in Sutton-Smith's study who were read to a lot, literary influences on story material do not emerge to any significant degree. It may be that in the school setting TV stories can be relied on as a common culture.

Josh and the other children always listened to themselves at the end of each story, indeed this seems to have been the whole point of the game for them. Becoming their own audience in this way was undoubtedly an excellent metalinguistic exercise for them all. It is clear that the children internalized a distant audience for their stories, not the one present during the telling, but the one who would listen to the tape afterwards, just as they always did, and that they saw this audience as the prime one rather than the parent who was sitting beside them. The tape-recorder has the potential to become a valuable aid to literacy, since, in order to learn to write, children have to be able to imagine a reader removed from them in time and place, just as they did in telling stories on the tape-recorder. If the children needed help, or dried up, or wanted to ask a question to be sure that the story was true to life, then they would change intonation, interrupt the story, and resume it again when the matter had been dealt with. The way in which they did this reflected that their concept of storytelling was of producing an inviolate text with clear boundaries separating it from the conversations of everyday life. Within those boundaries, usually established by the use of conventional openings and closings, the language the children used was 'different'. This book is a study of those differences and of the role of literature in their formation.

To conclude this introduction to the study I shall present some simple tables showing the bare facts about the data collected from each child.

Table 1.1 *Stories recorded from each child*

	Robert	Jimmy	Justine	Josh	Sundari
Total no. of stories	26	20	30	86	19
Age	3: 7–4:1	4:9	4:1–5:2	5:0–6:1	5:4–5:7

These figures compare well to the numbers of stories collected in Sutton-Smith's study. He collected stories from 350 children aged 2 to 14, and part of his intention was to elicit large numbers of stories from individuals. Approximately one-quarter of the children in his study told between 10 and 20 stories. Here each child tells 19 or more. The very first story session I recorded from Josh showed me that on the same storytelling occasion, when the child is telling one story after another and the conditions and setting of the recording do not change, there can be enormous variation in the stories in almost every respect: length, complexity, number of characters, use of language, and so on. This convinced me at the start of collecting the material that I needed many stories from each child if I were to be able to discover what their narrative competences were, for one story could never be regarded as representative.

Table 1.2 *Number of words and mean length of the narratives*

	Robert	Jimmy	Justine	Josh	Sundari
Total words	3854	2308	2613	24164	7195
Mean word length	148	115	87	331	378

These are very large samples of narrative material from such young children. Though it is clear that the two 5-year-olds tell longer stories than the three younger children, we must be cautious in reading anything of great significance into these figures when comparing one child to another. The number of stories and the words produced seem largely fortuitous, reflecting the children's willingness to narrate at that moment. Robert and Justine's stories are longer when they are retelling known stories, but this is not the case with Josh and Sundari who both tell very long invented stories. All Sundari's stories tend to be fairly long, but Robert and Justine have some play stories ('tiny' stories and 'stories for babies') which by definition are very short, and which reduce their mean story lengths. For the mean word length of stories there are comparative data from a study by O'Donnell, Griffin and Norris (1967). They elicited story retellings from 30 kindergarten children of mean age 5:10. They give a mean length of response of 209.4 words, with a range of 82 to 442.[2] The children in my study tell stories that are much shorter and much longer than this so that there is a much greater *range* of story length, even for Robert, who was two years younger than O'Donnell's subjects (see Table 1.3). Mean word lengths for narratives tell us very little.

Table 1.3   *Range of story length for each child*

Robert	Jimmy	Justine	Josh	Sundari
15–447	35–413	14–304	39–1756	176–701

Even the expected relationship between age and story length does not hold up with these five children, for while Josh and Sundari do seem to confirm that older children tell longer stories (though not always, as the range figures show), the figures for Robert upset the age/length relationship. Developmental studies give the impression that there is somehow an age 'norm'; in fact, though, that norm has been calculated from a very particular set of circumstances, i.e. the conditions for story collection set up by the experimenter. Given the opportunity to narrate as often as they liked, the five children showed great versatility. Some strategies, like the play stories I have referred to, reduce story length. Conversely, Josh fills his stories with dialogue and Sundari has invented narrators who address the 'audience' and sing songs, both strategies which increase story length. What is important to note is that such young children are capable of sustained utterances of this length. It is difficult to see what contexts other than storytelling monologues would give them the opportunity for such uninterrupted speech.

An implication for storytelling in school is that it may be misleading to form opinions or even to carry out assessments of children's oral narrative competences on the basis of one or two stories only. Even in the same storytelling session a child can tell a very short, simple story and follow it with something much longer and more complex, and vice versa. Storytelling needs to be a normal and frequent classroom activity if it is to give us a true picture of what children can do with words. The major purpose of this study is to show that if we manage to persuade children to tell stories fairly often we may find that linguistic, narrative and literary competences of very complex kinds are revealed to us, competences which are not so readily observable in other forms of child discourse.

NOTES

1. Sutton-Smith and his team carried out a large-scale study of children's invented narratives during the 1970s. Stories were collected in kindergartens and schools, so that the context for storytelling was very much more social than in my own study. Sutton-Smith (1979) gives

details of the large numbers of children involved and the numbers of stories collected from each. The stories themselves are to be found in Sutton-Smith (1981).

2. This study needs to be set alongside two other large-scale projects – those of Loban (1963–76) and Hunt (1964; 1965). All three looked at sentence (T-Unit) length in relation to age and syntactic structure. O'Donnell and Loban included children of kindergarten age, which provided me with a basis for comparison. To elicit the language Loban used an interview/question technique, while O'Donnell asked his subjects to retell the story of a short film. O'Donnell's subjects produced higher mean sentence lengths than Loban's, a result which O'Donnell ascribed to the higher socio-economic rating of his group. An alternative view, which I argue in Chapter 5 of this book, is that the difference in scores could be largely accounted for by the difference of discourse types: conversation in Loban's study, narrative in O'Donnell's.

Chapter 2

Sources of Story Material

once upon a time there was a very rude boy he said 'bum' and he said 'go
away' Mummy said one morning 'You have to go by yourself 'cos you're big
now' so he went by himself soon it was getting dark so he went out to
(the) the cinema (a-)and he watched the film and it was (P) (er) (P)
'Superman' (um) in Notting Hill Gate and then he went home to his own
house (and th- and-and-) and it was the next floor of Joshua's Daddy's
house but then he went out in the middle of the night and there was this
sound going 'Do-dee' [sung notes like a police siren] he looked all
around nobody was there in a small street where it had lots of holes he
looked down one of them he looked down the other they were all
alike but he looked down the next one and what was there? just a
surprise thing his daddy was there he had (um) a music box sort of went
[sings a tune] and Daddy said 'Hello but that wasn't a musical box it was a
very bad monster that lives in this hole I've killed it now but it can make a
noise (I've- and I've-) and I've killed it and it can't get alived and it can't
make that noise' so I went (the-the-little-um-er-) their little house behind the
police station they got back in time for the police and the police said 'What
did you do with that monster?' 'We killed it' and they said 'Why?' (well
he-) so the police said 'Oh you were trying to kill it (so-but-) but you must
kill it' said the police so he went and killed (the) the dragon 'There' said
the police 'Now you can come home with me for tea and you can sleep
with me and every morning I shall give you (er-er-um) break-no every night I
shall give you (er-um) breakfast-(no) [*Adult*: Supper] (no-every) every night (I
will) I will give you supper and every morning I shall give you breakfast (P)
and that's the end that's how he always went very rude and
bad *(Josh story 17 5:0)*

The identification of the sources of story material from children as young as these were
is no simple matter. It may seem a deceptively straightforward procedure to discover,
with the help of parents, explicit or even partially disguised references to books, TV

programmes or the events of everyday life. A quotation from a book is particularly easy to recognize if one is familiar with the book from having read it aloud many, many times to the child. For example, in Josh's story above there is a direct quotation from a text he knew well: 'their little house behind the police station'. This links Josh's story unmistakably with the Ahlbergs' *Burglar Bill*, just as Josh's story 2, quoted at the head of the last chapter, was linked to the same book by a reference to Bill's words when he steals something. I, and the other children's parents, were able to keep an eye on this sort of thing, and thereby to obtain valuable clues about the origin of a particular motif or idea in a story. And I was grateful to have such demonstrable and verifiable evidence that books were sometimes major models for the children's stories. Useful as they are, these unmistakable signs of books in the stories are the merest surface manifestation of far more complex deep structures, structures which, when unravelled, reveal the nature of the relationship between the children's narrative and literary competences on the one hand, and their experience of books and written language on the other. I shall return to these deep structures in Josh's story 17, but first I want briefly to discuss story retellings, which also appear from time to time, and the ways in which these too give us clues to the sources of material in invented stories.

Of the five children Josh and Robert retell stories from books more often than the other three children. However Justine retells a couple of stories too. By this I mean that the child attempts to tell the story as closely to the language of the written text as he or she can recall it. Sundari, on the other hand, uses many elements of book stories in her narrations, but always employs them for her own inventive purposes. Identifiable elements from books are not present in Jimmy's stories, nor does he retell any book stories, but this does not necessarily imply that books have had no influence on his narrations. Robert recorded two complete retellings of *Burglar Bill*, but does not transfer its language or motifs to his invented stories. Josh never retells *Burglar Bill*, yet he quotes from it, or uses ideas or language from it, in a large number of his early stories. For example, in story 38, told when he was 5:3, Josh is apparently inventing a fairy-tale about some rabbits, a wolf and a bear. On the surface the story seems to have very little relationship to *Burglar Bill*. Yet in the middle there is a quotation from Ahlberg's text:

> soon they went to bed   downstairs there was a noise   it is a noise that they have heard before   (it's) it's of the big wolf carefully stepping in (*Josh   story 38   5:3*)[1]

In the original text Burglar Bill and the baby he has found abandoned on a doorstep go to bed in the middle of the night, only to be wakened by a familiar noise, the noise of a burglar breaking into their house. It seems that Josh has no problem in spontaneously changing the intruder, Burglar Betty, into a wolf, the baby into some young rabbits and Bill himself into the rabbits' mother – for Bill is a substitute mother for the baby in the Ahlbergs' book and much of its humour stems from that. It's as though that central section of the original story, which is the most tense and exciting part, is instantly transferable by Josh to equally exciting parts of his own invented tales. Indeed, in many of Josh's invented stories where he has a sound coming out of the darkness in the middle of the night, the traces of the *Burglar Bill* narrative are lying beneath his words. Story 17, to which I shall return by and by, is another example of the same borrowing process. However, in Josh's story 38 matters are not as simple as that, because Josh takes his characters and some elements of the plot from at least two other stories he knew well from books: *The Wolf and the Seven Little Kids* and *Snow White and Rose Red*.[2] Josh even quotes from *Snow White and Rose Red* in much the way he quotes from *Burglar Bill*. So now the picture of the ways in which the children borrow from books becomes more complex, for they seem to take the parts – in the original language – of stories that have most impressed them and recycle these into something apparently completely new. The way in which the children are able to stitch together this and that from several books, and sometimes to add events from their own real lives, or from TV or from a poem heard in school, is quite unrehearsed and almost automatic, as though they know that what you have to do to become a storyteller is *do what other storytellers have done*.[3] The spontaneous nature of these changes and borrowings implies a two-way traffic between the stories the children have heard again and again because they loved hearing them and the stories the children are telling themselves in their own heads. I believe the implication is that children hear their favourite stories as *metaphors* for their own concerns, their own emotions, their own lives. When they tell their own stories the metaphorical processes of their reception of stories is revealed in all the borrowings they make.

When I began this study I would think of the children's references to books as 'borrowings', but over the years the term 'transformations' seemed a better way to describe what they were doing. I have come to regard the stories as large but intricate tapestries, woven from threads of many colours and textures, drawing together into a new tableau the metaphorical representation of myriad events and words from both real life and fiction. Although the retellings from books that appear in the data are very interesting, and although they offer very valuable insights into the language and narrative structures that have been most memorable and thereby most important to the children, nevertheless all five children prefer to invent their own fantasy stories; made-up stories are much more typical of the data than story retellings.

A very simplified way to describe the metaphorical process to and from known books and invented stories would be thus: the child is drawn to a particular story because it gives him or her pleasure. Parents who read to children will know that some stories have to be repeated again and again and that the child never seems to be able to get enough of them. The pleasure comes from all the various affective satisfactions children derive from their play – perhaps the joy of recognition that the story tells of something, in disguised form, that the child knows to be deeply true of his or her own life and experience. The story is a metaphor for the child's affective and social living and she wants to hear it over and over. The child will not tolerate any changes to the story language, since language is what the story *is*. To change the language would be to change the story, to make it into something else. When the child comes to make up a story herself she reproduces the metaphorical processes which were implicit in her reception of other stories, showing how the stories she has heard have made sense to her in ways which are very finely tuned to her personal experience. This summarized description of what must be a very complex process is much too simple, and the reader who is interested in the theoretical aspects of such metaphorical processes in language acquisition is referred to the next chapter, in which I shall explore these issues more fully. One thing must be remembered, though, and that is that the child's engagement in this sort of metaphoric process in storytelling is mediated entirely through language, through what it is possible for words to represent. I hope this will not be taken to imply that I think the pictures in children's story-books are not as rich in possibilities of representation as words are. One could hardly argue that, for in many illustrated story-books for young children the opposite is the case – the pictures very often do much more work than the words. I stress the language of stories here because when my children came to do their telling, words were all they had available to them. This is even true of Jimmy who *drew* a picture of his story before he told it. However important the visual medium was to Jimmy, and to the other children, when they sat down in front of the tape-recorder they could only rely on language to tell their stories.

Let us return now to Josh's story 17, which opens this chapter, for it provides a very rich illustration of the kinds of interaction between books, life and metaphorical processes I have been talking about. Much of story 17 comes from Josh's actual life. His father did work in London and live in Notting Hill, and they had seen *Superman* together at a cinema nearby. However, his father's house was not 'behind the police station', for that is a direct quotation from *Burglar Bill*, one of those surface references which are so helpful in discovering the sources of an invented story. Perhaps a brief resumé of Ahlberg's story would be helpful here so that readers can see exactly what Josh does with the book material.

This is how the story goes. Burglar Bill lives by himself and spends his life stealing things, everything he needs from jars of marmalade to toothbrushes. One night he 'steals' a big brown box with little holes in it that he finds left on a doorstep. When he gets home he hears a noise like a police car coming from the box, and when he opens the box discovers a baby inside. Bill does his best to take care of the baby in the way a good mother would, and after taking the baby for a walk in the park at night, they both settle down to sleep. They are awoken by the sound of an intruder, who turns out to be Burglar Betty and who is very apologetic for breaking into a fellow-burglar's house. Spotting baby clothes drying in Bill's kitchen Betty triumphantly identifies the baby as her own by the traditional device of the birthmark! She had left the baby in the box temporarily while she was busy breaking into a house. Burglars Bill and Betty see the error of their ways and reform, returning all their stolen property to its rightful owners before they marry on the last page, thus giving the story a fairy-tale ending. Those who know the text will appreciate the paucity of this summary, for in its language and its illustrations the book is very rich, meaningful and funny.

There are many parallels with *Burglar Bill* in Josh's story 17:

- Bill always steals in the middle of the night; Josh goes out in the middle of the night.
- Bill hears a strange sound, like a police siren, which is coming from a big brown box; Josh hears a siren-like noise.
- Bill lives in a 'small street'; so does Josh's Dad.
- Bill's big brown box has lots of holes in it; Josh's small street has lots of holes in it.
- Bill finds a baby in the box; Josh finds his Dad in one of the holes in the street.
- The siren-noise was coming from Bill's box, and from Josh's Dad's hole in the road.
- In the end Bill reforms, returning his stolen goods to (among other places) the police station. At the end of Josh's story his father is replaced by a policeman.

- Bill takes on the father's role for Betty's baby, and the policeman takes on a father's role for Josh, offering him food and shelter.
- Betty has abandoned her baby, albeit accidentally, while Josh is sent away by his mother at the beginning of his story for being rude.

Josh's story 17 is framed by transformations from a second story Josh knew well: Maurice Sendak's *Where the Wild Things Are*. The rudeness of the boy and his abandonment by his mother are a transformation of Max's 'wild' behaviour at the opening of Sendak's book, followed by Max's isolation and his journey to the land of the wild things. The monster in Josh's story hints again at Sendak's tale as a source. The supper at the end of Josh's story recalls the supper still waiting for Max at the end of Sendak's, and, reminded of it, Josh recalls his story opening in the coda 'That's how he always went very rude and bad'.

Though *Burglar Bill* is a very funny story it deals with some strong and powerful themes: questions of right and wrong, loss of identity, abandonment and the danger of death, gender roles, marriage and parenthood. Josh enjoyed it hugely and had heard it many times over a long period. It makes many disguised appearances in the first 40 stories he told, so there can be no doubt of its power for him. The story celebrates what is potentially anti-social and rude in a safe and humorous way. It closes with a conventionally moral fairy-tale ending. Ahlberg narrates it very formulaically; actions and speeches are tripled in the oral tradition manner. Josh not only transforms themes, settings and images from *Burglar Bill*, he also transforms the *how* of Ahlberg's storytelling, the narrative discourse – the ways in which the author has used language to make the story work. For example, Josh uses the tripling device:

1. he looked down one of them
2. he looked down the other
   they were all alike
3. but he looked down the next one
   and what was there?[4]

More important, Josh has learned, from *Burglar Bill* and other stories, that if you want to make a story exciting you must draw the listener's attention to the dangerous parts of the narrative. One way to do this is to set up mysteries and questions and then suspend the action for as long as possible, keeping the listener straining to find out what happens. In story 17 Josh does this over eleven successive clauses in which he slows his listener down by using detail and questioning the narrative. At the same time he manages to narrate this section of the story entirely through the eyes of his central character. Labov (1972), in his analysis of 'danger-of-death' stories told by black adolescents, calls these suspenseful sections of stories *evaluation*. He suggests that evaluation is what makes a story reportable and worth listening to. Barthes (1970), in a more literary analysis, sees this technique as representative of one of five codes by means of which cultural experience is implicit in the structure of narrative texts. The code of mysteries and puzzles, of questions and answers, he calls the *hermeneutic*, describing it as a major structuring device of classic 19th-century realist texts. Barthes sees the hermeneutic code as manipulative of the reader's response in much the same way as Labov sees evaluation as a major means of focusing the listener's attention. These are *discursive* ideas of what narrative is, in that they regard listeners'/readers' responses as part of the communicative activity of storying. I shall later employ the analytic systems of Labov and Barthes to explore the structure of the children's narratives. The point being made here is that transformations from books operate very deeply inside the structure of some of the stories; surface 'borrowings', such as a quotation or a character, simply lead us to uncover these deeper transformations.

There remains the question of what power *Burglar Bill* held for Josh, or, for that matter, for Robert, who retells it at great length twice.[5] I think it would be intrusive and irrelevant to attempt to match aspects of the children's lives, personalities and social situations to the sense they made of this story. Stories deal in what *might* be, in possibilities, in hypothetical scenarios.

In story 17 Josh takes the metaphors of parents and children from *Where the Wild Things Are* and *Burglar Bill* and presents a kind of mirror-image of the original stories, reversing the roles of fathers and children, burglars and policemen in a very personally meaningful interpretation of both his own world and the world of the book. If we regard story 17 as this kind of metaphor, a very early form of art in fact, then the illogicalities of Josh's tale make more sense. The noise in the road may be a siren, may be a music box, may be a monster. The *danger that it represents* needs to be extinguished by a strong father figure who may need to become a policeman in order to take on the responsibilities of killing the monster *and* caring for a little boy. If we look at the story as this kind of metaphorical exploration then killing a monster twice has a logic of its own, for it enables us to pass from the father to the policeman and then back to the father, creating a meaningful idea of what a father is. At the same time Sendak's story proposes the idea that the wild things, or Josh's monster, are the feelings of anger and rage Max experiences when his mother locks him in his room, and this is another possible reading for Josh's monster in the hole in the road.

It must be clear now that Josh's text is what the structuralists describe as *polysemic*, i.e. capable of several layers of interpretation. Discovering the effects of book stories on the children's oral narrations is a matter of uncovering these layers in their narrative discourse. The second half of this book presents the discoveries I made about the children's narrative competences when I analysed their stories using systems that are capable of revealing the deeper structures that I have sketched here with Josh's story 17. Books were not the only sources of story material, however. By taking each story in turn, and noting all the sources named by parents as generating story material, I was able to draw up a set of story source categories.

SOURCES OF STORY MATERIAL IN THE FIVE CHILDREN'S STORIES

Autobiography

This comprises any identifiable references to any aspect of the child's home life, such as setting details, local place names, or characters who are recognizable as siblings or school friends. We have had an example in story 17 where Josh mentions Notting Hill, the film *Superman*, and his character's father's house, all of which were drawn from Josh's real life.

This is actually a deeply problematic category, for if the children do make references to their actual lives they are usually transformations from life to a fictional form.

Sundari, for example, has a story about a man called Sona who has two little daughters of five and seven, an exact parallel to her own family, using her own father's name. However, her story is clearly fictional. All the children often have a main character of the same gender as themselves, of the same age, and, sometimes, as in story 17, with the same name. These characters may engage in activities which are drawn from life, but the fact that they are third person characters, *referred to by their narrators as if they were somebody else*, establishes that the children are in the *fictional* field.

Usually references to life, which are extraordinarily sparse – after all these are what parents can be expected to recognize – are mixed in with fictional elements. Josh tells several stories where a boy called Josh and his friends, who are given the names of Josh's actual school friends, have adventures which are magical and fantastical. In a sense all the stories must be autobiographical, as indeed is the work of every writer of fiction. The children can only allude to what they know. Even the wildly imaginative elements of their stories are representations of their experiences of other stories. In another sense, as I have tried to show in my discussion of Josh's story 17, the children often tell stories which are deep metaphorical versions of aspects of their feelings and lives. What is important is that the children do not recount straightforward auto-biographical events. They choose fantasy. Direct allusions to some aspect of real life are much rarer than allusions to books. But transformations from life are a part of most stories they tell.

Immediate surroundings of the storytelling

Occasionally one of the children incorporates into a story an object s/he has caught sight of during the telling. For example, at the beginning of one story session Sundari happens to be holding a pair of roller skates. So she makes roller skates a central theme of the story, even providing some sound effects on the tape. In another story Sundari catches sight of talcum powder and scent bottles on her mother's dressing table. She very quickly transforms these objects to make a point about her story character, a boy called Cletcher: 'and he had girls' things like talcum powder and perfume he loved to put it on' (*Sundari story 7*).

This is a very opportunistic category of source material and is rarely used, except on a few occasions by Sundari. She manages to incorporate these objects into her story in such a way that the listener would not know that the immediate context has supplied her with a prop. However, her mother was able to supply the information.

TV and films

Josh and Jimmy had seen superhero films both on TV and in the cinema. Josh tells a story in which Superman, Batman and Robin, and the Incredible Hulk are all com-bined. Strangely enough, though the actions of the story are what we might expect, the telling itself is one of the most literary, in its language style, in the study. Josh also tries, early in his storytelling, to retell the film *Star Wars*, but the telling is very confused and trails off into one of Josh's very few failures to get a story off the ground.

He also starts his longest story, story 39, with a rough retelling of the film *Mowgli*, which he had very recently watched on TV. However, he soon abandons the film and moves into story material drawn from other sources. There is one retelling, and many more transformations, of *The Wizard of Oz*. Josh had seen the famous film, but I had also read him the book and its sequel, *The Land of Oz*, a chapter at a time for a few weeks. Because Josh usually transforms elements from *both* books in his invented stories, I am inclined to think that the books were more influential than the film.

Wherever Josh does try to retell a film story, the result is much less well-structured than when he uses a book for a retelling. I think this has a lot to do with the repeatable, nature of books, which must be an enormous aid to the child's ability to recall the text, and with the kind of visualizing children must do when listening to stories, a visualizing which is certainly part of their inventing when they tell their own stories. Josh, in fact, once told me that he couldn't start a story without a picture in his head.

There is the further fact that the children's own storytelling had to operate entirely in the medium of words, so it was probably natural for them to use stories told in words as models. Jimmy makes the odd reference to *Star Wars* characters in his stories, but does not tell the story of the film. Justine makes occasional references to TV shows, but only as part of setting material. Indeed, I would not have noticed them unless her father had pointed them out to me. Josh tells three long and very well-structured stories with Dracula as a main character and Frankenstein as a minor one. The idea of Dracula, who is given fairly comic treatment by Josh, may have come from children's cartoons, but I think is more likely to be taken from one or two rather lurid comics which Josh treasured. Even in this instance the Dracula story is transformed and mixed with several others taken from books, so it is by no means a clear matter to state that this or that story comes from a film.

Sundari did not have access to TV, but Jimmy, Josh and Justine must have seen some TV on most days, and even Robert saw some. In spite of this, allusions to TV are very rare. Sutton-Smith (1981) found that TV was the major influence on stories collected from children of equivalent age in his large-scale American story study. My children were chosen for their rich experience of book stories, reaching back to their first or second year of life, at a time when TV stories, if they had seen them at such a young age, would have made little sense. It may be that their idea of what stories are was established in the medium of written language before they came to see films on TV. Also my children told their stories at home, usually with a parent present, a parent who had often read stories to the children, so that they may have responded to the request to tell a story with something that represented the normal story-reading situation between parent and child. Sutton-Smith collected his stories in kindergartens, and the children would tell stories to one another in small groups. In that context TV stories may have been the ones most children held in common, the ones they understood other children would recognize and know. At home, on the other hand, my children may have assumed that what they shared with their parents were written stories. Whatever the truth of it is, it is certain that TV stories are very rare, whereas stories taken from book sources are very frequent.

Radio

This category accounts for the playful newsreadings and weather forecasts in the data from Josh. Radio 4 was the medium for receiving the news in our house, in the mornings and the evenings. Josh therefore heard the news every morning and every evening while he was eating breakfast and supper. I took the news seriously and would insist that we listen to it.

I cannot find influences from radio in the other children's material. At a deeper level, Sundari's very sophisticated and communicative style of narration is quite close to the format of the pre-school children's radio programme *Listen with Mother*, though Sundari's mother does not cite this as an influence.

Returning to Josh's news broadcasts and weather forecasts, it is interesting to note that, once again, the material is not directly retold, but transformed to his own purposes. Indeed, he turns weather forecasts into humorous poems which explore the human body in an entirely metaphorical way.

Oral stories

Two kinds of oral storytelling influence the data. First there are oral stories invented and told by parents as a kind of family ritual. Josh's father used to make up very funny and tightly-structured stories about a character called Jumper-Bumper. On one occasion Josh actually retells one of his father's stories. Robert, too, tries to tell Sandy and Paul stories, modelled on a series his father made up for him. Once or twice Jimmy alludes to some characters from the Scots oral tradition of storytelling in his family, though he never actually retells such a story. Though there is no directly perceivable influence, both Sundari and Justine were told oral stories by their fathers. It is very striking that with these five children their mothers tended to read to them and their fathers to invent oral stories. It is impossible to estimate the extent of the influence of this kind of storytelling on my children's narrations. Because the influence of books is so great I think it is as an indirect influence that oral storytelling is very important. Each child had in existence a model of what s/he was required to do in response to the request to make up a story. In this respect their fathers must have been very powerful examples for them, so that storytelling seemed a perfectly natural activity.

Originally I invited 10 children to take part in this study. I ended up with five because for various reasons the other children did not find storytelling a very natural activity. It is quite possible and even likely that they lacked the model of the storyteller in their backgrounds to give the activity some sort of credibility. One child giggled so much during recordings that his mother gave up trying to collect stories from him. Another child shut himself away by himself and recorded unconnected, dream-like sequences which were very difficult to follow. A third child read aloud to his mother from reading scheme texts, so obviously the idea of *telling* a story had not been grasped.

This is a study of book influences on children's spoken language, but it must be said very strongly that the home-grown models for oral storytelling which were part of the children's culture must have played a large part in making the children suitable subjects for this investigation.

Rhymes and verses

Sundari includes many songs and rhymes in her stories, and they are often identifiable, traditional or popular children's songs. In one story she makes use of the witch's song from *Macbeth* but she changes it to make the ingredients of the cauldron even more horrific. Sundari actually sings in her stories and usually makes up the words to well-known tunes. In one or two stories she sings the entire narrative.

Josh also invents poems and rhymes. At first these were lyrical, in the present tense as opposed to the past of his stories, and always about the sea. I feel sure that these were influenced by poems he heard on the BBC schools radio programme *Poetry Corner*, which he enjoyed and would tell me about. However, I cannot identify particular poems which influenced him in a direct way. Josh later takes well-known rhymes, like '*Twinkle, Twinkle Little Star*' and lampoons them, often in a daring and rude way.

There are no poems or songs in the data from the other three children. As is the case with all the source categories I found, Josh and Sundari transform poems they have heard rather than recite them. At a deeper level poetry may have had a very strong influence on Sundari's narrative style, which is frequently very lyrical indeed, including fairly extended passages which, if taken out of the stories, could stand by themselves as poems. Of all the children, Sundari's concept of story was closest to poetry, and furthest from the action-packed plot-centred narratives of Josh and Jimmy. Josh and Sundari had undoubtedly heard a lot of poetry in their early years and I think it greatly influenced their choices of words and phrases. In Chapter 4 I examine the vocabulary of the stories, focusing on the strange and bizarre uses all the children seemed to see as part of narrating. It may be that this was the largest kind of influence that poetry had on their stories.

Toys

As far as I know all the children possessed toys, including teddy bears and cuddly toys which were very important to them. Jimmy and his brother had a collection of small teddy bears that they would weave endless games around. Jimmy and Josh also collected the little plastic figures of *Star Wars* characters. Sundari tells a long, lyrical, beautifully formed story about a little girl who plays on the beach with her dolls, but this turns out to be drawn from two book stories rather than Sundari's own dolls. Teddy bears are characters in one of Jimmy stories. Apart from this, toys do not feature in the story material, nor are they often part of the children's subject matter. Again, I find this as surprising as the paucity of material drawn from TV.

School

Josh and Sundari were attending the reception classes of their first schools at the time of the storytelling. Jimmy attended a play group, and Justine a nursery school for the latter half of her telling. Robert attended kindergarten. In spite of this, school plays very little part in the stories at all. Occasionally Sundari uses an incident from school, and Justine retells a long story she had heard at school. Josh uses the names of his school friends as characters in several stories. Otherwise school is absent.

Drawings

In a distant way the pictures in story-books may have provided the children with many of the images in their stories, but there is no way of identifying or quantifying this sort of influence. On one occasion Josh uses a picture on a record sleeve to open a retelling of *Hansel and Gretel*, and Sundari, in her opportunistic way, uses a picture of a little girl with a watering can. As usual Sundari incorporates the picture so skilfully into her narrative that I would not have known it was a source without her mother's telling me.

Jimmy would draw his stories before he told them, and his mother sent me several of the relevant drawings with his tapes. Jimmy and his brother Malcolm were passionate in their pursuit of drawing and painting at this time. Their father was an artist. The two boys devised several interesting ways to make their pictures (which were not cartoons) narrative. Malcolm, for instance, would paint pictures with arms or tentacles coming into the side of the picture, suggesting things happening beyond the picture's boundary. When Jimmy told the story of his picture he was naturally led to description of what he could see, and this meant that sometimes his story lacked events. On one occasion his mother prompts him to say what happened in the story, I cannot attribute the tendency to tell stories in which nothing happens solely to drawing them first, however, for Sundari also tells several stories which are all description and where nothing happens, and she did not draw her stories.

Dreams

It is impossible to trace this category, but it was almost certainly present. Jimmy's mother makes one explicit reference to a dream as a source of one of Jimmy's stories.

Books

All information relating to book sources was supplied by the children's parents.[6] Robert makes 19 references to books, drawing on 11 titles. Of these the most important are the Ahlbergs' *Burglar Bill* and Galdone's *The Three Little Pigs* (each retold twice), Goodall's *Creepy Castle* (a wordless picture book), Bannerman's *Little Black Sambo* and Rice's *Sam Who Never Forgets* (each retold once), and several *Topsy and Tim* stories (Adamson). Robert retells book stories more often than he transforms them. Justine makes 9 references to books in her stories. She retells *Topsy and Tim Go to Hospital* and *Hansel and Gretel*, and alludes to several books in her invented stories, though she tends not to transform them in such a sustained way as Josh and Sundari do.

Though he had just as much story-reading in his infancy as the other children, Jimmy makes no identifiable references to books in his stories. However, he draws on a wider range of other sources than the other four children, including drawings, toys, oral stories, films and dreams. This makes me wonder whether for some children visual media may be more important influences than aural ones.

Sundari draws on at least 15 books in her stories. She does this in a variety of ways; she quotes a line, or transforms a story ending, or makes use of a character or a motif. Like Josh she plunders several books for her invented narratives. Among the most influential books for Sundari were Aitken's *A Necklace of Raindrops*, Perkins' *King Midas and the Golden Touch* and Lear's *The Quangle-Wangle's Hat*.

Sundari nearly always fictionalizes herself as the heroine of her stories. The fictional Sundari is shy, quiet, often lonely and sad, sometimes hated and treated badly by her family. None of this resembles the real Sundari's life at the time, but is like the little girls of the stories she most enjoyed. Walkerdine (1990), in a discussion of comics written for little girls, talks about the large number of stories in which girls do not have, or do not live with, their parents. She presents this as an example of the way in which girls are often fictionalized as 'victims'. Certainly fairy tales, with which Sundari was very familiar, and which appear in several of her stories, have many examples of girl heroines who are impoverished, orphaned or badly treated – *Cinderella*, *Snow White* and *Rapunzel* are classic examples.

Josh tells more stories than the other children, so he has a greater number of references to books – 78 in all, drawing on 38 titles. *Hansel and Gretel* is retold 8 times, based on two quite different original texts, both of them heard on gramophone records which Josh would listen to obsessively during the first six months of the storytelling period.[7] The books which are transformed most frequently are *Burglar Bill* and Baum's *The Wizard of Oz* and *The Land of Oz*.

On the whole it is true to say that the stories which most impressed themselves on the children's narrations are the powerful stories, the stories which deal with major fears and strong emotions, however humorously or exotically they are told.

It needs to be said that in spite of the eleven sources of material I have given for the stories the subject-matter of most is the children themselves, not in terms of events which happened to them, but in terms of the ways they felt about things, or their extensive explorations of their own family situations. In this sense all the stories must be profoundly autobiographical, even those which are retold from books, since these have obviously been repeatable for the child because of their meaningfulness. The metaphorical processes I referred to earlier are present in the children's listening to stories. The children make up those stories to reflect their own life situations. And they are present in the children's telling and transformation of stories, for the children recreate books and life into a new metaphor for their experiences.

It is surprising how little factual autobiography is included in the data, particularly when one reflects on the infant school practice, which is still common, of asking children to tell their 'news' as a basis for story writing, or drawing, or practice in oral narration. Tied to the facts of what actually happened most children must be quite limited in what they can say, especially if life at home has been going along in a humdrum way. How much more productive to liberate children from the facts by asking them to make up story material, or to tell their own version of a story the teacher has read to the class. Fiction offers the children an opportunity to escape the intrusive gaze of others on their actual lives, while at the same time giving them the scope to talk about what is deeply meaningful to them in a disguised, metaphoric form.

I have avoided any in-depth survey of the themes of the children's stories. I know that they are often of great interest to practitioners, but they will emerge as this book goes on, for I shall quote from many stories in part and in full. There have been earlier extensive studies of the content of children's narratives, notably those of Pitcher and Prelinger (1963) and Ames (1966). Using the same data base, two stories each from 137 children aged 2 to 5, the researchers use psychoanalytic ideas to interpret the material, though they say little about the cultural context of the storytelling or about the language used to tell the stories.[8] The themes of my children's stories are very similar to their findings. Violence is a strong theme for all the children, so are birth and death, eating, fights, threatening adults (particularly witches and mothers) and animals/monsters.

In the course of subsequent chapters many stories will be illustrated and analysed in different ways, so the reader will be able to see what the children were interested in talking about. On the whole the children do not tell pretty or dull or sanitized stories, but deal in metaphorical form with major fears, such as abandonment, punishment, pain and death, the anger of parents, the jealousy of siblings, loneliness and helplessness. However, the stories are by no means woeful in tone. Often these themes are given comic or exaggerated treatment, and endings tend to be happy. The children use traditional stories, particularly fairy-tales, to disguise and make safe the affective concerns of their narratives, and it is true to say that their stories come closer to the fairy-tale form than to any other. One does not need to be a psychoanalyst to see that story reading and telling perform serious and powerful functions in children's lives, just as other kinds of symbolic play do. Unfortunately, some of the material children are offered as reading material in school, particularly material which is expected to teach them to read, lacks power and affective depth, as Bettelheim and Zelan (1982) and many others have pointed out.[9]

I shall close this chapter by quoting another full-length story, this time from Sundari. Like Josh in story 17, Sundari makes transformations from both books and life here. She uses Perkins' version of *King Midas and the Golden Touch* to accentuate the victimization of her girl heroine, the fictionalized Sundari.

> Hello my name is Sundari I would like to tell one story it goes like this once upon a time there was a little girl (P) she was so sad she didn't have a mother and her pet was only a tiny little kiwi (P) she was so sad (P) she just *loved* to tell stories she sang little songs so sweet I'll tell you one it goes like this [sings in a soft mournful voice] 'one day a sad girl sang a song weary when it came they [unclear words] they [unclear words] little girl' and here is a person to tell another song Hello my name is Angeli I'd like to tell one little song it goes like this   'Oh I weared on the step how I weary went and I weared on the step so-o weary as I weared on the step there was nothing I could which was weary' (P) the little girl's name (P) was Sundari (P) she had nothing to play with she was only about one month (P) she quickly snatch-ed up a biscuit but no use (gold) turned to silver you see 'cos everything she touched turned to silver and gold she snatched up another biscuit that was OK it didn't turn into gold so she snatched and snatched up all her food she was *such* a poor girl (P) it came to life again when she ate she ate so soundly nobody could hear her nothing could [unclear word] turned to silver and gold when she

drank it turned to silver water   she was glad (P) but as she came nearby
a forest when she was walking out (P) Sundari just fell   she looked up
again   there was a *bad* lion   he *killed* her   he was so sad when she was
dead   here is a story she sang in her sleep from Angeli   it goes like this   'A
poor little girl   she was so sad to see   a we-a-ry girl which was her   she did
love her-er mummy when she had a-a mummy   but now she was killed by a
lion'   and that is the end of the story (*Sundari   story 2   5:4*) (*Sundari's
emphasis*)

NOTES

1. J. and A. Ahlberg, *Burglar Bill*, London, Heinemann (1977). 'Suddenly he wakes up. Downstairs there is a noise. It is a noise that Burglar Bill has heard before; the noise of someone opening a window and climbing carefully in.'
2. I read these stories aloud to Josh from the version of *Grimm's Fairy Tales* by Amabel Williams-Ellis (Blackie, 1959). This is not illustrated, so Josh had to focus on the *words* as I read.
3. Referring to Flaubert's processes of composing *Madame Bovary* Mario Vargas Llosa (1986) writes:

    A novel is not the end result of a subject taken directly from life but, inevitably, the product of an aggregate of major, secondary, or seemingly insignificant experiences which, dating back to different periods and circumstances, some buried deep within the subconscious and others of fresh memory, some personally lived, others merely heard of at second hand, and still others garnered from reading, little by little converge in the writer's imagination, which, like a powerful blender, will break them down and transform them into a new substance to which words and a particular ordering give another existence.

4. In *Burglar Bill* Bill steals from three houses in succession, then, in an ellipsis of story time, finds the big brown box at the sixteenth house.
5. For a full-length transcript of one of Robert's retellings of *Burglar Bill* see Chapter 7, pp. 95-6.
6. For a list of all the children's books referred to throughout my text see the bibliography on pp. 213-14.
7. See Appendix A, pp. 200-3, for full transcripts of Josh's retellings of *Hansel and Gretel*.
8. The story collection which is the data base for these studies is very large, yet Ames found that themes of violence predominated for all ages and both sexes. She also found that young narrators have means at their disposal to 'distance' themselves from the violent nature of some story material, thereby protecting themselves. Bad things happen to characters other than the protagonists, deaths are reversed, and so on.
9. Bettelheim and Zelan's book, *On Learning to Read* (London, 1982) is a psychoanalytic treatment of children's reading problems and processes.

Chapter 3

Metaphorical Processes in Language Learning: A Theoretical Chapter

Most of the remaining chapters in this book are devoted to the different analyses I made of the story material from the five children. There is so much to be said about the very rich and complex stories the children told that I could only do justice to what is in them by means of a multi-layered analysis. Accordingly, in the ensuing chapters I explore the stories at the level of the word, the sentence, the plot structure and the structure of the discourse, and I conclude by looking at stories as reflections of children's thinking. This chapter, however, is largely theoretical, as is Chapter 6. In it I shall explore and discuss some of the ideas about language, play and narrative that have been most helpful to me in deciding what I wanted to look for in the stories and from what sort of perspective or angle I would do the looking. It was difficult to fit this kind of linguistic material into the patterns of existing studies of child language. For this is essentially a study of the *language* of the stories – they consist of nothing else – and its relationship to written and literary discourses. Narratives are rarely foregrounded in studies of child language acquisition, and when we turn to studies of the development of narrative competences we find that there is no focus on the language of the stories the children tell. Yet it seems very important to attempt to bring language and narrative together, for I shall show in later chapters that the children's experiences of stories and storytelling generate a whole array of very complex linguistic and discursive structures. Sentence structure has been the main focus of child language acquisition studies, but the analysis of the syntax of sentences tells us very little about how stories are put together. When the studies reach beyond the sentence level to look at discourse they tend to focus on children's developing ability to hold conversations, which again is problematic for data such as these stories, which are monologues. Narratologists have rightly perceived that sentence-by-sentence approaches will not fit stories and that a model of overall structure is required for narratives, yet in the burgeoning field of narrative schemata studies plot structure has been the whole focus while the language which tells the stories has been virtually ignored. What I needed were theoretical perspectives which would bring together what we know about language acquisition, what we know about the acquisition of discursive practices, and what we know about symbolic play; in other words theoretical perspectives to unite the cognitive, the social and the affective in ways that would *include* storytelling monologues in mainstream language development studies, rather than leaving them out on a limb as a special case.

The children's stories of this study are forms of verbal symbolic play. There can be no doubt about that as one listens to the tapes. As they narrate the children show their pleasure in their own inventions; they mock, laugh, joke, exaggerate, sing, whistle, make strange noises and give their characters funny voices. They invent worlds peopled by lions, bears, rabbits, monkeys, witches, giants, robbers, policemen, heartless mothers and small children. They make liberal use of magic and coincidence, extreme forms of punishment, a great deal of violence and much fear and suspense. Free from the constraints of holding conversations with real interlocutors, their utterances can be much more extended than is usual for young children, for here they themselves are simultaneously addresser and addressee throughout. To tell their stories the children use tacit knowledge, knowledge they are not aware that they have, of the ways narratives get told. This knowledge is a learned part of their cultural experience and is based on what they have heard, both spoken and written, in the past. Their knowledge of how to tell a story is not only grounded in all the other stories they have ever heard, but also in their everyday social experiences, the conversations they have listened to and participated in, the games they have played, everything they have observed and heard. Their 'rules' for constructing narratives incorporate all their syntactic and communicative competences into a larger, narrative competence.

The concept of competence is a very useful one here. The idea that children have unconscious knowledge of complex rule systems for constructing sentences and taking part in conversations can be usefully applied to the production of a verbal narrative.[1] Stories structure experience just as sentences do, and are acts of communication just as conversations are. Narrative competence will include syntactic and conversational competences. The concept of competence not only enables the researcher to draw parallels between language and narrative but also invites discovery of what is systematic, repeatable, generalizable.

Perhaps at this point it would be useful to summarize the original Chomskyan notion of competence, from which our ideas about communicative and narrative competences have developed.[2] Chomsky's (1957, 1965) theory was abstract and formal. It sought to explain linguistic universals – those aspects of language which are held in common worldwide – by regarding grammatical structures as psychological processes which are part of our innate mental capacity. Competence is defined as underlying, unconscious knowledge of the rule systems for generating linguistic behaviour, and it puts language as a system into the mind of each individual language user. Can narrative be similarly considered as a formal structure with 'rules' for story reception and generation that are parallel to the syntactic structures of language? Narrative can certainly be regarded, like language, as a universal structuring device, and there is no doubt that all societies and communities, literate or not, have their stories. Child language study tells us that infants produce their first narratives along with their first sentences.[3]

From the point of view of the present study one factor which favoured the notion of a competence for narrating was the unrehearsed and spontaneous quality of the children's narrative production: they told their stories in an entirely undirected manner, without pre-planning or help from adults. Later chapters will show how complex the children's knowledge of narrative was, yet they could not have brought that knowledge to the surface in an explicit way. Their knowledge was of the tacit, unconscious kind – knowing by doing. Although listening to themselves on the tapes must have been of great value to them, at their inception the stories were not worked out in advance. It seems then that they were employing the kind of knowledge which functions below consciousness. The children were remarkably unwilling to discuss their stories, given that there were plenty of opportunities for them to do so before and after the storytelling. Many snatches of conversation have been caught on the tapes, but if there are any remarks about their stories from the children themselves they tend to be dismissive.

There have been many studies of narrative structure which have sought to reveal a human, innate capacity for the reception and generation of stories. Since the whole field of narrative structure is central to this study I shall discuss it extensively in Chapter 6. At present it will suffice to refer to one or two studies, simply to show their limitations for the researcher who sees story not only as a cognitive structure but as an affective and discursive structure too. Propp's (1928) folklorist study of 100 Russian fairy-tales, for example, and Levi-Strauss's anthropological study of myth (1955) both showed that traditional narrative texts lend themselves to formal structural analysis, and both these studies pre-date Chomsky. Post-Chomsky psychological analyses have tended to treat language and narrative as structurally analogous: both are universal and both are produced and comprehended on the basis of a finite number of structuring rules. Indeed, as I shall show in more detail in Chapter 6 the terminology of transformational linguistics has been imported into these studies so that narrative 'syntax' and 'grammar' have been described by means of re-write rules, tree-structure diagrams, idealized stories and so on. Most psychological studies of narrative 'grammar' are text-based. A grammar is written to describe the most basic and typical folklore texts, and is then matched to corresponding psychological schemata revealed in child and adult retellings of the test story under controlled conditions. Nothing could be further removed from the relaxed, spontaneous play sessions from which my story data emerged.

However useful these studies have been in illuminating our understanding of the mental organization of experience, it has to be said that existing descriptions of story schemata are simply not complex enough to account for the stories in this collection. The specially devised narratives of typical story recall/comprehension experiments take no account of the meaning a particular story may have for an individual, as though stories were not forms which delight and please us or frighten and appall us, but sets of 'facts' which we happen to remember because they are arranged in a special order, called narrative. In these studies lexical choices make no difference – all that matters in the story is what happens. Yet it seems almost too obvious to be worth stating that our responses to stories depend not only on what happens in them but also on the way they are told, and this is likely to be more the case with young children who will often get tremendously upset if the words of their favourite stories are changed. Psychological studies of story grammar (examined more extensively in Chapter 6) tend not to take into account children's cultural experience of stories, and even the social setting of the storytelling tends to be controlled in experimental conditions.[4] The story grammar studies are bound within a very narrow concept of what a story is; it is usually regarded as a strictly ordered set of plot moves rather than as a discursive practice. I want to explain and describe how listening to highly meaningful and elaborated stories, read aloud in the intimacy of home and family in the early years, can generate extraordinarily complex linguistic and narrative structures. What is needed is a view of language learning which can locate the affectivities of verbal symbolic play *inside* what is already known about the development of language structures and narrative competences.

Where can we begin to look for such a theory? We might start with the child as a speaking subject and the kinds of unconscious knowledge s/he reveals in storytelling. The Chomskyan notion of competence posed real problems for those whose interest lay in the analysis of actual child language. 'Competence' is an entirely theoretical idea, locating grammatical structures inside the mind of the infant in a kind of 'idealized' form, whereas the language that we actually utter is too imperfect (subject as it is to all the false starts, hesitations, memory lapses etc., of ordinary interaction) to yield a true reflection of our linguistic knowledge.

Dell Hymes's 'communicative competence' extended the Chomskyan model to include rules for language use, units of language which were larger than sentences – whole conversations and other discourses – and relationships between speakers who are positioned in social situations in different ways (Hymes, 1973). This more liberating theory, which linked social experiences and relationships directly to the development of implicit knowledge of linguistic structures, ought to have led to the inclusion of storytelling monologues in the field of potentially interesting child language data. However, adding on the 'context' to linguistic structure does not seem to have made much difference to our knowledge of how it is that some children become very accomplished storytellers.

One of the difficulties has been to allow affects a role in the constitution of competences. Early on in the post-Chomsky development of psycholinguistics Ruth Weir (1962) recorded her infant son's pre-sleep monologues. She was ahead of her time in using a functional framework for analysing Anthony's utterances and in acknowledging the pleasures and satisfactions of his wordplay. Yet even she tended to avoid the meaning of what he was doing in talking to himself at night, somehow seeing the spin-off of his activity – practice in phonological patterns and syntactic rules – as its driving force.[5] Yet it is no more likely that syntactic practice lies at the generating centre of these pre-sleep monologues than that my children's oral stories were felt by them to be good opportunities for practice in the structure of narrative.

Narratives do make their appearance in sociolinguistic studies, such as Halliday's account of the language development of his son Nigel (1975), yet he is curiously sparing in giving credit to affects like excitement in the generation of Nigel's first story.[6] As we shall see, it was only Labov who turned the tables by placing major emotions – fear, danger, excitement, pleasure – at the very heart of what made a story worth listening to. He related those emotions to a fundamental category of narrative structure, the category he terms evaluation, the aspect of storytelling which reveals the narrator's attitudes and feelings about the events narrated. For Labov, stories which lack the evaluative elements are purely referential, lists of happenings. Without the elaborations a skilled storyteller can give to the story events there will be little response to, or interest in, what is recounted. This is an entirely discursive concept of narrative and an account of narrative structure which includes aspects of my children's competences that are missing in story grammar studies. (Labov's analysis is treated in more detail in Chapter 7.)

Of course other branches of psychology do give a central place to affects in development. There has been a psychoanalytic tradition of analysing children's stories, represented, for example, by Pitcher and Prelinger (1963) and Ames (1966). While these studies are fascinating they are not very helpful in the search for a unitary theory of language development, since they reduce everything to theme and content, which are interpreted in the classical Freudian manner to yield evidence of the repressed affects and conflicts of infancy. Words are treated merely as the vehicle bearing the traces of unconscious drives. If the linguists have tended to neglect meaning, the psychoanalysts, at least in this tradition, have tended to neglect language, yet meaning and language must be inextricably linked when the context is verbal play.

Other psychological studies of imaginative play also give a central place to affects. Vygotsky (1978) tells us that 'the central attribute of play is a rule that has become a desire'.[7] This compact statement, with its apparently contradictory juxtaposition of 'rule' and 'desire', perhaps needs some amplification. I think that what Vygotsky means is that our play is subject to rules or laws or guiding principles. Our behaviour in imaginative games can never be random or arbitrary, for when we act out roles in pretend play, or make one thing stand for another, we do so according to strict criteria of our own making. But at the same time we are not merely practising skills or rehearsing our knowledge because the fact that we are playing means that we are engaged in activity entirely for its own sake and for the pleasure that it gives. By its very definition, play is entered into voluntarily. 'Rule' and 'desire' are thus locked in interdependence, for on the one hand we ourselves choose to conform to the criteria which must be adhered to to make the game, while on the other hand we derive the greatest pleasure from what is freely entered into with no consequences for our lives in the 'real' world.

Storytelling is a play activity which can demonstrate how this works. The children in this study tell their stories earnestly, with effort, straining to utilize all their knowledge to make the stories work. For example, they sometimes use long, grammatically complex sentences and have to struggle not to get themselves into a syntactic muddle, or they risk using words and phrases whose meanings they are not quite sure of in the interests of making the language sound like story language. They often push themselves to resolve their stories properly or to cleverly disguise the fact that they cannot do this. Yet at the same time they are telling stories for fun, because they want to, and enjoying the licence of their freedom from the constraints of more mundane language interactions – especially with adults. Vygotsky explains the link between pleasure/desire and rules as a *paradox* of play, for the child at once plays because she feels like playing, yet also, in voluntarily submitting herself to rules, she renounces what she feels like doing. For this reason Vygotsky claims that children exercise their greatest self-control in imaginative play, and that the feelings of mastery which are contingent on that self-control are the major source of pleasure and satisfaction in playing. Although he constantly gives primacy to the social basis of learning, Vygotsky's account of play has some Freudian undertones, for he sees wish-fulfilment as a motivating force of pretend play, thereby placing an affect at the very heart of what play is.

Affective forces are also central to Piaget's (1951) account of symbolic play, and he refuses to separate the affective and the intellectual in the inception of all symbolic thought, including play, even in the most scientific and logical modes of reasoning.[8] Vygotsky (though he does not use the term) even refers to play as a means of constructing a new, fictitious subjectivity – 'play gives a child a new form of desires. It teaches her to desire by relating her desires to a fictitious 'I', to her role in the game and its rules'. Unfortunately neither Vygotsky nor Piaget applied these ideas to children's verbal symbolic play. In their storytelling children's unconscious desires are implicated in several ways, in the affects which dominate the themes of *what* they tell, and in the fictitious 'I' (or several fictitious 'Is') who desire to become the storyteller, bringing all their mastery to bear on *how* they tell.

The theories outlined above do not originate in specific studies of child language. When we do look at linguistic studies it is striking how often play and affects are lurking in them without receiving any special attention from the linguists. For example, there are several accounts of baby-talk (BT), or Motherese, the register used by some mothers (for it is not universal) in adaptation to the limitations of their infants' speech. Brown (1977) tells us that BT is not only adaptive to the limits of the baby's comprehension, but it also has the function of expressing affection. Ferguson (1977) also includes emotional expression as a major element of BT.[9] Yet most studies of BT take these central affective forces for granted, perhaps regarding them as too obvious to warrant attention. The tendency of most studies of BT is to stress its linguistic structures, while the infant and its mother, and the situation within and between them as speaking subjects, are virtually ignored except insofar as they supply an external context. Vygotsky warned against the intellectualization of play, that is, the tendency to regard play as consisting only of its intellectual spin-offs. Studies of BT seem to do just that, though, when they regard what is fundamentally a warm and expressive act of communication as solely an exercise in linguistic adaptation. The point is that the affects of BT are *inside* the communicative structure, not an 'added-on' contextual feature.

This is probably a good place to return to the children's story material, and to see how these ideas map onto what is under scrutiny here:

> Hello   there's going to be a story today(P)   one day there was a little fairy who lived on a mountain   one day there was an earthquake(P)   and it knocked the little rock off the mountain with the fairy on it   she was crying and crying when this happened   she was so sad she told a nearly crying story nearly nearly nearly   she would never stop talking about the rock(P)   she was so quick(P)   and it was so lonely where she lived   (it was) it was humble in the sea   one day the tide came out(P)   and she got washed onto the beach   and soon she [two words unclear]   and the little rock was made into a statue(P)   she *loved* sitting on the little statue(P)   the statue was of *her*   she looked so nice with a shining crown shining little bracelets all nice shining things a shining wand shining rings   they were all shining(P)   she couldn't tell everything   she did so much   nor can I   it's nearly the end of this story 'cos it's not a long story   it's a quick story not talking fast though talking slowly and wearily along   I'd better get on with the story now   the fairy flew about hedges in the night and joined her other fairy friends   one day she was so frightened of a thunderstorm (P)   she cried her heart off   but her heart wasn't really off (P)   that is the end of the story
> (*Sundari story 10 5:6*)

There are some interesting uses of both words and sentence structures in this story. For example, there are two passive verb forms, and a modal 'would'; there are some colourful lists, poetic repetitions and some interesting word choices – 'humble' and 'nearly crying story' are unusual and draw attention to themselves. There are several changes of tense and a first-person narrator. The story has a shape, with a beginning, middle and end, and is framed by formal opening and closure. The act of storytelling calls forth all these competences in Sundari, yet describing all these features would not amount to a satisfactory account of what Sundari is doing here. She is obviously making every effort to tell her story in language she regards as special and 'other' than everyday language. She is thinking quite hard about what she is doing too – note the number of pauses, which are usually at least three seconds long, often considerably longer. The effort Sundari is making can be regarded as a form of Vygotsky's 'rule', but we need to remember that, impressive though these linguistic and intellectual concomitants of Sundari's verbal play are, *they are not the thing itself but only part of it*. The other half of Vygotsky's paradox is the desire. Sundari's fictitious heroine could certainly be seen as a form of wish-fulfilment, an invented subjectivity for Sundari herself. But the same is true of Sundari's narrator, the 'I' who addresses us in between telling us what happened in the story. This is another 'fictitious I', another subjectivity for Sundari to experience by playing with it. So Sundari's 'desire' lies in both the *what* and the *how* of the story – the events she narrates and the narrating that tells them, thus both constitute the linguistic and narrative competences she reveals here. And what of the context? Sundari was alone during this recording session, but she addresses an imaginary interlocutor, perhaps ourselves listening to her tape in the future. So her addressee is inside her head during the storytelling, a fiction like the fairy and the narrator. Perhaps the context of this story is all the stories Sundari has ever heard, together with several life experiences we have no way of knowing about. These will certainly be constitutive of her story and language, but in a very general and distant way. If we regard Sundari as playing out the practices of a specific communicative discourse in which she is able to position herself as both the storyteller and the story that is told, then we can locate the context of this utterance not only in the external features of its setting but inside the narrative discourse itself. Sundari's verbal play gives her the scope to create a fictional fairy, a fictional storyteller and a fictional audience. The rules of the game – describing the fairy in a vivid, even poetic way, finding the right words (even if this means taking risks with strange words like 'humble'), making the sentences melodic, communicating with the imaginary listener, directing the progress of the story, and so on – are what give her the pleasure, and her pleasure in the mastery of such rules generates the competences she displays. Supposing we look at some types of linguistic interaction, not as sets of structuring rules which are co-variant with an infinity of outside contexts, but as processes which are fundamentally metaphorical?

I believe the metaphorical dimension of language and language use may be the missing link in some of the linguistic studies I have referred to earlier in this chapter. It isn't enough to attribute Sundari's storytelling competences solely to her cultural experiences, vital and constitutive of her stories as these undoubtedly were. It is certain that Sundari's everyday social discourse has helped her in the communicative aspects of her story, and also that her experience of hearing other oral and written stories in the past have helped to show her how stories get told. But Sundari's stories must surely also be constituted by her *inner* experiences, by her desire to construct other selves in storytelling, selves which only come into being from the facility of language to represent things metaphorically. What Sundari has learnt is that it is pleasurable and exciting and interesting to play with the linguistic system as a way of making metaphorical experience. Work by Walkerdine, Urwin and their colleagues (1984) has taken us some way towards a theory which unites the insights of modern linguistics with the metaphorical dimension of language and its affective roots, the kind of theory which would help to account for what is going on in Sundari's narrating. I shall briefly outline the major ideas on which they have drawn, and then I shall go on to suggest that metaphorical processes are deeply enmeshed in the kind of fantasy story material which is the subject of this book.

It was Freud who charted for us an unconscious where drives and desires can be hidden from our conscious awareness, yet, of course, Freud pre-dates modern structural linguistics. The affective unconscious of Freud and the linguistic unconscious of Chomsky (the idea of competence) are tied together in Lacan's proposal that the human mind 'is structured like a language' (1977).[10] Lacan argues that in the psychoanalytic situation the only medium available to the analyst for interpretation is the patient's speech – the 'talking cure' – and that therefore Freudian theory is essentially a theory about language. This view of Freud's ideas finds some support in Freud's own texts. In *The Interpretation of Dreams* (1900) Freud compares the ideas in dreams to sentences which lack the necessary conjunctions to make coherent sense, or which are entirely substantive and lack a grammar.[11] Dreams, then, are unconscious languages which, during analysis, are reconstructed. Language also plays a part in the content of dreams; in the process of condensation and displacement, by means of which hidden desires escape censorship, language assumes the disguises it typically wears in jokes, puns and slips of the tongue. The 'talking cure' is not so much an analysis of dream content as of the language which speaks it.

Looking at the unconscious as *linguistic* in this way raises some major questions about the nature of language itself. We know that the language of dreams and poetry can be highly ambiguous, but surely words are also capable of standing in a more direct relation to reality, of denoting our experiences? Using the linguistics of Saussure (1916) and Jakobson (1960), the psychoanalyst Lacan proposes that there is no secure bond between a word (a signifier) and its referent (the signified). He regards words as marks of *separation* or *difference*, because they take their meanings not from a relationship to reality, but from their contrast to other words. This suggests that linguistic structure itself is constituted by just such a movement from meaning to meaning as Freud's methodology for dream analysis uncovered in the unconscious. Lacan regards language as a signifying chain, along which we can only articulate meanings by recourse to other signifiers – or words. The slipperiness of meaning is not confined to poetry and dreams but is an implicit part of linguistic structure as a whole.

Lacan made use of Jakobson's description of the two major, intersecting dimensions of language, represented as horizontal (metonymic) and vertical (metaphoric) axes, to argue that language represents separation or difference. Along the horizontal axis, best seen in the linearity of writing, words take their differences from one another by means of grammatical rules and phonological distinctions. Along the vertical axis words are selected from sets of possible meanings, so the principle of difference is a semantic one. Jakobson's formulation of a metaphoric dimension of language structure was intended to explain how language works in the poetic function, but Lacan argues that this is a dimension of all speech. Linguists have traditionally studied the combinatorics of syntax and phonology and have neglected the metaphoric – the capacity of language to represent double, disguised or hidden meanings.

If Lacan's reading of Freud and Jakobson admits a metaphorical principle to language structure, what of the affective dimensions? Lacan's concern is with the construction of subjectivities early in life: how do we achieve a sense of self? He suggests that we construct ourselves and our worlds only as *speaking subjects*.[12] In early life the infant is a genderless, shapeless mass who can have no sense of the boundaries between itself and its mother's body. To become a social being several kinds of 'splitting' are necessary: the inner must be distinguished from the outer, the conscious from the unconscious, the present from the absent and so on. These distinctions are achieved through the onset of language, for it is then that the child is able to perceive itself as an object which is signifiable, and to take up positions and roles in signifying relations. For Lacan the moment of splitting is symbolized as a 'mirror-stage'. Gazing in delight at its own image in a mirror enables the child to construe itself as a unified whole and, simultaneously, to acquire a sense of mastery over itself since the child has the illusion that it can completely control the mirror image. This masterful, controlling ego is an 'ideal I' which, Lacan suggests, is turned 'in a fictional direction', and it comes into being at the point where the child is able to separate itself as a subject from the external world.[13] Separation is also the mark of linguistic structure, which matches exactly the formation of subjectivity in the child in its ambiguity, in the constant elusiveness of meaning, in the separation of signifier and signified.

The affectivities of the gender identities involved in the Oedipus complex are at the centre of Lacan's view of language. The narcissism of the mirror-stage and the development of a gendered being necessitate language learning. In acquiring the rules and definitions of language the instinctual drives of the body and dependence on the body of the mother must be repressed, hidden in an unconscious, which linguistic structure, with its ambiguities and disguised meanings, parallels.

Urwin (1985) regards these aspects of Lacanian theory as too phallo-centric, and proposes some modifications which reflect our current knowledge of child language. She instead suggests that subjectivity is constructed not through the linguistic system *per se*, but through *discursive relations*. Children experience language through specific social practices – the school, the family, the hospital, and so on, in whose discourses they are able to adopt particular roles, according to their cultural opportunities. Storytelling could be regarded as one such discourse, a space where children can try out emergent subjectivities in the medium of language. Urwin also suggests that the Lacanian mirror can be constituted by the 'significant adults' surrounding the child.[14] Baby-talk, and the rituals and formats between mothers and infants, mirror the child's subjectivity back to her. Of course stories are ideal candidates for such mirroring – the reader will recall Josh's story 17, with which I opened the last chapter, where *Burglar Bill* is recast by Josh in an extraordinary mirror-reflection of the original story. According to Urwin, the mother does not hold proto-conversations or use BT with her baby to rehearse the rules of turn-taking or grammar, though these are spin-offs of the activity. She is rather reflecting the child's subjectivity in an imaginary relation, by means of which the child will come to know that things are signifiable. This formulation combines affectivity, social relationships, language and discourse, in the constitution of the subject, and places Lacan's 'fictional direction' at the centre of development. I would add that play is the favoured space for these processes to develop in infancy – Vygotsky, coming from rather different psychological traditions, affirms that an 'ideal I' is constructed in imaginative play.

The idea that there is a metaphoric dimension of all language which plays a central role in the construction of subjectivity in language acquisition suggests that child language needs to be studied from this point of view. Studies of children's use of metaphor, construed as the traditional figure of speech, show that young children produce more metaphors than older ones, but that the metaphors are often bizarre and unconventional (Gardner *et al.*, 1975, 1978).[15] Rumelhart (1979) suggests that initially children cannot distinguish between literal and non-literal uses of language because at the beginning *all* language is unconventional – the conventions must be learned. He calls for a new account of language, one which acknowledges that at the beginning the interpretation of language depends on 'top-down' kinds of mental organization, rather than a 'bottom-up' accretion of terms. Rumelhart's insights arise from his work on story schemata, which show that we understand stories not by adding up the parts but by bringing to our perception of stories a mental model of how stories work.[16] Gardner *et al.* too, suggest that stories, with their multiple layers of meaning, may be good candidates for the examination of metaphorical processes. Walkerdine (1982)[17] also proposes that metaphoric processes are implicated in children's discursive practices. Again the context is play. Walkerdine observes that in their role-play children show that they know the conventions of many more discourses than they can have participated in in everyday life: teachers and pupils, mums and children, doctors and nurses, and so on. She finds that these roles are adopted spontaneously, without forethought or negotiation, just as the children in my study told their stories. Walkerdine suggests that it is the opening move into a new discourse which signals to its participants all its practices – 'once upon a time', for example, may elicit story forms. Walkerdine believes that children are able to call up such discourse practices spontaneously through the operation of an associative, metaphorical principle, and that the 'context' for such linguistic interactions lies *inside* the practices themselves. For Josh and Sundari, in story 17 and story 2, it is certain that the discourse they are engaged in is as important to them as the referential aspects of their stories; form and meaning are united because *what* they are telling becomes fused with *how* they tell it.

The ideas that I have sketched here are necessarily oversimplified, and there are yet more threads which could be drawn into an exploration of language/discourse as metaphor.[18] One rich field is the anthropology/ethnography of verbal play forms from around the world. Research in places as far apart as Burundi, Turkey, St Vincent, Hawaii and New York shows verbal duelling, rapping, sweet-talk, ritual insults and the like, to be linguistic mirrors/metaphors for the values, status relations and world view of whole communities. These linguistic forms subvert the referential functions of language, disguising meanings which are primarily to do with sexuality and power in a complex array of metalinguistic and poetic formats which constitute not only the 'rules of the game' but the message, the very point of the play.[19] Kirschenblatt-Gimblett (1976) describes this sort of verbal play as an escape from 'the tyranny of a certain kind of meaning' i.e.: dictionary definitions and literal meanings. Edmund Leach (1964) pointed out that typical forms of verbal play are concerned with socially suppressed taboo areas. He proposed a very Lacanian 'Leach theory' which locates taboo in the border zones between distinct categories for naming the environment. In other words taboo lies between and beneath the definitions of language.[20] Stories, too, are forms of verbal play, and certainly the five children in this study used them to explore what is forbidden, dangerous, and unmentionable.

Freud's description (Freud, 1920) of the Fort/Da game will be a helpful way to bring together the themes of this chapter. He observed that an 18-month-old boy, at the onset of language acquisition, had one obsessional game. After his mother had left him, he would throw away from himself small objects, while at the same time uttering a long, drawn-out 'Ohh' accompanied by an expression of satisfaction. This sound was understood by Freud to be the German 'Fort' ('Gone'). After the child had thrown out the toy, a cotton-reel tied to a piece of string, he would pull it back in again, this time uttering the sound 'Da' ('There'). Both parts of the game afforded the child much pleasure. Freud read the game as the child's means of coping with his mother's absence, and noticed that he played the 'Fort' part of it more often, even though it paradoxically represented the unpleasant part of the experience – his mother's going. Freud concluded that the child's pleasure in 'Fort' lay in the sense of mastery he achieved in it, for the game allowed him to control and take on the role of the powerful adult in his life. Lacan discusses the Fort/Da game, but for him the child achieves his mastery *linguistically* by repeating the contrasting phonemes 'Fort' and 'Da'. In this sense, it is linguistic structure itself, constituted as it is by *difference* (the contrasting words) which offers the child the opportunity to gain mastery. Urwin's reading places the emphasis not on the linguistic system itself as the metaphoric mirror, but on the ways the child in his game can assume a role in a discourse which reverses the usual power relationships in his life. Opportunities for these kinds of mastery are present in the discourse of storytelling. The children can achieve mastery of their own existential problems, simultaneously mastering the story discourse, and taking on all the powerful roles they do not have in their real lives.

Children as young as those in this study are highly dependent on adults for every aspect of their living, but in order to learn and develop they need also to experience the feelings of control exemplified by the Fort/Da game, to mirror for themselves subjectivities which are powerful, and in order to do this in story they need to master the medium of language. In storytelling the mirror-world created by the storyteller is a world of words. In Josh's reversal of *Burglar Bill* it is what he can make the words do that counts, not what he makes the characters do – for the characters are fabrications only of words. This is why merely to tell what happened would not be enough. What is important is *how* the story is told. What I first noticed about the language of the stories is that it had *style*, characterized by a kind of excess with words, with unusual lexical choices, ringing phrases, complicated sentences, formal modes of address between characters, exaggerated narrators' voices. Yet the verbal excess is not a kind of adornment to the story events; *the verbal excess is the story*, whether what it relates is bizarre (fairies knocked off rocks by earthquakes, fathers hiding in holes in the ground), or mundane and ordinary. Margaret Meek (1991) gave me the insight that the power of stories seems to be involved in excess of every kind, but this excess in the end consists only of words. For me, it is as though, as they tell their most powerful stories, the children are plugged into some hidden force within the linguistic system, which links them through some electricity or magnetism to what is most meaningful in their experience.

The theoretical issues which I have touched upon in this chapter are intended to provide some explanation for the linguistic operations the children were involved in, and some rationale for the different kinds of analysis I describe in the ensuing chapters. Because the process of reflecting their affective drives in stories accords with the capacity of language to represent meanings metaphorically, all the analytic systems I use focus on the story language, rather than on the themes or story content. Making this study primarily a multi-layered analysis of language means that I have not focused on the interpretation of the meanings of the stories. This may seem paradoxical, as in this chapter I draw on the work of a major interpreter of meanings – Freud. But I have adopted Lacan's view that Freudian theory is essentially linguistic. Thus rather than hunting for definitive meanings for the stories I have tried to show what kind of discourse practice the children are engaged in, and what it is that storytelling can show us about what very young children can do with words.

NOTES

1. Here I am thinking not so much of Chomsky's Language Acquisition Device, the mental blueprint for linguistic structure, as of language learning proceeding on the basis of regularities which are perceived and tried out in social settings. I use the term 'competence' because the children's stories were full of such regularities, or conventions, which they had taken in and were able to produce unconsciously. My analyses in later chapters show the experimental nature of their use of story conventions, which fits the idea of hypothesis-making and testing.
2. Dell Hymes (1973) saw the concept of underlying processes as Chomsky's major and most important principle. He also asserted (p. 283) that 'affective and volitional factors' should not be separated from cognitive aspects of the theory of competence.
3. For example, both Pitcher and Prelinger and Sutton-Smith and his team were able to collect stories from children as young as 2 years old.
4. There are exceptions. Bennett (1980) found that in Hoopa Indian stories what counts as a resolution would not be regarded as one by narratologists outside Hoopa culture, thus showing that story structures are culturally variable.
5. Weir's monologues bear a striking structural resemblance to the *stories* collected from younger children in Sutton-Smith's study, and to a *narrative* spoken by $2\frac{1}{2}$-year-old Lem in Shirley Brice Heath's *Ways with Words* (p. 170). The 'chain' linking of elements, the sound play, the interiorized dialogues and the circular rondo-like structure, characterize all these examples and suggest that Weir's data might be regarded as early narrative – though she herself asserts that the monologues were not narrative in structure.
6. Halliday acknowledges that the semiotics of verbal play is a neglected area (1975, p. 87). He shows how Nigel's stories were built up through dialogue, and how they draw on both past events and stories told to Nigel. However, he tends to intellectualize Nigel's verbal play, focusing on the development of cohesion and information structure.
7. I cannot possibly do justice in this chapter to Vygotsky's highly condensed account of the development of imagination through early play and its implication for future higher-level mental operations. Of all the theorists I have mentioned in this book Vygotsky's description of imagination in play provides the most convincing explanation for the precocity, the ahead-of-development aspects, of my children's storying. Vygotsky's basic argument is that when children start to make one thing stand for another in play they begin to separate the meanings of things from the things themselves, thereby heralding a radical restructuring of their mental relationship to reality.
8. Piaget finds many aspects of Freud's theories of childhood development consistent with his own, but takes issue with the Freudian notion that the unconscious is the site of repressed affects. Piaget instead explains the unconscious character of much play as

springing from the elimination of the need for accommodation, and the primacy of assimilation. Although Vygotsky uses terms like 'wish-fulfilment', 'desire' and 'pleasure' he does not cite Freud at all in his account.

9. There are several other studies of baby-talk, e.g. Rogers (1976); Garnica (1977).

10. 'I have tried to suggest that the study of language may very well . . . provide a remarkably favourable perspective for the study of human mental processes' (Chomsky, 1968, p. 84). Lacan says something similar: 'What the psychoanalytic experience discovers in the unconscious is the whole structure of language' (1977, p. 147)
    There are several brief explanatory accounts of Lacan's theories. For readers who would like an introduction to Lacan's ideas, Wright (1984) and Coward and Ellis (1977) are particularly recommended.

11. Segments of dreams are referred to as 'clauses' and dream thoughts as having 'main' and 'dependent' clauses (pp. 425, 430, 450).

12. 'It is the world of words that creates the world of things . . . Man speaks then, but it is because the symbol has made him Man.' (Lacan, 1977, p. 65).

13. The illusionary 'ideal I' of Lacan's mirror-stage is an echo of Vygotsky's 'ideal I' which emerges in imaginary play.

14. See D. W. Winnicott, *Playing and Reality*. Winnicott sees the mirror-stage as a metaphor for the ways in which the mother, in handling, holding, and presenting objects to the baby, is 'giving back to the baby the baby's own self' (p. 138). See also Melanie Klein's essay 'Development Of A Child' in *The Writing of Melanie Klein*, 4 vols, Hogarth Press, London 1921–45. For Klein all accommodation to external reality is grounded in fantasy and affect. She sees fantasy as the earliest kind of mental operation, preceding language. Winnicott and Klein worked with children and developed play as a major therapeutic tool.

15. In his 1975 study Gardner used a traditional experimental methodology. 141 subjects, aged 3 to 19, were asked to complete a simile at the end of a story. We do not know how meaningful the subjects found the story. Tying the subjects down to one simile must have been a severe limitation on their composing. Gardner's concept of metaphor in this study is close to the Aristotelian one: a formal figure of speech. In the 1978 study Gardner changed from this concept, suggesting that stories, with their multiple layers of meaning, might be better candidates for the investigation of metaphoric capacities in children. He now observes children's spontaneous utterances in their *play*. Gardner notes in the 1978 study that 'there is a virtual void in the semantic sphere' of child language study, and argues that metaphor is so central to our use of language that it ought to be included in mainstream language acquisition studies.

16. This is a very interesting argument. Rumelhart points out that children have no way of distinguishing between literal and metaphorical terms in the early stages of language learning; the interpretation of literal language at the beginning must therefore depend on 'knowledge well beyond the definitions of the terms involved' (Rumelhart, 1979, pp. 81–2).

17. This is a very important article. It proposes that children's thinking in the early years is fundamentally metaphorical, and suggests that in language study there has been too great emphasis on the metonymic axis of language (the combinatorics of sentence structure) and not enough emphasis on the metaphoric. She gives some support to the Rumelhart/ Gardner position that metaphoric processing can be most clearly observed at the *discourse* level of utterances, particularly in role play (Walkerdine) and story (Rumelhart/ Gardner).

18. See Miller Mair (1976), which modifies Kelly's account of personal constructs as a 'psychology of man as a maker and user of metaphor' (p. 264). She regards metaphor-making as a way of 'entering the unknown through the gateway of the known' (p. 261). Kelly sees man as the scientist because he requires 'as if' thinking in order to learn, but Mair points out that 'as if' thinking is exactly what we do when we use metaphor (p. 273).

19. No student of play and language should ignore the rich studies of verbal duelling from around the world. Particularly illuminating are: Conklin (1964); Frake (1964); Abrahams

(1972a and 1972b); Albert (1972); Brown (1972); Dundes Leach and Ozkok (1972); Kochman (1972); Labov (1972); Mitchell-Kernan (1972); Bricker (1976); Gossen (1976); Sherzer (1976); Watson-Gegeo and Boggs (1977).

20. Leach (1964) suggests that the infant initially sees the world as an undifferentiated mass, and constructs an environment by naming the categories of things. What is *not* named (i.e. suppressed) is taboo.

Chapter 4

Learning to Use Words

concrete tinsel starfish snowdrifts chores furious sprinkle
decided cackled glittered appeared realized perished
radiator lanterns dynamite insects icicle normally actually
scolded mechanical-digger ordinary rusty tombstone astonished
dismay glowed disguise gnashing skill surrounded bargains
injured vanished hobble delicious instrument bagpipe cone   talcum
powder perfume precious stones jewels gobbled snatched
skeleton knight Vikings Scandinavia returned bored evil

The story data show that the five children had wide vocabularies of interesting and exciting words. The list above is composed of words taken at random from all the five children's stories, and each word was used conventionally in its context. Some of the words have a distinctly bookish feeling about them: 'dismay', 'astonished', 'perished' and 'scolded' are not as common in everyday conversation as they are in the pages of children's story-books, and indeed those particular examples were all transformations from book texts the children knew well. In many ways, though hundreds more examples could be added to it, this is not a particularly remarkable list. Teachers and parents know that children are capable of learning and using words which are very technical and scientific – the names of dinosaurs, for example – if the domain of those words is an interesting one. My belief is that if we think about children's vocabularies at all we are apt to think that rich ones consist of rather unusual or 'grown-up' terms used correctly. In the course of reading these stories many hundreds of times I have formed a different view. The words children know and can use properly and have command over are indeed evidence of their vocabularies, but the words that are used creatively, or experimentally, or playfully provide us with very useful evidence of several aspects of competences in action. They show us that children are prepared to invent, make up, transform from one grammatical function to another, define, explain and take risks with *language which is in the process of being acquired*. That children are prepared to do all these things with words is a reflection of their enormous interest in them, of their desire for mastery of new terms, of their appreciation of aspects of words other than their denotative meanings – the sound quality of them or their analogous aspects, for example. When we start to look at children's *creative* uses of words we see many examples of unconventional or even mistaken terminology, yet these 'errors', like miscues in reading aloud, are capable of revealing to us the active processes of learning in a way that the finished knowledge of conventionally used vocabulary never can. We can also see that denotative meanings are not the whole story in vocabulary acquisition, for the children often explore language in the ways that poets do, choosing words that are appropriate to the tune of the discourse, that have some aesthetic value, and that have enjoyable sound qualities. In this chapter I want to discuss not the words which automatically strike us as precocious, but those which are used in a slightly off-beat, disorderly or original way. The examples I shall give show that the children have at their disposal a whole range of means of making their narrative discourse ring true. In demonstrating these techniques I shall argue that creativity in child language is not only a matter of transforming combinatorial rules, as the psycholinguists have shown us, but is also a matter of bringing associative principles into play in assonance, alliteration, puns, jokes, repetitions – in other words, Jakobson's metaphorical dimension of language.

There are several important issues surrounding children's acquisition of new words. One of them is about the top-down/bottom-up view of language learning. Are words added to lexicons one by one, which is probably the commonsense view, or are they acquired often in larger chunks, perhaps as collections of terms surrounding particular semantic domains, or as *kinds* of words which are perceived to belong to particular discourses? If there is evidence of the latter, the 'top-down' view, then it accords with the proposals of Rumelhart and Walkerdine (see Chapter 3, p. 33), that associative, metaphorical principles are involved in children's competences in story and role-play discourses. Certainly I might expect data like these stories to yield such evidence. After all, the many story retellings in the data show that though the book language is often transformed to suit the child's competence at that stage of his/her development, nevertheless the words of the original seem to be recalled by the children as a whole linguistic unit – the act of telling the story brings all that vocabulary into play. We know that children take on new terminology if they meet it in meaningful contexts, and undoubtedly a great deal of new language must be acquired in this way; children learn all kinds of strange names for new chocolate bars or icecreams which they have particularly enjoyed, for example. But we need also to remind ourselves of the Urwin/Walkerdine argument of the last chapter, that the context for role-play language lies inside the discourse itself. I am suggesting that the children use words like 'perished' or 'dismay' because the practice of storytelling discourse calls up, spontaneously, that kind of vocabulary.

Another issue relating to children's idiosyncratic uses of words focuses on their tendency to employ a word from one grammatical category in the service of another. There are some interesting examples of this in my data. In her story 2 Sundari has her second narrator sing a song:

Oh I weared on the step   how I weary went   and I weared on the step so-o weary   as I weared on the step there was nothing I could do which was weary

Here Sundari has formed a verb 'to wear' from the adjective 'weary'. In another example Jimmy (*story 4*) transforms the noun 'icicle' into a verb participle 'icicled':

> it was a icicle car for icicled snowball person

In a long story ending, transformed from a book, Sundari summarizes all the actions of the narrative in a series of 14 negative constructions. Here is an extract (*story 7*):

> not play the bagpipes   not do the tambourine   not see the clown clown
> clown   not go on the swings not go on the fire-engine   not pick apples   not
> see the pigs   not see the horses   not swing swing   not see-saw-see-saw

Here she has used 'swing' and 'see-saw' as both noun and verb.

Although the children make use of their implicit syntactic competence here to manipulate grammatical forms into new words, they are doing it in a playful, even poetic, context; the grammatical transformations are part of the patterns of their word-play. Sundari's 'not swing swing' is grammatically conventional, but it is followed by 'not see-saw see-saw', a completely logical extension of the 'swing swing' but more original. Jimmy's 'icicled snowball person' is an unusual noun phrase by any standards, yet though it is original, it combines both explanatory power *and* poetic image. The invention of a verb 'to wear' is not accidental, nor a grammatical 'mistake'. Sundari enjoys the word, and likes to repeat it in different forms (it appears in several other stories). These three examples all involve the use of repetition because the children are attending to both *meaning* and *sound pattern* in their narrating. Clark (1982) looked at children's linguistic creativity in transferring words from one part of speech to another. After a lengthy analysis of children's coining of innovative denominal verbs, Clark believes that the children are not making intentional analogies but applying grammatical rules. For example, when the child uses a phrase like 'I'm going to pliers this out' for taking spaghetti from the pan with tongs, the child, believing 'pliers' to be the conventional term, transforms it into a verb by using syntactic knowledge. If this is the case the child is not making a deliberate analogy but a kind of semantic 'error'. I believe that this is to miss the point. My view is that when young children do not know the conventional term required they invent or coin new terms by combining grammatical knowledge with an associative or analogic principle. The new term will be syntactically appropriate, but will also, by its *metaphoric* or *phonological* properties, or both, be strongly associated with the intended meaning. I do not believe children think this through. It is a part of spontaneous play or experimentation with language – a way of discovering, on the hoof as it were, what language can do.

We know from a study by Hudson and Nelson (1984) that even very young children (aged 1:8 to 2:4) tend to 'over-extend' word-meanings analogically, using the word 'ball' for the sun, for example. Having first checked that the children knew the conventional names for a familiar set of objects, the researchers attempted to elicit re-namings in the course of pretend play. Additionally, mothers kept records of the children's spontaneous analogic extensions. The experimenters were able to identify 27 per cent of the children's re-namings as analogic. It seems that metaphorical principles are involved in language learning from the very beginning.

It must be said that in my data grammatical over-extensions are much more frequent than analogic ones. Most common are past tenses of irregular verbs formed by the addition of 'ed': 'goed', 'fighted', 'bursted' and 'litted' (as in 'he litted the cannon') are typical. Very ordinary verbs like 'to go' and 'to light' usually have correct past tenses but over-extensions still appear *alongside* these. More interesting are the children's experiments with irregular past tense forms, producing expressions like 'I've *sawn* [seen] them before', 'he *dag* [dug] through' and 'he pulled his knife out all of a sudden and *dagged* [stabbed] him'. There is certainly an analogic element in coining the verb 'to dag' to mean what is done with a dagger. Other past tense forms create difficulty for the children because they are part of unusual (for them) grammatical constructions: 'he was took off to hospital' and 'it can't get alived', in the first case an unfamiliar passive construction, and in the second the combination of a negative with the verb 'to come alive'. Also familiar in the literature and fairly common in my data are confusions about plurals. In one story Josh uses both 'mouses' and 'mices' alongside the conventional 'mice'. Other over-extended plurals are 'foods', 'wolfs', 'breads', 'yourselfs', and the reverse, '*a* water'. Another category of unconventional grammatical forms is related to the unfamiliarity of the *discourse* the children are engaged in. For example, '*there comed* the ball of the fairy'. Josh normally uses 'came' for the past tense of 'to come' but here he is trying a rather literary word order. Perhaps he had in his head the echo of a similar construction from one of his other stories: 'now *there glowed* a little light in the sky'. The latter was borrowed from the nativity play at school!

From time to time malapropisms appear in the stories. When they do they tend to be phonologically similar echoes of the correct term for the child's intended meaning. Rhyming is one principle for choosing the wrong word. 'Mr Whitelaw *required* [enquired] in the Commons' 'he looked through his *kaleidoscope* [telescope] and what did he see?', and, in a mock newsreading from Josh, 'from *Nonsenseland* to *Conscienceland*'. In other instances it is less easy to see the source of the child's mistake; for example, 'It was *humble* in the sea' (Sundari); 'Poppies will make them *grant*' (Josh); a 'her necklace *rustled*' (Sundari); 'he went through the town snatching *foolish* money for poor people' (Josh). Interestingly, there are fewer examples of these bizarre usages from the three younger children, though, in two story retellings from books, Robert, the youngest child, produces 'and they saw some breathing' and 'suddenly he heared a smell'. A simple explanation could be that the younger children utter fewer words *in toto*, so that there are fewer examples from them of many of the verbal phenomena described here. Another explanation seems more likely, since the younger children nevertheless produced very large samples of language. Perhaps they were less experienced in the narrative discourse of children's literature, and therefore less aware of the ways in which book language often sounds 'different' from everyday speech. After all, it would be reasonable to expect the 3- and 4-year-olds to make more linguistic 'errors', because they will be less experienced language users than 5-year-olds. But here, the reverse is true. Words like 'grant', 'humble', and 'foolish' are not very likely to be the common currency of 5-year-olds' conversations, but in books fairies and witches are always granting things, the sad little girls preferred by Sundari may well be described as 'humble', and 'foolish' is a very common term for characters in folk-tales.

Semantic errors of this kind occur infrequently, even when the two 5-year-olds are at their most adventurous and playful with words. Usually the language of the stories is characterized by usages which are not so much 'incorrect' as rather unusual or unconventional. These usages make the language of the stories colourful and interesting, but they are unlikely to be used by adult writers. Here are some examples:

> It *wasted* things [of a 'baddie'] (*Robert*)
> *Normally* he escaped (*Jimmy*)
> Now we are going to *collect* a 7-year-old (*Sundari*)
> Robin's got a *chest-ache* and Batman's got flu (*Josh*)
> some balloons *for smacking* (*Robert*)
> a *nearly crying* story (*Sundari*)
> lots of money to earn their *lives* (*Josh*)
> their hair was just looking *outspreaded* (*Josh*)

While all these examples are permissible, both syntactically and semantically, they are unusual enough to draw attention to themselves. Knowing what the conventions are, sadly, turns much of our adult language into cliché. Here we have children's creativity in using words before they know what the clichés are. Sundari's 'nearly crying story' is perfect for the kind of tale designed to bring a lump to the throat, and she stresses this by following the phrase with 'nearly nearly nearly'. Presumably the listener to such a story just manages to told back the tears! Josh's 'chest-ache' is not only a legitimate, if uncommon, complaint, but it also avoids repetition, being presumably in the same semantic domain as Batman's flu. To 'collect' a 7-year-old, along with all the other ingredients for a witch's stew, has a suitably sinister ring to it, and 'smacking' vividly describes what children like to do to blown-up balloons.

In considering original usages such as these – original in the sense that the children would not have heard these words used like this before – the question of intentionality arises. Did the children consciously intend to use language in original ways, or are these 'accidental', chancing to be grammatically and semantically appropriate? Certainly Josh's 'to earn their lives' may have been intended to be their 'livings', but the other examples have no such precedent phrases. In any case the terms in question seem too well-chosen to be accidental in any way. Meaning seems to have a greater priority than convention, and, not knowing the conventions, they coin terms like 'outspreaded' and 'chest-ache' on the basis of the words they already know. After all, we do talk about things being 'spread out', and we do use terms like 'back-ache' and 'tummy-ache'. And when Sundari's witch declares that she is going to 'collect a 7-year-old', she has already 'collected' all the items for the witch's brew in *Macbeth*. Using the same verb for 'dogs' tongues' and 'frogs' legs' as for a 7-year-old girl powerfully reduces the 7-year-old to something evil and rather disgusting.

In his study of the oral autobiographical stories of black adolescents in New York, Labov (1972) found that noun phrases consisting of collections of attributives were very rare. They do not appear often in the stories of the three younger children in my study, but are more frequent in the data from Josh and Sundari. Some of these phrases are standard for fairy tales: 'the wicked old witch'/'a big wicked grey wolf' (*Josh*). Phrases such as these are formulaic. They appear so frequently in the stories the children had heard that they are taken over and slotted into their own stories at the appropriate point. But the children are also able to invent their own attributive phrases, using a variety of techniques. Exaggeration is one way of amplifying a description. Robert, in retelling *Burglar Bill*, adds a couple of 'bigs' to the phrase 'a big brown box with little holes in it': 'a big big big brown box with little holes in it'. Another phrase he repeats several times in his version of *Little Black Sambo* is 'a big big tiger in the whole wide world'. Josh brings a whole collection of adjectives to his description of a giant: 'a big big fat tall heavy giant'. Some attributive phrases are conventional but not formulaic: 'a big deep road' (*Josh*); 'a little soft tune' (*Sundari*); 'a very nice pink door' (*Sundari*); 'the old rusty streets' (*Josh*); 'a furry white dog with lots of furs on it' (*Sundari*).

Other descriptive phrases are more detailed and original, sometimes requiring the addition of a dependent clause:

a special dentist underground who was magic (*Josh*)
flat round stones painted brown like biscuits (*Sundari*)
two bottles of nice fizzy tonic water—lemonade   lemonade sort of tonic water (*Sundari*)
a very high bit of a big wall that a castle would have (*Josh*)
special blocks and iron bars what the wolf couldn't break (*Josh*)
but they knew that there was a little house covered with sweets in the wood that had a big pine tree with wooden faces (*Josh*)

These attributives are both complex and exact, and involve the children in the production of sentences with a long grammatical span. They are not direct transformations from books, but they certainly employ the kinds of extended description to be found in books. The instances where the children do transform unusual descriptive passages from book texts indicate that it is books which have shown them how to do this. For example, one text of *Hansel and Gretel* which Josh knew very well reads:

as morning approached the little dewer man spread his dewdrops all around

This is transformed by Josh to:

as morning approached the little dewer man spread his dewdrops to meet the day

And, from another version of the same story, also known to Josh, the original has:

some white pebbles, which lay scattered around the house, shone like newly-minted silver coins

Josh's version is:

and he saw newly-coined silver money in the house

Both transformations are creative, in that Josh is able to render the original meanings in his own language.

The children are very creative in the invention of compound nouns, making verb participles and nouns do the work of adjectives:

pirate shipwreck has become the treasure under the sea (*Josh*)
he had to hobble over the *walking bridges* like this (*Sundari*)
she always got it even all the *marry things* [dressing-up clothes for wedding] (*Sundari*)
crawling insects (*Justine*)
a *woman lady* (*Robert*)
the *biggest bally bomb* in England (*Josh*)

When I asked Josh about the adjective 'bally', while he was telling his story, he explained it as 'a round one the same shape as a ball'. The clarity of this explanation shows a high level of metalinguistic awareness of his own word coinages.

Completely original word coinages, which are not transformations from one part of speech to another (as in 'bally'), occur in several stories where the children show that they enjoy playing around with pretend words. Their comments on their own inventions show that they know explicitly about the arbitrary nature of words, and that words have meanings which are agreed by convention and use. Usually some explanation of the new word is contained in the sentence where it appears:

> a big thing was after them *called a chooyda* (*Jimmy*)

> and he lived in a funny place *called hala* (*Jimmy*)

> I'm going to tell you another story about a boy this time a boy *called Clet-cher* a very funny name I made it up (*Sundari*)

> and they had two little babies the first one called *Mmmubble* and the second one called *Trrruggle* they're silly names aren't they? (*Sundari*)

Sundari bases a whole story on Edward Lear's *The Quangle-Wangle's Hat*. She does not use Lear's nonsense words but invents her own, giving explanations at the appropriate points in the narrative.

> Once upon a time there was a tree (not) but not an ordinary tree (P) a tree with eyes and ears and a mouth and a very round nose and this tree had legs and arms not ordinary arms (P) but brick arms it was called the quoggly woggly tree and it walked all about with the other quiggly quoggly trees and the quoggly quoggly trees now the quiggly quoggly trees are the girls and the quoggly quoggly trees are the boys

Sundari seems to have two strong perceptions about language in this story opening. One is that if you are going to invent words you must invent the things they denote – imaginary words must describe an imaginary world. (Jimmy also only uses invented words for his made-up monsters and their worlds.) The second perception is that nouns are sometimes differentiated by gender. The story continues:

> and this tree had a shopping basket called a cocking casket 'cos this was called this land Psulwa

At this point Sundari shows that rhyming with the original word is a principle for inventing a new one.

> (P) and they all sang a little song called 'Quiculapa it goes like this [sings] 'Qua-ku-ba-quo-pi-ko-ko-pe-ko-pe-quo-pe-ko' and it goes on like that and they have pencils called giggles goggles (P) see this land is a funny land and the hills and mountains are called kiggley coggles and they have houses shaped a diamond (P) with (P) triangle windows and square doors not oblong like you do have square ones (P) and they have (P) doormats on the very top of the house (P) and they have roses shaped as a (P) foot and they're called coggley cogs (P) and there was a girl who lived next door she was very frightened (P) she said 'Maybe I'll be one of them' so when she went in the house she turned to one and her house and all the things turned in it (P) and all the flowers even all the big ones in the world

> were called coggley coggle coggles boggles (P) and there was a bad witch
> called Sogulla what she done was sogged things

Here for the first time Sundari invents a verb, using the story technique of making
characters' names and actions match.

In another story about a witch Sundari explains a name in the same way: 'and her
name was Porridge she was called Porridge because she ate porridge'. Here it is
obvious that 'Sogulla' and 'to sog' are derived from the adjective 'soggy', a word Sundari obviously enjoyed in the same way as she liked the word 'weary'.

> but she didn't sog ordinary things she sogged the sky called the coggle kye
> (P) she sogged (P) the chairs called the pears and she sogged all sorts
> of things 'cos you see the tree but not the ordinary trees (P) loved soggy
> things so she turned everything soggy (P) and their houses I might have
> told you them but I think I've forgotten were called coggly woggly wogs
> (P) as I've got two names if I've told you if I haven't (P) they have got
> two names I'll just tell you the other one shoggly shoggly shogs (P) and
> they had radiators called cadi caculs and their lights weren't lights they
> were lanterns but called piggly poggly pogs (P) and when they saw little
> insects called poolze they said 'tiddly tiddly widdle' all of the words in here
> are funny aren't they? (*Sundari*)

Sundari's 'funny' words on the whole follow the pattern of Lear's, with two rhyming
words of two syllables followed by a third non-rhyming word of one syllable (e.g.
Quangle Wangle Quee/Piggly Poggly Pogs).

The children's explicit knowledge that words have definitions is not only reflected
in their invented language, but also in their conventional usages. Very often a term
brings some kind of definition or explanation along with it. In one story Josh addresses
his imagined audience:

> 'Do you know why they were poor? because they had no money'.

In another story he offers his audience a synonymous phrase:

> and then (he -um (P)) Fereyal nearly got his life cut off *'cut off' that's
> another word for getting his life cut down*

Justine offers the listener a proper definition for a word she thinks might be
unfamiliar:

> and then a monster came to that road a huge monster *it was called a
> hooligan and that is a dragon*

In a retelling of *Hansel and Gretel* Josh takes over a piece of dialogue between Gretel
and the witch which is specifically concerned with the definition of terms:

> Gretel: you leave my brother alone
> Witch: now is that any way to talk to a friend?
> Gretel: *a friend doesn't tie someone up with a rope*

A rhetorical device often used by Sundari in addressing her audience is the narrator's
assumption that words will not need explanations because the listener already knows
them:

as you know what also means
now you know what annoyed means

Other terms are not defined but defining characteristics are given alongside the word:

one day the two girls had a other *instrument* and they played it like this *it
was called a piano* (Sundari)

In a story of Josh's God and St Peter are discussing the properties of heavenly clouds, which are solid and encrusted with jewels. St Peter says:

Oh I thought clouds were *just ordinary clouds that you could fall through*

Josh explains a rainbow as well as referring to one:

except it was rainy and it was sunny so a rainbow came

Occasionally the children lack terminology necessary to tell the story. In a story about mummies in a museum Josh has to be explicit about the cloths mummies are wrapped up in:

and we pulled the string he came whizzing out and then he was just to
bits he wasn't to bits he was just in a piece of string and a *piece of that
flat rope that they are tied up in*

In a retelling of *Hansel and Gretel* Josh gets into a muddle because, although he has an understanding of the term 'wife' he seems to have forgotten its counterpart 'husband', a term he uses correctly in many other stories:

(and- and suddenly) and suddenly (they they um-um) their wife died and
they had to get a new one and married her but as she became her wife she
got much more wicked and didn't like the woodcutter (and) for being her
wife . . .

It is quite possible that the confusion here is one of pronoun use rather than husband/wife terminology, but if that is the case it certainly does not happen in other stories. Six months later this passage, in yet another version of *Hansel and Gretel*, is rendered as:

(and) and then their mother died and (after) after their mother died at Easter
their Daddy married a new one but this new one wasn't very kind

In the oral tradition of folk-tales, which gets written down in many stories for young children, lists of various kinds play a prominent part. Items may be grouped together on the basis of similarity, or on the basis of difference, or sometimes a group of words belonging to one general semantic domain will contain within it much that is diverse and different. Eric Carle's picture book *The Very Hungry Caterpillar* is a good example. While all the things the caterpillar eats on different days of the week can be linked together as 'food', nevertheless the food items are as distinct from one another and as interesting as the author can make them. Children enjoy classifying things as belonging to superordinate or subordinate groups, and my five children do this in their storytelling. They seem to be good at putting words from the same semantic domain together, sometimes as synonyms, but more often as items in a related group. We have already seen an example of this in Sundari's nonsense story, where, in order to describe topsy-turvey houses, she uses the terms *oblong*, *square*, *diamond*, and *triangle* all in one sentence. In a series of stories about an under-the-ground terrain Josh uses three different terms – *passageways*, *tunnels* and *underground* – and in one of his retellings of *Hansel and Gretel* he borrows a set of words to describe ways of crossing over water: *bridge*, *boat* and *stile*. It is logical that when children hear stories with specific settings and themes they should take on whole groups of words together. Foodstuffs, as in Eric Carle's story, are one example. Josh has the witch in *Hansel and Gretel* put 'pancakes and sugar and eggs and wine' on the children's supper table, though the original version has 'milk and pancakes with sugar, apples and nuts'. In another invented story a bear goes shopping for dinner:

> 'shall I get (some) some turkey for you for dinner in the market and some carrots and brussels sprouts and potatoes and turkey? Do you like that?' 'Yes, and some stuffing'

Justine particularly likes lists. In one story she has a mother bird listing for her baby all the dangers outside the nest:

> she said 'there's wolves out there and foxes and ugly lions (and) (P) and other sort of things that will eat the birds (and) (P) and crawling insects (P) and spiders and witches (P)

Still on the topic of eating, she has a monstrous bird in another story consume the entire world. In this list there is a pattern as she moves from items which are close to the child to those which are more global:

> Do you know what? he ate all the houses up too the concrete and all the books and all the curtains and all the glass and all the tinsel (and all- and-and) and all the teachers and all the schoolchildren and he ate their school he ate islands and water sea and star-fish and fish like that (and) and everything even the whole world

Another category of items for lists is treasure, again familiar in stories for children. At the end of an adventure story Josh has the Mayor give rewards to all the boys who took part:

> he gave Joshua his chain and David (um-his) his cup and he gave Jimmy (P) (his) his golden plate and he gave Malcolm (um) his magic ring and he gave (um-um) (P) [*Adult*: Paul?] Paul Grimmer (P) (um-um) a golden magic necklace

Here is another list from Josh, this time the contents of a pirate's treasure trove. The items are not all precious, but, in Josh's eyes at least, they are all glamorous:

> do you know what they saw (in) in their treasure box?   necklaces perhaps and perfume (and a broo-) and a brooch (and) and a crown (and- and beautiful- and) and all sorts of lovely things to have and lipstick

Though these kinds of list appear in written stories the children knew they tend to fill them with items of their own. In a retelling of a non-fiction book, *Vikings* by S. Oram, Josh gives a list of weapons:

> but for fighting they had helmets, weapons (and) and shields

In an invented story where some robbers find weapons in a castle the list is:

> (they) they found pistols and rifles and spears and all sorts of other weapons

Sundari invents her own list of different dances:

> she did tap dancing ordinary dancing Dutch dancing all kinds of dancing   I'll tell you all the ones if I remember (P)   she did (P) Swedish dancing (P)   she did maypole dancing um) all kinds . . .

> they did outside dancing   they did (tap) tap shoes   they was tapping (on the) on the concrete   and (P) they did somersault dances cartwheel dances head-over-heel dances all sorts of dances

The names of most of these dances are unconventional, and are made up by Sundari on the basis of her knowledge of how dances are named.

The children use groups of words belonging to a particular semantic domain to give coherence to the information structure of their narrations. This is especially true of the imitation newsreadings and weather forecasts invented by Josh. In his first newsreading Josh uses language that he obviously does not understand but which he knows belongs to the news:

> the *prime minister* says (er) *Mr Michael Foot* has *presented Mrs Thatcher* (er-er) to go to *Ireland* for her *produce*

A few months later, in newsreadings and weather forecasts, Josh is using the same kind of language for comic effect:

> in *Australia* there has been a *failure*

> Fulham won Newcastle yesterday and the other day Newcastle won Newcastle

> somewhere in *Australia* a hundred *bargains* has been cut off by *Thatcher   Mr Whitelaw required* in the *Commons* today and said 'I beg this' (very plummy voice) 'we have lost hundreds of pounds'

> at *London* it was *lovely and warm*   at *Newcastle incidentally* the (trem-the temp-tremp-temp) temperature has gone up to (sixty) *sixty degrees*

Lists are not only used for comic effect but also for the power of the juxtaposition of certain items to shock:

> and they went into a toyshop   Julie had a dolly   David had a mechanical dig-ger   Joshua had the biggest bomb in the world

Sundari uses the same technique in adding human parts to the animal ones she has transformed from *Macbeth*:

> and what she ate in her porridge was frogs' legs dogs' tongues (P) and (P) tch-tch-tch hedgehogs' prickles   and (P) it was horrid porridge   and they ate *people's hair and people's legs*

What conclusions can we draw from these rather unusual uses of words, and are there any implications for education? The examples I have given here certainly do imply that words are often absorbed as packages of whole sentences, or phrases, or lists and that children put them together into categories or chunks of their own. Children who hear a lot of stories read from books, or a lot of news broadcasts may well start to use some unfamiliar words before they understand what they mean. These children show great awareness of the phonological properties of words, producing rhymes and rhythms effortlessly. They know how to manipulate their grammatical knowledge to form new words, or to coin unusual noun phrases. They also have explicit knowledge that words have meanings, that meanings are conventional, and that unconventional words will need to be accompanied by definitions. The children take great pleasure in words, repeating their favourite words and playing with them. They are prepared to take risks with new words which they take every opportunity to try out.

Perhaps the major implication for school is that children need to be surrounded by rich language, adult language, written language and do not need to be as protected from unusual or 'difficult' terminology as some teachers of young children think. They do not need language to be confined to what is familiar. If they are to become interested in and excited about words they will need the stimulus of constantly meeting new ones, especially in their books.

This is not to say that children will benefit from reading books which are full of incomprehensible words. But when there is a strong story, especially one which is familiar to the child (as in folk- and fairy-tales) children can hold onto the story while taking in all kinds of strange words and the structures of language in writing.

Another implication, one which applies to every aspect of this study, is that children need many repetitions of their favourite stories. This gives them the chance to unpick the details and learn the meanings for terms which were unfamiliar at first. If the text is read unaltered, with no changes to make it 'easier', the children also have a chance to hear rhythmic, patterned language which has a poetic structure.

It is through playing with rhythms and patterns that the children in my study were able to explore language and learn to take risks with it. Songs and poems seem to have been tremendously important to Josh and Sundari. They both invent little verses from time to time, as though the invitation to narrate naturally led them in this direction. The last story session of all from Josh which I included in the data collection took place when he was 6:1. He started to retell *Hansel and Gretel*, then abandoned it half-way through, and moved into a retelling from a story called *Ferreyal and Debbo-Engal the Witch*, an African folk-tale which strongly resembles *Hansel and Gretel*, and which I had read him a few times. He stays extraordinarily closely to the original text using new phrases like 'with practised skill'. The last line of the story is 'the python perished', a pleasingly alliterative phrase, which he remembered and followed with 'and that's the erished – the end'. This little bit of word play then leads him on to a whole string of nonsense poems, weather forecasts, newsreadings and anything he could think of to lampoon. Play with words employs all kinds of linguistic knowledge, and, because it's play, there are no 'right' and 'wrong' consequences. Children need this if they are to discover the pleasure of making language do what *you* want it to do. There are probably spin-offs for reading competences, too, for in their meticulously carried out study Bradley and Bryant (1984) show that phonological awareness (as in rhymes, rhythms, and patterns of words) is a clear predictor of later reading success in 5-year-olds.[7]

   As teachers we need to show our own interest in words, our own pleasure and delight in them. We need to receive children's strange usages and experiments positively, seeing in them an affirmation of the child's linguistic awareness and the creative nature of competences.

   In this chapter I have tried to show that children's word choices are significant and can tell us a lot about the child's ability to use language inventively and to put to use what has been first encountered in books. But there are many other aspects of the children's narrative discourse which lie well beyond the level of the word. Just as the children are experimental with words, so they are experimental with phrases and sentences. One of the questions I asked myself at the beginning of the study was whether the children's obvious sense of style meant that different kinds of sentence structure were associated in their minds with different kinds of discourse. This is the topic of the next chapter.

Chapter 5

Special Features of Phrases and Sentences

1 once upon a time there was a little girl
2 and her name was Mandolin
3 (she liked) she said to her mother 'Mumma Mumma I would like to (P) have a picnic'
4 and what she took was a paper bag which her mummy had wrapped up (P) with some (P) stones in painted like raisins round stones (P)
5 and she took them and put them into her bag (*Sundari story 1*)

My study was not intended to be an exploration of syntactic competences, a well-trodden field, yet from the beginning I felt that the sentences in the children's stories were often unusual in several respects. I noticed quite a high incidence of multi-clause sentences with several embedded dependent clauses, like the fourth sentence of Sundari's story opening above. I knew, too, that sometimes these grammatically complex sentences were constructed in rather sophisticated ways for such young speakers; for example, starting a sentence with a noun clause in the subject position, as Sundari does in the same sentence. I found that word order in phrases and sentences was often as 'strange' as the children's lexical choices; book language echoed through structures like *and still the town she hated* (Sundari) where the common subject/verb/object is rearranged. I also observed that the children had at their disposal many ways of expressing negatives, again giving a rather literary style: *but not any sound could they hear* (Josh). Possessives, I found, were usually expressed in the common way by the possessive 's': *her daughters' throats, God's palaces, their father's cottage*, yet Josh particularly often preferred a genitive construction with 'of': *that was the house of a very bad woman.* I knew from the extensive literature on language acquisition that I should not be surprised at children's grammatical competences, but I also knew, from the work of Perera and others, that the discourses of writing often entailed unfamiliar constructions which were acquired through reading and education.[1] I set out to discover whether I could find any connection between the discourse of narrative and particular features of the children's language at the phrase and sentence levels.

I was aware that a full grammatical analysis of 46,000 words, single-handed, was not a possibility, and would preclude my using other more productive and relevant analytic tools. I knew, too, that the children's language could be striking and unusual when it was not grammatically complex, for stories consist of strings of sentences where short structures can be as effective as long and complex ones. Consider this story opening from Josh:

1 there was a farm
2 it had many horses in
3 and it had many calves and sheep
4 now all the small pigs were in their barns
5 it was a rainy day (*Josh story 2*)

None of these sentences is remarkable for its grammar, yet this passage has the measured rhythm and careful lexical choices I associated with talking in the manner of books. Here Josh makes little use of the connective 'and', but there were some stories which used it so frequently that one sentence would constitute the entire narrative. Making a T-Unit analysis of the story material overcame this problem. Hunt (1964, 1965) defined a T-Unit as consisting of 'one main clause with all the subordinate clauses attached to it'. A main clause connected to another by 'and' would therefore become a new T-Unit. Sundari's story 1 and Josh's story 2, quoted above, are divided into T-Units. The reader will see that three of Sundari's T-Units and one of Josh's start with the connective 'and'. This procedure was simple, well-defined and particularly helpful for my narrative data, where one could expect extensive use of common connectives like 'and', 'so' and 'then'. It would also give me a reference system for a very large data collection.

Using a T-Unit analysis to make discoveries about the children's syntactic competences had the advantage that there were several large-scale studies which had adopted this procedure, thus giving a basis for comparison: Loban (1963–76), Hunt (1964, 1965) and O'Donnell, Griffin and Norris (1967). Loban and O'Donnell *et al.* had included children of kindergarten age. All the studies had focused on the development of sentence-combining transformations, and they established a correlation between length of T-Unit and syntactic complexity (O'Donnell *et al.*, 1967).[2] T-Unit length (i.e. syntactic complexity) was also found to increase with age. If the children in my study were using unusually long T-Units several factors might be implicated. Perhaps they were exceptionally advanced language users. In that case I could expect the mean T-Unit length of their language to correspond to the scores of high ability language users in the other studies. Loban had carefully divided his subjects into high and low ability language users, so there were comparative data.

Another more interesting hypothesis was that long-T-Units might be related to the particular discourse of this study: narrative. The earlier studies had rigorously controlled their data collection to minimize the effect of the large number of variables inherent in eliciting language from children. Little attention had been given to the context for language production in these studies, to the extent that Loban had used an interview/question technique with the younger children in his study, while O'Donnell had asked his subjects to retell the story of a short film. O'Donnell did make a passing nod towards the possibility of variation in different discourse modes (p. 87), but he was content to ascribe the slightly higher T-Unit scores of his subjects to their superior socio-economic rating (p. 46).

A later study of 16-year-old pupils' writing by Rosen (1969) gave grounds for hypothesizing a strong link between discourse mode and T-Unit length. Of Hunt's study of writing Rosen comments (p. 172): '[Hunt] does not consider the possibility that for one and the same writer there might be significant differences in T-Unit length as he engages in quite different verbal strategies'. Rosen also observed that for the same pupil there could be a greater difference in the mean T-Unit lengths of two pieces of writing than Hunt found in a four-year maturity gap. I was aware, therefore, that *range* of T-Unit length, varying with the speaker's intentions and the discourse in operation, was as important as T-Unit length *per se*.[3]

The technicalities of T-Unit segmentation need not concern us too much here, but it is worth outlining the very simple procedures involved. Basically the total number of words in a story is divided by the total number of T-Units to give a mean T-Unit length for each narrative. However, nothing is quite as simple as that, and some rules were needed for what would count in the word total and what would not:

- *Garbles* are placed in parentheses and excluded from the word count. Garbles are unintentional false starts and groping for words which are characteristic of some adult and child speakers. Garbles are not related to syntactic proficiency, but in a transcript they can distract from the overall structure of the narrative. Here is an example (*Josh story 18*):

  he was walking down the street (P) (and he was – and he- he- and-and-and Joshua and Julie- Julie and David- Julie right in the middle of-holding)

  In this example only the underlined words are included in the T-Unit, which thus consists of six words.
- False starts, and non-deliberate repetitions, are excluded from the word count (*Josh story 1*):

  (the) the bad people threw nails on (till) till he died

- Audible pauses, such as 'um' and 'er' are excluded from the word count.
- Contractions, such as *'don't'* are counted as one word. In earlier studies these counted as two words, because the focus was on syntax *per se*. I count them as one because my focus is on *writing-like* syntax, which would tend to use the uncontracted form.
- Compound and hyphenated words are counted as one word, though other studies count them as two. However, I saw no harm in a conservative word count to strengthen the hypothesis that these children use long T-Units.
- Dialogue is included in the analysis. It was excluded from the earlier studies because of the distorting effect of one-word utterances. I decided to count these as one-word T-Units even though they would reduce mean T-Unit lengths. Dialogue in narrative constitutes a discourse within a discourse. Skill in using it is as much part of narrative competence as syntactic complexity. Where dialogue is tagged with narrative as in *The boy said 'yes Daddy'*, the tag and the first main clause of dialogue is counted as one T-Unit. Subsequent main clauses of dialogue in a continuing speech become new T-Units. For example (*Josh story 32*):

37 and she said in a loud in a grumbling voice 'I'm going to get that boy (16)
38 'I'm gonna leave that boy in that cage (to-when-he) till he's fat (11)

39 and when he's fat I'm gonna eat him' (8)

- All conversation with adults before, during, or after narrations is excluded from the T-Unit analysis. The children indicated clearly when they were temporarily leaving the story by quite dramatic changes of intonation.
- The data from Josh include some distinct genres (poems, news broadcasts, weather forecasts and one pre-sleep monologue when he was unaware of being recorded). The poems are excluded from the T-Unit analysis of narratives, since they are announced by Josh as 'poems' not stories. The other prose forms are included, since they are narrative in form. Separate analyses of these genres were made. Poems and songs in Sundari's stories *are* included in her analysis because they are an intrinsic part of her story, often continuing to tell the tale. Indeed, Sundari sings one entire story!

I shall now present the results of my analyses in the order in which I arrived at them, thereby reflecting the evolution of my thinking. Each analysis arose from a hypothesis generated by the results of the previous analysis. The initial hypothesis, based on my observations of the children's language in their stories, was that *they would be found to produce unusually long mean T-Unit lengths in their narratives.* To arrive at final mean T-Unit lengths I combined word totals and T-Units totals for all narratives told on the same storytelling occasion. I then calculated a mean T-Unit length for those stories taken together. In turn I further combined total words and total T-Units for the same month of storytelling, giving me a mean T-Unit length for that month of storytelling (see Table 5.1). The advantage of this progressive analysis is that it clearly showed variations within storytelling sessions, between storytelling sessions and from month to month as the child got older.

On the face of it, these results are quite startling, placing pre-school children, who had not been regarded as linguistically precocious, several years ahead of their age in

Table 5.1 *T-Unit analysis of narrative monologues of five children*

	Josh	Sundari	Justine	Jimmy	Robert
Age	5:0–6:1	5:4–5:7	4:1–5:2	4:9	3:7–4:1
Total no. stories	73	19	30	20	26
Total words	24164	7195	2613	2308	3854
Total T-Units	2910	799	305	281	585
Mean T-Unit	8.3	9.0	8.5	8.2	6.7
Range of mean T-Unit length	6.1–13.3	5.9–13.6	6.2–14.2	6.4–15.0	5.1–9.7

Table 5.2

	Age range/mean age	Mean T-Unit length	Range of T-Unit
Loban, 1976	5:0–6:0	6.8	6.00–8.00*
O'Donnell *et al.*, 1967	5:10	7.07	4.00–9.5

*high-ability group

development. The results certainly do not 'match' those of other T-Unit studies. The comparison of my results with Loban's and O'Donnell's shows the scores for my five children to be considerably higher, even though three of my children are between one and two years younger than their subjects (Table 5.2). Since the earlier studies collected data from children across the age range, the comparison also places each of my children several years ahead in development. It is also noticeable that the ranges of T-Unit length are much greater for my children. I tended to favour the context and the discourse mode in my study as the explanation for my results, since my children seemed to be both well ahead of Loban's higher ability group, and well ahead of O'Donnell's higher socio-economic group (of whom my children were probably the equivalent). My analysis, in fact, was producing similar findings to Rosen's analysis of writing: a greater *range* of T-Units for one subject than for a whole age range in the earlier studies.

I had noticed during the analysis that dialogue sections of the stories often contained very short T-Units, which tended to reduce mean T-Unit length scores for that story. Using exactly the same procedures as for the overall analysis, I then marked all T-Units in the transcripts containing dialogue separately, and performed a specific analysis of these. The new hypothesis was that *dialogue T-Units would be shorter than narrative ones*, indicating that the children had instinctively conceptualized the difference between speech and non-speech narration. These results are given in Table 5.3.

Table 5.3

	Josh	Sundari	Justine	Jimmy	Robert
Narrative minus dialogue	8.5	9.4	8.3	8.2	6.2
Narrative with dialogue	8.3	9.0	8.5	8.2	6.7
Dialogue	7.4	7.0	13.4	8.0	5.8
Difference between dialogue and narrative	− 1.1	− 2.4	+ 5.1	− 0.2	− 1.0

Table 5.3 shows that the hypothesis is correct for Josh, Sundari and Robert, is unconfirmed for Jimmy, since it makes virtually no difference to mean T-Unit lengths in his stories, and is reversed quite dramatically for Justine. When I scrutinized the dialogue sections of Jimmy's and Justine's stories I found that they had used dialogue very sparingly indeed compared to the other three children. In fact, dialogue represents just over 5 per cent of Justine's T-Units, and just under 8 per cent of Jimmy's, whereas for Josh and Robert dialogue constitutes more than 20 per cent of the T-Units and for Sundari more than 16 per cent. A close inspection of Justine's data showed that the high T-Unit mean for her dialogue sections is explained by just two stories in which characters do *not* have conversations but rather make speeches. By this I mean that there is none of the *turn-taking* of conversation represented in Justine's stories. A similar pattern was found to be true of Jimmy's stories, where there are several narratives containing only one long speech from a character. I speculated that in real conversation children would always be involved in a reciprocal situation, whereas in the representation of speech in a story dialogues would need to be more explicit since words and intonation alone would need to take on the burden of the situational context. Would the children's conversations with their parents give different, shorter

Table 5.4 *T-Unit analysis of conversation for four children*

	Total words	Total T-Units	Mean T-Unit length
Josh	1606	307	5.2
Justine	609	120	5.0
Jimmy	171	28	6.1
Robert	795	196	4.0

T-Unit lengths than those of the representation of speech in stories? A third hypothesis thus appeared: that *the T-Units of ordinary conversation would be shorter than dialogue T-Units in stories*. Unfortunately, there was no conversation at all on Sundari's tapes, but for the other four children I separated their conversation with parents and performed a T-Unit analysis of it, using exactly the same procedures as before (Table 5.4).

It is now clear that there is a considerable drop in T-Unit length between narrative as a whole and conversation. The difference in mean T-Unit length between the two is as follows:

Robert: −3.3   Jimmy: −2.1   Justine: −3.3   Josh: −3.3

Only one score, Jimmy's, comes within the *range* of mean T-Unit lengths given by Loban for high ability language users, the others are a little below. Loban based his findings on conversational data. All four are well within the range given by O'Donnell, whose data were narrative. If the children's scores seem low compared to other studies, it must be remembered that conversations in different settings, with different interlocutors and different functions, will almost certainly vary. In these conversations, all with parents, there is quite a high question/answer content, and, as answers to questions are often elliptical, this could give shorter T-Units. However, the children's scores for narrative show that very long T-Units were within their competences, indicating that the discourse mode might make a difference.

At this point I began to scrutinize the data from Josh, which contained a number of distinct discourse categories. There were imitation news broadcasts and weather forecasts, 13 invented 'poems', and one pre-sleep monologue which took a narrative form. My next hypothesis was that *T-Unit analyses of these genres would show a possible relationship between length of T-Unit and discourse category* (Table 5.5).

Table 5.5 *Mean T-Unit lengths in all discourse categories from Josh*

	Total words	Total T-Units	Mean T-Unit length	Total monologues
News/Weather	834	85	9.8	5
Poems	738	82	9.0	13
Narratives without dialogue	19663	2305	8.5	69
Dialogue in narratives	4501	603	7.4	69
Pre-sleep monologue	328	50	6.5	1
Conversation	1606	307	5.2	–

The mean T-Unit length for news/weather broadcasts is very high. It is identical to the mean given by O'Donnell for his subjects in Grade 7 (age 12/13). The *range* for Josh of 8.8 to 13.3 is almost the same as O'Donnell's range for Grade 7 *writing*. For narrative, Sundari has the highest mean T-Unit length of the five children. One might be justified in supposing that Josh's competences in T-Unit length were less well-developed than hers. However, given the opportunity to use another genre, Josh produces a consistently higher score than all the children's narrative scores.

The summary of Josh's mean T-Unit lengths for genre categories is suggestive of differences of formality both in the situation of the utterances and in Josh's perception of the structure of each kind of discourse. Conversation and pre-sleep monologues are informal discourses. In the first, a shared context between mother and child allows for utterances to be elliptical and unelaborated. In the second there is no interlocutor at all, neither a parent nor (to Josh's knowledge) a tape-recorder; the child is talking entirely to himself and imposes little structure on what he says. Although he is telling himself stories he knows, they all blend into one another.[4] At the other end of the formality/informality continuum are the narratives, poems and news broadcasts. Here a certain amount of role-playing is implicit in the situation, for the child has to invent himself as newsreader, poet, storyteller. He must signal these roles by using the formal characteristics which his experience tells him marks these genres.

The results of these T-Unit analyses suggest that the children perceive the need for elaboration in their utterances to differ according to the conversational situation (dialogue or monologue), and according to the genre chosen. The models available to the children for stories, poems and news broadcasts were *written* forms, even though they had all been communicated orally by reading aloud. In Loban's and O'Donnell's studies length of T-Unit correlated with syntactic complexity, and I needed to find out if my children's sentences were long because they were grammatically complex, or if other factors accounted for variations in T-Unit length.

My procedures for looking at the construction of the children's sentences were again simple. I defined a long T-Unit as one consisting of 12 or more words. Because the large amount of data from Josh would unbalance my findings I used only the first 30 stories from him. This gave a total number of T-Units which was comparable to the data from Sundari: 799 for Sundari, 777 for Josh. I then scrutinized all the T-Units from all the five children consisting of over 12 words to see if a set of categories would emerge which could explain their length. Ten categories emerged clearly:

1. *Dependent clauses*

   but the boy did play on his ice skates on the ice which was a puddle which was ice turned in ice (22) *Sundari*

2. *Narratized speech* (sometimes called indirect speech)

   his mother and father said he could go to the fair one day (13) *Sundari*

3. *Reported speech*

   'Now' said the nurse 'You never do that in the middle of the night' (15) *Josh*

4. *Passive*

a little Bo-Peep story was a long time ago told by a little girl (14) *Sundari*

5. *Co-ordinating clauses*

but Spiderman just stayed there (and) and got the Incredible Hulk into his rubber sack (and) and took him along (to) to the police station (22) *Josh*

These five categories all involve some kind of grammatical transformation. However, children's stories borrow from the oral tradition, which has other ways of making long T-Units:

6. *Lists* (of nouns or attributes)

he ate islands and water sea and star-fish and fish like that and everything even the whole world (18) *Justine*

7. *Formulae* (ready-made phrases taken from songs and stories)

so when she had the baby they went all rolling rolling over the hills and over the mountains and far away over the chimneys and far away (27) *Sundari*

8. *Repetition*

they went as high and low and high and low and high and low (14) *Sundari*

9. *Topic*
This category is identified by Loban (1963, p. 14).[5] The subject of the T-Unit is given twice, so either the first or second mention of the subject is redundant.

so *they* went to the master *the policeman and the two Paddingtons* (12) *Josh*

10. *Unclassified*
Some T-Units are 12+ words long but do not fit any of the above categories. Usually they contain one or two attributives.

well other police there was a wicked old witch in that forest (12) *Josh*

It will be obvious to the reader that these ten categories will sometimes overlap, and that this categorization cannot therefore be a strictly scientific enterprise. A T-Unit can contain a dependent clause and a list for example. In such cases I had to decide which of the two categories gave more length to the T-Unit, and this was usually fairly obvious. Having given all the T-Units of over 12 words a category I was able to draw up a table showing where the length of the children's sentences tended to come from (Table 5.6).

Table 5.6 shows clearly that, even for the youngest child, Robert, the majority of the long T-Units is accounted for by grammatical complexity. This confirms the relationship between length of T-Unit and syntactic structure found in the earlier studies. For all the children *dependent clauses* are the dominant category.

Of course, young children do not think in terms of long and short T-Units, though they sometimes spin out their lists and repetitions in a fairly deliberate way. Perhaps it is more helpful to think of the ten categories in terms of the oral and the written. A high degree of syntactic complexity, use of the passive, and of reported and nar-

Table 5.6   *Analysis of T-Units of 12+ words into 10 categories* (figures are a percentage of the total T-Units of 12+ words)

Category	Sundari	Josh	Justine	Jimmy	Robert
1	56.4	52.0	60.4	58.1	34.7
2	0.6	3.1	2.3	4.6	–
3	4.2	8.3	9.3	4.6	4.3
4	0.6	–	–	–	–
5	4.9	26.0	4.6	6.9	21.7
%	**66.7**	**89.4**	**76.6**	**74.2**	**60.7**
6	22.6	5.2	18.6	18.6	17.3
7	5.5	–	–	–	13.0
8	3.0	–	–	2.3	6.5
9	–	2.0	–	2.3	2.1
10	1.8	3.1	4.6	2.3	–

ratized speech, are not exclusive to written language but are strongly associated with it (O'Donnell, 1974).[6] On the other hand, lists, formulae and repetitions are characteristics of the oral tradition of narration (Ong, 1982).[7] The analysis of Robert's 12+ T-Units suggests that he, younger than the other children, is closer to the oral tradition, while they are moving towards the language of writing. In Robert's stories the oral tradition is reflected in his choice of stories to retell: *Burglar Bill, The Three Little Pigs* and *Sam Who Never Forgets* are high in repetitive oral formulae. The authors' use of these traditions in their writing provides children a perfect bridge from oracy to literacy.

The non-appearance of a category in Table 5.6 does not mean that it is not within the competence of the child. The outstanding example of this is in the data from Josh, where no passives appear in 12+ T-Units in his first 30 stories, though they do occasionally appear in shorter T-Units and in later stories. However, in Josh's news broadcasts passive constructions appear in 4 out of a total of 16 T-Units of 12+ words. There are 8 passive constructions all together, the other 4 consisting of shorter T-Units. Here are some examples:

> and she *was found dead* in the bath because that little person (P) who smashed into Finchale Hall got her (19)

> somewhere in Australia a hundred bargains *has been cut off* by Thatcher (12)

> Mr Whitelaw said that all the rates of Thatcher's money *must be taken* to Carol Fox (16)

Passives occur rarely enough in Josh's narratives, and in those of the other children, for one to be justified in assuming that this is a later syntactic development and not yet fully in the children's competences.[8] Yet *here it is associated with a specific genre*; it only appears in news broadcasts, not weather forecasts, which, in their turn, have their own syntactic characteristics. This is quite an important finding of the T-Unit analysis, for its implication is that if we wish to evaluate children's linguistic competences we must give them the opportunity to operate in a range of discourses.

Every T-Unit of 12+ words in Josh's imitation weather forecasts seems to follow a grammatical formula which will be recognizable to anybody who has ever listened to a forecast. The future tense is consistently used, though it is rare in narratives, which on the whole employ the past tense. There are also large collections of noun phrases which are about location ('at the South and West ear of Australia') or are attributive ('some more rain and cloud', 'very nice and warm').[9]

I want to be very clear about the implications arising from these rather laborious analyses. If we are interested in children's syntactic competences, the findings show that for these five children narrative discourse entails the use of sentences with long grammatical spans and complex structures. Other discourses will certainly give opportunities for utterances of similar complexity, but narrative discourse appears to be a rich seam. However, the mark of the good storyteller lies in variety and range of sentence structure. The children can be very powerful storytellers when they are using a whole series of short simple sentences, or representing the chatty elliptical nature of speech in the dialogue sections of their stories. It is pointless to value syntactic complexity for its own sake – after all a story told in long, complex sentences can be a very dull affair. In these narratives the syntactically complex sentences seem to be linked to two major narrative functions. The first is the necessity for the story to be explicit, for everything to be fully explained. The following T-Units are good examples of the explanatory force of certain multi-clause sentences:

> and she gave her some egg sandwiches which were really the stones and which the bread sandwiches were really little flat round stones made like a little biscuit which she put colours in brown as well (*Sundari story 1*)

> (and the) and then – who was very pretending in being very kind (who was) who put Hansel off to bed (she was) – she cackled to herself (*Josh story 44*)

Both stories are about wicked witch/mother figures, and in each of these very complex sentences the storyteller is concerned to let the listener into the secrets of the story. In different ways Sundari and Josh are contrasting the appearance and reality of things by combining them in one utterance. This involves Sundari in a sentence with four dependent clauses, and Josh in an unusual structure containing two unrestricted dependent clauses. What I am saying is that *syntactic complexity of this kind always expresses complex narrative functions.*[10] In a very well-structured and explicitly told story Justine has a little girl who speculates about eating the chocolate kittens she has bought for her brother's birthday:

> and then she just said to herself in a whisper like this (P) she said 'I wonder if Timothy would mind if I just got one kitten? (*Justine story 26*)

Narrating her characters' thoughts necessitates two conditional dependent clauses embedded in the structure of reported speech. Since this book requires lengthy and frequent quotation from the children's stories, the reader will not lack opportunities to find many other examples like these. It seems obvious to state that storytelling entails a fair amount of explanatory language, but equally complex sentence structures arise from the children's use of rhetoric.

If the T-Unit analysis tends to confirm Walkerdine's assertion that children know how to operate a number of different discourse modes by the time they start school, scrutiny of many of the longer sentences (including the grammatically more simple ones like lists and repetitions) shows that metaphorical processes are involved. In other words, grammatical complexity often arises from the children's achievement of poetic effects. The following sentence from Sundari is not only narrative and explanatory, it is also poetic and lyrical, both in its sound patterns and its lexical choices:

> she liked doing things playing about at the beach on sunny days when cool wind was blowing making sandcastles playing with her little necklace with people on it and some little raindrops falling from the people and bags on it what the teddy-bears were in what the people were holding (*Sundari story 12*)

The reader may recognize the influence of Joan Aitken's story *A Necklace of Raindrops* here,[11] and it is true to say of the story data as a whole that more tightly structured and complex sentences tend to occur in stories which are strongly modelled on a book. When we start to consider the children's uses of rhetoric the limitations of T-Unit analysis as a window on the children's narrative competences are clear. Analytic tools are required which are capable of throwing some light on the children's techniques of communicating story to a listener, for the grammar of single sentences, interesting as it can be, tells us nothing about this. The later chapters of this book are concerned with the structure of narratives rather than sentences. For the remainder of this chapter I would like briefly to focus on aspects of phrase and sentence structure which seemed unusual, and on syntactic structures which caused difficulty and pushed these young storytellers to the limits of their competences.

Negative constructions in the stories seem particularly varied and often archaic or literary in style. I noticed that particular grammatical features belong to the style of particular storytellers and varied negative constructions are especially strong in Josh's stories:

1. but not any sound could they hear (*Josh*)
2. she was no mother but a wickedest witch in the forest (*Josh*)
3. may you never have to go out here again (*Josh*)
4. but there's no way to take him down (*Josh*)
5. when they could eat no more they slept in a little bed (*Josh*)
6. and the little fish have no hiding places (*Josh*)
7. so there was naught left in that house (*Justine*)
8. the little girl was not only bad but she was also good and kind (*Sundari*)
9. she would never stop talking about the rock (*Sundari*)
10. there's nothing to be done (*Josh*)
11. so they couldn't have comed to see the witch else she would cast a spell (*Josh*)
12. the skeleton was no longer seen (*Josh*)

These short negative sentences sometimes involve some complex grammar, for example the use of the passive in 12, the modal verb in 9, and the 'no . . . but' and 'not only . . . but also' constructions of 2 and 8 respectively. Example 1 has a rather unusually literary word order.

The children often order their words in sentences in ways that sound bookish. Sometimes this is a feature of particular stories. All the following examples are taken from one story by Josh, a story about several comic-book/TV superheroes which is nevertheless told in an extraordinarily literary style:

> now *there glowed a little light* up in the sky
> and then *down came Superman*
> we *never can* get help
> and *out came the Incredible Hulk* bashing them down
> but *not any sound could they hear*
> and *there they lay* sleeping
> *how surprised they were*

Sundari also has many examples in her stories, though this kind of inversion of word order is less common with the three younger children:

> but still *the town she hated*
> you sing *so merry those tunes*
> and they *one day said*
> *so dirty and horrid the porridge was*

I believe the fact that the younger children do not do this sort of thing with word order reflects their relative inexperience in the language of literature.

The use of a genitive construction with 'of', in preference to the ordinary possessive 's' is a characteristic of Josh's storytelling language, though all the children do this occasionally. In some instances there is a grammatical reason for choosing the 'of' form, as in this example from Sundari:

> and there was so much goodness of the animals

Since animals already has a plural 's', Sundari avoids confusion by using the 'of' form. Ordinary possessives using the 's' form appear frequently enough to confirm that this construction was well within the children's competences ('their father's cottage', 'God's palace') and the double possessive ('the next floor of Joshua's daddy's house'). Some 'of' constructions do not really have an alternative possessive 's' form:

> but of their stepmother she had died (*Josh*)
> they were really truly of their home and going to it (*Josh*)
> and that was naughty of his kind (*Robert*)
> they weren't of a very rich family (*Josh*)

In other sentences the use of the 'of' form instead of the possessive 's' has the effect of leaving the most interesting information in the sentence to the end:

> there comed *the ball of the fairy* (*Josh*)
> that was *the house of a very bad woman* (*Josh*)
> this little cottage was *the house of Hansel and Gretel* (*Josh*)
> once in *the palace of God* (*Josh*)
> there were *the treetops of little Bruin's mousehole* (*Sundari*)
> they gave *the broom of the witch of the East* to the wizard (*Josh*)

Most of the quotations from Josh here come from his retellings of *Hansel and Gretel*, and some of them are to be found in the original written versions his retellings were modelled upon.

In her discussion of the reading difficulties experienced by older pupils when they encounter textbook prose, Perera (1984) suggests that sentences which begin with dependent noun clauses pose problems for inexperienced readers, because it takes longer for the reader to get to the main verb. Though Josh and Sundari do not produce textbook sentences, there are several instances where they have a noun clause in the subject position. This is particularly characteristic of Sundari, who utters such sentences more frequently and more successfully than Josh. For Josh they are sometimes a source of difficulty. Here are some examples from Sundari (*story 1*):

> and *what she took* was a paper bag which her mummy had wrapped up (P)
> with some (P) stones in painted like raisins round stones
> *what they really were* were flat round stones painted brown like biscuits
> and *what she did* was ate all the stones up

These noun clauses are brief, but we might expect that the repetition of 'were' in the second example would cause Sundari to falter. Josh attempts similar constructions:

> *the only thing he could do* was hide on another steamer
> and *all that they had* was the floor left
> *all that he done to them* was threw them in the water
> *what she really meant* was push (Han) Hansel and Gretel in the oven as well
> as Hansel

These last two examples from Josh are slightly less sure of themselves than the others. He is unsure of the correct verb form to follow 'was' in the third example, and in the fourth the first 'Hansel' is redundant, though it is difficult to say whether this arises from his use of an unfamiliar sentence structure or not. Like the children's use of the passive, this construction is unusual in the data.

One of the most interesting things about the sentence structures in the stories is that the children attempt syntax which is not quite within their competences. Josh and Sundari feel a real compulsion to keep the story flowing, holding the floor without interruptions or breaks. Sundari's narrating is punctuated by pauses, some of them very long. She is obviously thinking of the next thing to say and the syntactic frame to say it in. There are very few garbles or syntactic mazes in her material. Josh, by contrast, rushes his stories forward very fast, and seems to work out the syntax aloud, so that there are many more garbles and mazes in his material. The important thing about the syntactic awkwardnesses which appear in the data is that on another occasion the child will have used that form correctly. It seems that much practice is involved in establishing a new syntactic structure to the point where it could be said to have been mastered by the child. The children's narratives reflect syntactic experimentation in action, and it should be noted that although they could not write yet, many of the structures they try out are those they will require in writing.

For Sundari one problem in using a whole set of conditional clauses is working out the appropriate tense. This passage occurs in a narrative told in the past tense:

> *they had brought a candle with them unless it-*

Here she breaks off, and changes the 'unless' structure to 'if':

> *if it gets dark and starts raining they can put it up*

Sundari has lost touch with the pluperfect tense of her main clause ('*had brought*') and puts her conditional clauses in the present. She goes on:

> *and if it's wasted if it blew out they had a torch*

Here, as she moves towards her main clause in the narrative past, she changes from the present back to the past in her second conditional clause.

Josh, whose competence with strings of relative clauses seems very firm in sentences like

> but they knew there was a little house covered with sweets in the wood that had a big pine tree with wooden faces

nevertheless produces a structure like this:

> they were in the room that they smashed the window in the hospital.

Presumably what he intended was something like 'they were in the hospital in the room where they had smashed the window'.

What seems to lie at the source of this sort of syntactic error is a belated desire to be explicit; Josh needed to start with the hospital rather than finish with it. In some sentences Josh seems to be consciously monitoring himself for explicitness, leading him to use redundant tags on the ends of his sentences:

> the firemen said they could put on all their clothes *the firemen*

Here Josh seems to be making quite sure that there is no confusion about the referent for 'their' in 'their clothes', for the possessive pronoun is potentially ambiguous; it could mean the clothes belonging to 'they' or the clothes belonging to 'the firemen'. In fact the story establishes that 'they' dress up in firemen's clothes. Other examples are:

> she saw some staring eyes *the witch*

> Julie and David slept with Joshua and they lived with Joshua *Julie and David*

Sometimes direct and indirect speech cause problems, though usually the children are very adept at handling the necessary grammatical transformations. In the following passage Josh starts a fairly complex sentence in the indirect speech form but abandons it and reverts to direct speech:

> but God said it was (alright) alright (um-St Peter) God said it wasn't
> alright   (he) he had to keep an eye on as well as God in the night   'and if
> the door opens you mustn't be frightened (and then) and get down the bed
> when Dracula came in

What Josh is trying to do in the indirect speech part of this passage is quite complicated; he has to handle a negative which he doesn't manage at first, and the referent for 'he' needs to be understood as St Peter, so Josh puts in the explicit 'as well as God'. He then reverts to direct speech, but cannot get the tense of the verb in the clause 'when Dracula came in' to fit the main verbs of the sentence.

There are some important aspects of the sentence syntax in the stories that I have not discussed here. Although I have shown that indirect speech was sometimes a syntactic problem, I have not covered the range of means within the children's competence for reporting speech. Similarly, I have not discussed the children's use of tenses and modal verbs. Ways of reporting speech in stories have implications for the storyteller's control of point of view, and tenses and modal verbs are related to the chronology, pace and duration of stories. In other words, these aspects of syntax need to be examined *at the level of the narrative* rather than the sentence. This I do very fully in later chapters.

What general conclusions can be drawn from these observations at the T-Unit/ sentence level? T-Unit length varies according to the discourse mode in operation. Where mean T-Unit scores are high, involving the use of complex syntactic structures, the discourses are those which entail specific features: explicitness and explanatory/ rhetorical power in stories, the passive voice in news broadcasts, the future tense and locative noun phrases in weather forecasts, and ellipsis in conversation. Just as the children use words experimentally in their stories, so do they try out word orders and sentence structures which are less likely to appear in everyday talk than in the language of writing. Telling stories gives them the opportunity to expand the scope of what they are able to make words do, makes the space for them to try out new structures and take the risk of getting them wrong.

Verbal play gives young children the chance to try out discourse modes which in real life they witness but do not take part in. The evidence presented here bears out Walkerdine's view that we as yet know too little about children's discourse knowledge in the context of play. That the children's syntactic competences seem to be unexpectedly sophisticated for their ages gives some support to Vygotsky's view that in play children are 'above their daily behaviour' and 'beyond their age in development'. The results of the T-Unit analyses imply that we could seriously underestimate children's linguistic competences if we evaluate them on the basis of one 'chunk' of language or one discourse mode. I believe that we should be particularly careful about assessing children's oral language on the basis of conversation with an adult. It is the *range* of discourse knowledge that we need to discover by having plenty of storytelling and role-play going on in classrooms all the time as a matter of course.

While T-Unit length and syntactic structure of long T-Units suggest that the narrative genres involve the children in language which is moving towards writing, T-Unit analysis can take us no further in the investigation of narrative competences. Let us consider one of Josh's weather forecasts, a discourse which showed up very specific grammatical features:

> it'll be sunny (at) on the mouth of Newcastle
> it'll be very rainy on the nose of Newcastle [*laughter*]
> and it'll be very nice and silly on the head of Newcastle
> and it'll be very (P) wet on the tinkle of Newcastle and it will be lovely and warm in the South of the ear [*laughter*]
> and it will be very nice and smudgey and soft and warm [*laughter*] (in the) in the West bum [*laughter*]
> it will be very nice and warm (at) (P) in the mouth of Newcastle (*Josh story 83*)

This discourse may be marked by a high use of the future tense and collections of noun phrases, but a sentence analysis tells us nothing about the personification of a place, Newcastle, as the human body, which structures the whole piece, and the parodic effect achieved by that personification. Yet it is this playful metaphor-making which underlies the syntax of this imitation weather forecast. While the personification of Newcastle is a specific, clear and deliberate metaphor, whole stories are also metaphors constructed by the child intuitively. The stories need to be analysed as total structures in ways which reflect the metaphoric processes involved in the practice of narrative as communicative discourse. There are many analytic tools available for investigating narrative structure, each of them predicated on a particular view or theory of what narrative is. The following chapter surveys some of the literature on narrative structure, with a view to selecting the analytic systems which will reveal the essential characteristics of the children's stories.

NOTES

1. Perera (1984) argues that the disembedded and impersonal style of much textbook writing can cause problems for inexperienced readers. Some important issues emerge from her analysis of textbook sentence structures. Do certain subject areas require a special decontextualized kind of discourse, or should the authors attempt more communicative styles? Does extensive experience of imaginative fiction help to prepare children for later, disembedded discourses, or does it raise the wrong expectations for these kinds of written language? My analysis of both the content and the sentence structure of young children's oral stories convinces me that book stories give children a good introduction to the language of a wide range of reading material.

   Moffett (1968) argues that in the early years when children lack the experience to identify the discourse of school subjects 'narrative must do for all'. I have argued elsewhere (Fox, 1989b) that storymaking employs all children's knowledge in domains as far apart as Mathematics/Science and History or Religion. The proper examination of these issues is a vast field. For definitions of 'essayist' (scientific) literacy see Scollon and Scollon (1981) and Olson (1977). For arguments that fictional prose requires the same mental operations as scientific prose see Tannen (1980). The most powerful case for imaginative fiction is made by Rader (1982).

2. Though the project by O'Donnell *et al.* (1967) was undertaken so long ago it is useful in establishing a relationship between T-Unit length, syntactic complexity and age. My criticism of it, which accords with Rosen's (1969) findings, is that the crucial contextual variable of *function genre/ discourse mode* was not considered.

3. Rosen argues that different functions and purposes for writing will demand quite different verbal strategies, which will affect T-Unit length. Since the Loban/O'Donnell studies appeared to give some support to the notion of 'linguistic deprivation' in groups with a low socio-economic rating, it was crucial to demonstrate the importance of context, function and genre. Labov's studies of ritual insults and narrative syntax in BEV speakers also confirm Rosen's view. My data show that function/genre are as important in the speech of young children as they are in the writing or speech of adolescents.

4. See Appendix D, p. 205, for the transcript of Josh's pre-sleep monologue. Josh, an only child, talked and sang himself to sleep for many years, though this was the only occasion on which I was able to record him.

5. In their stories the children seemed to operate on the principle: when in doubt name the subject of the sentence twice. I believe this is accounted for not only by the children's linguistic immaturity, but also by the need in tape-recorded story monologues to be as explicit as possible. Loban (1963, p. 14) calls this category *topic*.

6. Of course, to focus on indentifying *clear* characteristics of speech and writing is to open another can of worms! I take the view, given some support in the work of Tannen, Brice Heath and others that there are oral–writing continua which overlap. The writing-like features of my children's oral stories fit the overlap theory. The idea of linguistic discontinuity between speech and writing tends to prevail if we regard literacy as one unified and monolithic state. If we see litera*cies* as plural and multifunctional, however, then the boundaries between speech and writing are less clear. See Street (1992).

7. While I agree that these features characterize oral poetry like *The Iliad* or the *Book of Genesis* most writers who propose an oral/literate divide miss the point that the writers of fiction for children put the oral tradition into literate form, thus creating an oral – literacy continuity.
8. Perera (1984) reports several studies of children's understanding of passive constructions (see pp. 124-7). There is some consensus that 'the full passive is one of the latest grammatical structures to appear in children's speech' (p. 125). However, none of the studies cited takes account of the discourse mode in operation. As Perera also points out that passives are rare in adult speech too, it seems likely that this is a context/genre dependent grammatical feature.
9. Josh's imitation newsreadings and weather forecasts are in Appendix E, pp. 210-12.
10. The basic argument of Labov's narrative syntax is that complex syntactic structures perform complex narrative functions. This is particularly true of the category of narrative structure Labov calls *Evaluation*. See Chapters 6 and 7 of this book for a fuller discussion of Labov's narrative analysis and the application of his categories to these data.
11. Sundari's story 12 is so rich and complex that I have used it to demonstrate the variety of Genette's (1972) categories of tense, mood and voice. The full transcript, together with the Genette analysis, is appended to the end of Chapter 10 (pp. 163-7).

Chapter 6

Narrative Competences[1]

What is a narrative? It is generally agreed that narrative is a fundamental means of organizing our experience along the dimension of time. Narratives appear early in language acquisition. We know this because story collectors such as Pitcher and Prelinger have been able to elicit stories from children as young as 2 years old. Barthes (1977) in his essay 'Introduction to the structural analysis of narratives', observes that narrative is 'international, transhistorical and transcultural', while Hardy (1968) calls it 'a primary act of mind' and suggests that all our living is shaped by it. Other writers see narrative as securely bonded with memory. Meek (1984) sees memory as the link which fastens together 'narrations and the annotation of time', and Langer (1953) suggests that memory shapes experience both as history and fiction. Fiction, she says, creates an illusion of 'a history entirely experienced' and goes on: 'This virtual history is in the mode typified by memory'. The universality of narrative has generated a large number of psychological and linguistic experiments in recent years. The aim has been to discover a model which will describe the structure of simple narratives and then to find out whether human cognitive structures match it. For the practitioner like myself who wants to describe children's competences for forming stories there is no shortage of possible analytic models. In this chapter I shall survey some of the existing accounts of story structure with a view to justifying the systems of analysis I chose for the children's stories.

As long ago as 1932 Bartlett published a study of memory in which he described subjects' recall of stories.[2] More recent psychological studies of narrative competences seem to have lost sight of some of his most important findings. In his story retelling experiments Bartlett found that his subjects worked from a general impression of the whole towards the construction of the details. He termed the mental frameworks for these whole structures employed in remembering *schemata*, which he described as 'active developing patterns'. He found that a step-by-step story recall was rare, but that the overall organization of a story persisted in the memory. With the passing of time, he found, his storytellers tended to omit, simplify or transform the story details, which sounds very much like what my young children did when they retold stories from books.[3] Most important from my point of view, Bartlett observed that the overall impression his subjects received was usually linked to an affective stance: doubt, hesitation, surprise, astonishment, repulsion are examples of typical affects. He concluded that narrative schemata have a 'personal flavour' and that what we remember is 'interest-determined' and that interests are a matter of temperament. If these observations seem obvious, i.e.: we tend to remember what *interests* us, nevertheless many psychological studies following Bartlett's work have managed to leave subjects' affective attitudes out of the experimental design.

Bartlett's discoveries about memory for story touch upon many of my own interests in developing theories of language and narrative that include the affectivities of play. He found that memory schemata involve mental operations like invention, condensation, elaboration, simplification and transformation. Some of these echo Freud's description of the processes involved in recounting dreams. Bartlett suggested that an associative principle, as in metaphor, is a function of schema formation, and that it is an affective quality which underlies the tendency to juxtapose, in schemata, materials from diverse realms. He commented that his theory of *active* schemata 'brings remembering into line with imagining'. The term 'active' is very important, for it implies that memory schemata are not blueprints which enable us passively to regurgitate material, but that we construct for ourselves what it is that we remember. Experimental designs, then, would need to take account of the affective variables and personality differences between subjects.

Bartlett's formulation of mental schemata for story recall needed to be matched by corresponding studies of simple story texts, then it would be possible to test his theories under controlled conditions. The work of Propp (1928) had indicated that some genres of story, such as folk- and fairy-tales, could be reduced to a set of elemental structural units. Propp found that though the surface characteristics of folk-tales varied (dramatis personae, language, locations, etc.) the actions of the characters in the stories, which he termed *functions*, remained constant. Folk-tales are only superficially diverse, but at a deeper level they have common structures formed from combinations of elements such as 'flight', 'lack', 'departure', and so on. In fact when he analysed these functions in 100 Russian fairy-tales he concluded that only 31 elements accounted for the actions in all the tales and for many others from all over the world. The implication was that the oldest and simplest forms of story shared a fundamental structural base. Many more recent developmental studies of narrative competences derive from putting together the work of Bartlett and Propp. Psychologists perceived that there might be a correspondence between the text structures revealed by the analysis of folklorist genres, and the kind of mental template for narrative structure suggested by Bartlett's schemata theory.

The search for a grammar of stories has been justified on several grounds: as a means of studying 'general features of human understanding' (Bower, 1976, p. 370), to discover 'what people will and will not remember from connected discourse' (Mandler and Johnson, 1977, p. 148), and to find out the implications for initial reading programmes (Glenn, 1980, p. 559). In order to describe the basic patterns of folk-stories, Maranda and Maranda (1971) modified Levi-Strauss's formula for the structure of myths. For simple narratives they described four structural levels, based on the hero's/heroine's responses to conflict. The pattern of increasing complexity was represented by a tree-diagram model like those used in transformational linguistics. When children retold the test stories, the younger ones could not recall the more complex structures. Each of the four stages was seen as an incomplete complex structure, and only children over the age of 9 were found to be in command of what the researchers call 'narrative combinatorics'. Rumelhart (1975, 1977) devised a similar grammar for story structure. Again the relationship of categories was represented by a tree diagram hierarchically reflecting the importance of the nodes. Here the 'gist' of the story was in the topmost nodes, while the details, considered less important in memory schemata, were spread in the lowest branches. Rumelhart stipulated that his grammar would only work for simple stories without several protagonists and without dialogue.[4] I found that it would be impossible to fit my invented fantasy narratives to these models of story structure, and in the following discussion I shall argue that these approaches are as limited for examining children's spontaneous narrative productions, as studies of children's syntactic structures are for describing their communicative competences.

One of the major problems is that on the whole children are not interested in listening to stories told in the irreducibly bare ways of story grammarians. Rumelhart's *The Man and the Serpent* (1975), for example, is a set of barren events, devoid of elaboration, colour, point of view or any discernible style. The assumption of the researcher–writer is that these aspects of story will distract from the 'gist' of the story structure. Thus a story is regarded as 'information'. Stein and Glenn (1979) also regard the essential information in a story as comprising what happened, and all other material – setting information pertaining to locations, adjectives and adverbs, ancillary characters – as less likely to be remembered. This idea of story as information is typified by Glenn's *The Peter Story* (1978, p. 232), where she shows that, for her, elaborating a story is simply adding more information to it, so that 'Peter got very excited. He decided that he really wanted to go' becomes, in its elaborated version 'Peter got very excited. He had heard that circuses had trained lions and that there were clown acts too. Peter decided that he really wanted to go'. In my view, children are unlikely to get particularly involved in either version, for they both lack life, colour and distinctive language – yet the topic is excitement! In these story grammar studies stories become 'problem-solving formats' (Rumelhart, 1977), or 'information' for 'retrieval' (Mandler and Johnson, 1977). No distinction is made between the events narrated (i.e. the story), the verbalization of those events (the narrative) and the activity of telling (the narrating) (Rosen, 1984).[5] Once we include the *language* of the story-telling and the *narrating style* in our account of story we have a discursive, communicative view of what a story is. But a model of story which confines it to the *events narrated* is a referential model, a Gradgrindish model, rejecting those very elements to do with expression and affects which may have a profound effect on the listener and condition what is recalled.

Cognitive studies of narrative competence seem to intellectualize stories in the way that Vygotsky suggested play was treated by many psychologists. The children in my study were always free not to tell a story, and when they did tell stories it was for pleasure and fun. It is impossible to discover how the children in the story grammar experiments construed the task or its purposes, for details of the context and situation are missing from the accounts.[6] This means that there can be no reflection of the person, and his/her attitudes and interests, in the matching of story to child. Yet in his original experiments Bartlett discovered that an affective attitude was a fundamental aspect of remembering. Would it not make more sense, if we want to find out what children remember of stories, to ask them to retell their favourite stories under more naturalistic conditions? The story retellings in my data show that even Robert at age 3 remembered many elaborative details *because he loved the story*.[7] Stories written for children, folk-tales or not, usually borrow heavily from the oral tradition, using all the formulaic mnemonic devices that have been remembered down the ages. Yet instead of making use of the ways in which real stories have been communicated to young listeners, the specially constructed stories of these experiments are written as impersonally as possible.

Leaving out the context, then, has led to the omission of dialogic aspects of storytelling which necessarily means that affective dimensions are missing too. I would argue that even more is left out of this conception of what a story is, for the notion of structure in these studies does not really include language. This may appear to be an invalid proposition since language is the medium used, but plot moves can be depicted pictorially, or as mime or dance, and narrative schemata can be derived from them. Rosen has argued (1984) that we need to look at narratives as *diverse* rather than as *unified* structures, in order to show why one version will be preferred or remembered over another. In Chapter 3 I briefly discussed the verbal play forms engaged in by adolescent males in many parts of the world. The structuring rules of these forms include features such as puns, rhymes and metaphors – features which have been treated very parsimoniously in the psychologists' versions of folk-tales. But we all know that when children listen to *The Three Little Pigs* we can rely on them to remember the wolf's words '*I'll huff and I'll puff . . .*' even if they cannot recall the plot in the right sequence.[8] Of course, seeing stories as a combination of plot moves means that story grammarians have not considered the metaphorical dimension of storying. We have already seen how the apparent illogicalities of Josh's story 17 arise from his metaphorical transformation of *Burglar Bill*. Stories are not one-dimensional channels of meaning but they encode multiple meanings, some of them lying beneath the surface or 'between the lines'. And listeners and readers *interpret* stories, that is they make them mean in their own ways. Bartlett's work showed that remembering a story was an *active* process of reconstruction, not a passive process of transmission.

Story grammars have not escaped criticism even by their own practitioners. Thorndyke and Yekovitch (1980) point out that the orientation and interests of the reader tend to be omitted, and that stories can be remembered in different ways. My children transform all kinds of images and motifs from stories they have heard into stories they make up, and these elements are by no means confined to plot moves. Black and Bower (1980) criticize story grammars because they ignore 'rich semantic relationships'; they argue that reading is essentially an interpretive act which involves personal styles of reasoning and particular and common kinds of cultural knowledge.

Existing studies of children's invented stories certainly face up to the semantic content which is absent from story grammars, but language or discourse is not a central concern. In two large-scale psychoanalytic studies of pre-school children's fantasy narratives (Pitcher and Prelinger, 1963; Ames, 1966), the same data are used, two stories each collected from 137 children, aged 2 to 5. In startling contrast to the story grammar experiments, Pitcher and Prelinger study stories in terms of ego-development, the differentiation of self from others, the development of social roles and skills, and the socialization of the drives of infancy. Formal aspects of stories are regarded as reflections of the concept of the self and the outside world. In this view stories take their forms from the differentiation of the main characters and their inner complexity, the degree of realism, and the ways thoughts and emotional processes are described. In my view these semantic categories come closer to a deep story structure than the syntactic categories of story grammars. A child's sense of the differentiation of itself from others, or of other people from one another, may have a strong relationship to the structural moves in a story. Take Josh and Sundari, for example. Many of Josh's stories are set in mythical universes whereas Sundari's settings tend to be more domestic. The space occupied by their characters affects the relationships within the story. Josh's characters tend to plan for *action* in co-operation while Sundari's heroines tend to be isolated and thoughtful. The psychoanalytic studies very usefully show us that fantasy increases with age, reflecting the greater security with the real world of the 5-year-old compared to the 2-year-old. Interestingly, since he came from a very different tradition, this accords with the view of the Russian poet Chukovsky (1925) on children's play with *language*; the more secure they are with denotative meanings the more able they are to turn them upside down in their verbal jokes. Ames found that children distanced themselves from potentially threatening aspects of real life by the ways they dealt with violent fantasy material. I found this to be so in my stories. Deaths and injuries are usually miraculously reversed or they happen to somebody other than the central character. Though the psychoanalysts certainly regard such fantasies as metaphors for repressed conflicts, they do not include the linguistic dimension in their analyses. It is through the medium of *words* that children create these metaphors, yet words are neglected as much by these researchers as they were by the story grammarians. The psychological and psychoanalytic studies I have referred to give us tantalizing parts of the whole. They tell us that logical plot structures develop with age and that in the meantime fantasy stories fulfil other, metaphorical, functions for young children. But in leaving language out of their analyses they are ultimately reductionist views of children's storytelling.

There are two major studies of children's invented oral stories which come closer to considering cultural, linguistic, aesthetic and affective aspects of storytelling than those I have discussed so far: Sutton-Smith and his team (1975–81),[9] and Applebee (1978).[10] These have broader aims than the story grammarians, for Sutton-Smith aims for a developmental psychology of the arts, and Applebee for an account of literary development. They take a multi-dimensional approach to narrative analysis because their conception of what narrative is is very broad. Sutton-Smith regards narrative as a good candidate for a model of the human mind, suggesting that the universality of story and its primacy in human history makes it likely that 'the most basic human mind is a storytelling one' (Sutton-Smith, 1981). Like Applebee his theoretical base is eclectic, drawing on ethnography, psychoanalysis and aesthetic theory, as well as psychology and linguistics. Both researchers use fantasy material made up by children. Sutton-Smith collected, under naturalistic conditions, one or more stories from 350 children aged 2 to 10 in kindergartens and schools. The researchers got to know the children over a long period and, within the constraints of the school setting, elicited the stories in the most free and relaxed ways. Sutton-Smith argues that storytakers need to be more like permissive play therapists than laboratory experimenters and his team actively sought children's engagement in the task. Older children wrote their stories, while the collectors scribed for the younger children. The researchers also attempted to collect large numbers of stories from individuals, acknowledging that this would give a truer reflection of narrative competence than the one-off storytelling. These methods yielded a rich story collection. How much attention, then, is paid to the story language?

Sutton-Smith stresses the sound play of young children's stories, to the extent that he sees them as 'verse stories'. He finds that prosodic features – alliteration, assonance, the repetition of words, rhythm – are greater determiners of structure than plot moves. Interestingly, he uses Lord's analysis of folk-song techniques (1973) to show how narrative competences in infancy develop analogously to folk-songs in the oral tradition, so that early stories are stitched together as theme and variation using prosodic formulae that the children have remembered.[11] Such formulae certainly make their appearance in my story material, and the reader will recall that in Chapter 5 I showed how certain of the children's longer sentences were structured as repetitions, or oral-tradition formulae, though my analysis also showed that grammatical complexity accounted for more longer sentences. Sutton-Smith notes that prosodic modes of story organization progressively give way to 'literate' modes, a logical plot structure. Walter Ong (1982) also argues forcefully that complex, logical plot structures develop with the rise of literacy, since they require the kind of prior planning that can only be accomplished through writing.[12] In the following chapter I shall show that my five children were able to produce logical plots, especially in story retellings from books and in 'verse stories' like the ones Sundari *sings* all the way through. This implies that hearing stories read aloud is a vital link in the move from one kind of story organization to another. While I accept this thesis I do feel that we ought to question the implicit devaluation of prosodic modes of story organization that is buried within the argument. While complicated story plots may well be dependent upon the prior planning made possible by literacy it is not logical to argue that the reverse is true, that literacy is characterized by them. Poetry is a very highly developed literary form and it is possible that some children are drawn to poetic prosody more than others, borrowing those features from stories in books just as they might borrow a complex plot. In this view prosodic organization of story material is not so much an indicator of narrative immaturity as a value in its own right, a value which could lead children in the direction of poetry. I believe this to have been the case with Sundari. Her stories are not filled with actions as Josh's are, but often with sound and word-play that revolves around her central characters and her narrating voices. Since there is no doubt about the intertextualities of her stories and the literary forms of her language, I can only conclude that the prosodic features of storytelling (written and spoken) interested her more than plots. Story researchers need to avoid the trap of overvaluing plot structure at the expense of other story features *which are also mediated through literature*. Sutton-Smith's insights suggest that *style* ought to be included in story analysis. However, in the multiple analyses he performs, developmental aspects of plot structure take priority over considerations of language.[13]

Applebee, too, analyses story structure in terms of the cognitive implications of plots, though his analytic system is original and in principle ought to be able to incorporate story language. Using the Pitcher and Prelinger data, Applebee bases his model of story structure on Vygotsky's (1962) stages of concept development. He focuses on the ways story elements relate to one another, starting with Vygotsky's *heaps* (elements randomly placed together with no links) and moving through the various kinds of *chains* to true narratives. Applebee identifies two major structuring principles:

centreing, an overall theme to which all the events in the narrative are related, and *chaining*, the links forged between one event and another. He claims that these two principles are at work in all the major literary forms – novels, poetry, drama. Here the concept of story is not limited to plot or 'gist' for the centreing principle includes the narrative discourse together with the story it narrates. In this analysis form and content are inter-related and equally valued. However, the Vygotsky structure lends itself better to an analysis of plot moves than to an analysis of the language which narrates them, perhaps because Applebee's interest lies in cognitive development.

In summary, while Sutton-Smith and Applebee take a refreshingly holistic approach to narrative analysis, neither in practice comes close enough to a focus on *style as part of structure* to supply an adequate model for my own data. They are ultimately interested in what is normative, but both have argued for case studies that would reflect individual differences in story style and the influences of literature on children's storytelling.[14]

To analyse the rich material in my data I needed systems that were based on original, spontaneous oral texts, systems which were capable of reflecting the rhetoric of the storytelling, and systems which construed narratives as discursive acts of communication. Labov and Weletsky (1967), and Labov (1972, 1982) come closest to such a system for oral stories.[15] They elicited oral narratives from black adolescent speakers of BEV (Black English Vernacular) in response to the prompt 'Were you ever in a situation where you thought you were in serious danger of getting killed?' This prompt was crucial, for it drew from the young males stories that they found so reportable that they seemed to relive the story events during the telling, using language that was expressive and natural rather than carefully monitored. For Labov reportability is *'the generating centre of narrative structure'*, a value that immediately places the emphasis not on plot moves but on *the way a story is told*. Reportability as a criterion of narrative competence places the *listener* inside the narrative discourse, so that monologic story forms become communicative acts. The emphasis thus shifts from what the story events do to what the narrator's language does. A story which failed to have a powerful effect on the listener would thus be deemed incompetent. Labov's interest lay in the relationship between linguistic skill and the membership of specific social groups, particularly those deemed to be linguistically inadequate by the dominant, educated community. The group of children in my study are in great contrast to Labov's. My storytellers are pre-school children, his are adolescents; my storytellers are steeped in the language of books, his are virtually illiterate; mine are white, his are black; mine are girls and boys, his are males only; mine invented their stories, his told narratives of personal experience. However, as far as story structure models are concerned these differences are surface ones. Labov claimed that the 'danger of death' theme is of universal and transcultural application, and that autobiographical stories taken from uneducated speakers would be simple enough to yield a basic narrative structure for all stories. Though I believe girls may well perceive the 'danger of death' theme differently to boys, a survey of the story material from both girls and boys in my study shows just as much death in the girls' stories as in the boys'. It has to be borne in mind that Labov's adolescents told stories which celebrated a particularly macho form of street culture, one far removed from Sundari's lonely heroines sitting on beaches playing with their dolls. Regardless of this, many of Sundari's stories are concerned with violent themes. In my view, though we need to bear in mind that girls may well orient themselves to narratives and narrating differently to boys (a topic surely for another book), if Labov's criteria for narrative competence are to be taken seriously it is the *reportability* of Sundari's stories we should be looking for.

Labov calls his narrative analysis a 'syntax' because he sees the constituent elements of story structure as directly related to the grammar of the storyteller's speech. Whereas the psychologists *borrowed* from linguistic analysis the terminology to describe plot structure, Labov actually analyses the clause syntax of the stories. He categorizes sections of the story as setting information, or as story events, or as the narrator's attitude to the events narrated, *on the basis of the language that is used*. For Labov the key to a well-structured story will lie in the language which tells it rather than in complications of plot moves. In his collection of oral narratives of personal experience, Labov shows that the referential parts of the story, which tell us what happened, employ simple declarative sentences, while the evaluative parts of the story, those which show how the narrator feels about the story, employ more complex syntactic structures. Since I am looking at linguistic competences which include both narrative and literary competences within them, this is a very useful focus for me. It should tell me whether the sentences I discussed in the last chapter are in fact associated with the evaluative aspects of the story or not. It should help to draw the children's linguistic and narrative skills into a complementary and interdependent relationship with one another.

In his study of 'danger of death' stories Labov defined the following constituents of narrative structure in the order in which they usually appeared in his stories:

Abstract: Introduction of story theme with an opening remark, such as 'Did I ever tell you about the time . . .'
Orientation: The setting information/background to the story – description of time, place, characters, etc.
Complicating action: What happened. This is the referential aspect of the story, but Labov's important contribution to narrative structure study is that on its own it is not enough to ward off the response, 'So what?'
Evaluation: The narrator's own stance on what happened, how s/he felt, the colour and emphasis given to the story that is told. Skilled narrators make the story powerful by their evaluative techniques.
Result/Resolution: The outcome of events. How the problem or danger was solved.
Coda: Closing conclusion, return to the present.

As a structure for stories this is deceptively simple. It has, like the psychological schemata I found so bare, a beginning, middle and ending, (*Orientation, Complicating Action* and *Resolution*). What is different about this story structure is the inclusion of and emphasis on *Evaluation* as the aspect of the story that gives it life and colour and sustains the listener's interest. Initially Labov saw a pattern in his adolescents' storytelling in which evaluation clauses usually followed the account of what happened – the complicating action. Later he found that evaluative elements could be freely distributed over an entire narrative, in the way that storytellers add setting details as the story goes on rather than placing them all at the beginning. The crucial difference between Labov's analysis and the others I have referred to in this chapter is that here at last great importance is attached to storytelling *style*, style which is not seen as unnecessary elaboration but rather as the lifeblood of the story. We need to be clear about what Labov is saying about narrative structure. He is *not* saying that complicating actions and resolutions are unimportant, indeed he claims that these are the essential characteristics of a narrative; if nothing happens there can be no story. But he found that a framework for narrative based solely on the narrative events did no justice to the linguistic skills of his young, black narrators.

Labov's work was carried out during the great controversy of the 1960s and 1970s which centred on the idea of cultural/linguistic deprivation or impoverishment. His careful analyses of the speech forms of the so-called 'deprived' groups, such as inner-city, semi-literate black adolescent boys, was intended to explode the myth of linguistic deficit as the explanation for educational failure. Thus the emphasis on the syntax of the structural units of the story. Labov's discovery was that the evaluation constituent of story structure involved his storytellers in very complex grammar. I have already shown, in the last two chapters, that my children make very distinctive lexical and syntactic choices, even though their genre of storytelling is very different from Labov's narratives of personal experience. The link between this study and Labov's is that in each case the stories collected are grounded in a very specific kind of cultural experience.

Several practitioners have applied versions of Labov's story structure to the narratives of children. The findings support Labov's view that storytelling competences develop within the framework of specific cultures and social settings. Kernan (1977), for example, finds that orientations and evaluations increase in quality and quantity with age, and that younger children's elaborations are simple and few in number. Menig-Peterson and McCabe (1978), on the other hand, find that all children from the age of 3½ use several types of orientation adequately, while Umiker-Sebeok (1979) confirms that the inclusion of at least one orientation element in pre-schoolers' stories increases from 16 per cent at age 3 to 100 per cent at age 5. It is clear that different narrating traditions existed in the different social groups featured in the studies. Bennett (1980) was able to show that a typical resolution in a Hoopa Indian story may not count as a resolution at all in non-Hoopa cultures. She compared Labov's analysis with Rumelhart's story grammar, and found that Labov's narrative syntax had the advantage of reflecting more clearly the stylistic and formulaic markers associated with different narrative traditions.

Using Labov's narrative syntax as a model of overall story structure for my story data has the advantage, then, of dealing with plot while including the elaborative, stylistic features which make storytelling discursive. Incorporated in the story structure now are the potential effects of the telling on the listener and the narrator's skill in manipulating those effects. Applying this model of structure also places affective aspects of story at the centre of the discourse, for as Labov claims (1972, p. 371):

> Evaluative devices say to us: this was terrifying, dangerous, weird, wild, crazy; or amusing, hilarious, wonderful; more generally that it was strange, uncommon or unusual – that is, worth reporting.

In choosing the Labov analysis we can relate both the telling and the told of the story to specific cultural experiences, in this case the experience of hearing books and stories read aloud.

Deciding that Labov's narrative syntax provided a closer fit for the kind of story material I had does not mean that it is an unproblematic system. Perhaps I can demonstrate what I mean by referring the reader to Josh's story 17 which I quoted in full at the opening of Chapter 2 of this book. In story 17, if I may recapitulate its sources, Josh has used material from two children's books, together with some autobiographical material. The hero is the fictionalized Josh, and the Daddy's house in Notting Hill and the visit to the cinema come from life. The major evaluation section of the story comes when Josh's narrator suspends the action, in the classic manner described by Labov, while the little boy searches for the source of the siren-like noise he can hear in the middle of the night. Let us quote this section of the story again to see how the Labov analysis fits Josh's storytelling, and vice versa:

12 but then he went out in the middle of the night
13 and there was this sound going 'do-de' (sung)
14 he looked all around
15 nobody was there in a small street where it had lots of holes
16 he looked down one of them
17 he looked down the other
18 they were all alike
19 but he looked down the next one
20 and what was there?
21 just a surprise thing his Daddy was there.

This section of the story combines some narrative clauses (complicating actions) together with setting details (orientations) and evaluation devices – the use of repetitions, comparisons, intensifiers and a question to create a feeling of suspense. While it is possible to show that these are all present in this section of the story, the *order* of structural elements set out by Labov is not at all clear because the elaborative material is not only present in greater quantities than in Labov's narratives of personal experience but it is included right through the story. This means that most T-Units have a multiple classification, which makes analysing the stories very complicated. This is not the only drawback. Though the house, the location and the cinema may have come from his life, Josh has borrowed from books the very techniques he uses for keeping the listener in suspense, as well as a lot of the setting details. The Labov analysis does identify the presence of these features but it cannot show us the intertextual nature of what Josh is doing. Labov's stories were selected on the grounds of their *non*-literary influences, so it is hardly surprising that his narrative analysis cannot take account of this source of story material. There is a further problem. The elements of story 17 that Josh has transformed from books are more than useful units for him to use in the construction of a fantasy story. They are also metaphors which he can turn into a total metaphor for his inner and social experience. The 'rude boy', the monster/dragon, and the supper at the end of the story, are borrowed from Sendak's *Where the Wild Things Are*. The noise in the street, the midnight setting, the holes in the ground, the search for a father, the little house behind the police station and the father/policeman transformation are borrowed from the Ahlbergs' *Burglar Bill*. The elaborations in story 17 add up to something much greater than the sum of their parts, an intricate metaphor or mirror-image of Josh's lived experience, and a re-reading of both stories. The Labov analysis has the advantage of showing, clause by clause, the elaborative competences of the storyteller in a dialogic context. This is what was missing from the studies surveyed earlier in this chapter. But his system does not synthesize the total metaphor created by those clauses, nor does it have a means of analysing below-the-surface themes and meanings. In this sense it is reductive.

All the analytic systems I have discussed in this chapter move from an oral model of language and narrative, as the most basic, universal and simple form. Literacy, if it is discussed, is quite understandably assumed to come later. But what of those children who have been absorbing the language of literacy all along, from the time they first learnt to take part in conversations? I can identify literary sources for the stories, as I did in Chapter 2 and throughout this book. I can indicate word uses and sentence structures that would be unusual in a conversational context, as I did in Chapters 4 and 5. I can show, as I shall in the following chapter, that the children can produce story structures which are fully formed according to Labov's criteria. But identifying special qualities of 'literariness' is more problematic. Labov intended that his analyses should provide evidence for the complexity, even superiority, of the linguistic competences of uneducated Black English Vernacular speakers compared to educated speakers of standard varieties. Paradoxically, while his category of evaluation is potentially literary (see Pratt, 1977),[16] the oral narratives from which his evaluation criteria emerge deny any special literary features in narrative discourse.

The question of literariness resolves itself around knowledge of story conventions which are not only linguistic (i.e. they are *uttered*), but also literary (i.e. they are *written*). Pratt's extension of Labov's analysis to literary works forces us to acknowledge the overlapping of the oral/literary, and to accept that the literary does not solely belong to writing. Without reopening the gap traditionally assumed to divide speech and writing, how can the range of literary structures within the oral competences of my five children be demonstrated? One solution would be to subject the stories to analyses designed specifically for literary narratives; in other words to read and analyse the stories *as though they were works of literature*. I shall use the Labov analysis to gain a purchase on the children's ability to tell a well-structured story, and shall follow Labov in showing how skilled these young oral narrators are in evaluating their narratives. But because this will not ultimately reveal the subtleties at work in the most accomplished stories of the two 5-year-olds, who after all had had a longer exposure to written fiction than the others, I shall devote chapters 8 to 11 to analyses originally carried out on classic, adult literary works, the systems devised by Barthes (1970) and Genette (1972). By using multiple analyses I shall argue that the children's literary competences are far greater than has previously been guessed at *and* that our current models for the analyses of children's narrative structures are inadequate because they are not sufficiently grounded in discursive, social, cultural and generic aspects of narration.

I shall conclude this discussion of different models of narrative structure by discussing post-structuralist notions of what it is about literary texts that makes it possible to read them in ways that are conventionally recognizable. I shall briefly draw on the work of Culler (1975), who is exceptionally clear in his definition and description of literary competences (*his* term), and shall leave the introduction of the work of Genette and Barthes until the relevant later chapters.

Culler regards literature as a semiotic system in its own right; the act of reading, or interpretation, depends on our experience of all the signals set up by texts, conventions which tell us, for example, that this should be read as a poem, or that should be read as a scientific report. In other words, our reading is the sum of all our previous reading allied to our knowledge of the cultural assumptions and values in which texts are embedded.

> A work can only be read in connection with or against other texts, which provide a grid through which it is read and structured by establishing expectations which enable one to pick out salient features and give them a structure.
> (Culler, 1975, p. 139)

The 'other texts' Culler is referring to are not only obvious relationships with identifiable literary works, in the way that Josh's story 17 uses images from *Burglar Bill* and *Where the Wild Things Are*. The intertextualities of a literary work stretch beyond such borrowings to the whole society in which that work is produced. We may or may not recognize the literary sources of Josh's story, but we will understand his references to parents, policemen, streets and cinemas because, in spite of the inclusion of fantastical elements (monsters), we share the world he is drawing upon. In fact this sharing is so natural that we tend to do it unconsciously, accepting that what the author sketches for us is somehow 'real'. Culler asks where this sense of reality, or vraisemblance, comes from, for by uncovering the systems which structure it we can understand how literary works achieve their effects, how they make our readings of them possible. Each structural system I have discussed in this chapter springs from the texts of specific genres: folk-tales for Propp and for most schemata theorists, myths for Levi-Strauss, narratives of personal experience for Labov. Those genres were selected for their simplicity and universality, making them good candidates for a description of a fundamental narrative form. Once we consider the structuring systems of Culler, Todorov, Genette and Barthes, however, we move away from the most simple folklorist forms to highly regarded and very complex works *written* by adults. If the children in this study can be shown to be engaged in operations which relate to the semiotic systems of literature then the argument for what they have learnt from books moves beyond the level of literary borrowings to structuring techniques which are more deeply and powerfully established in their competences for narrative.

Culler suggests that there are five levels of vraisemblance, that is, five ways in which a sense of the 'real' is structured into literary works. The very illusion of reality and naturalness produced by these layers of structure prevents us from perceiving their operations. Literary competences lie in knowing how these systems work. The young children in this study were experienced readers so it ought to be possible to detect the signs of literary competence in their concepts of what stories are and how they work. I shall sketch here Culler's five levels of vraisemblance, showing how they are applicable to Josh's story 17. However, that is a relatively simple story compared to others produced both by him and Sundari. Those stories are analysed extensively in later chapters using categories derived from Genette and Barthes.

First Culler proposes that literary works draw upon a socially given text, the ordinary everyday world with people in it, who have minds and bodies, who move and think, eat and sleep. This text is so 'inherently intelligible' (p. 141) that it is taken for granted by readers. In Josh's story 17 it is present in the realistic figures of the boy, the father, the policeman. It is violated by the monster in the ground who is killed twice. Culler says that the introduction of such 'unreal' elements in a story does not invite us to deny the realistic aspects of the story, but simply to transpose the setting to 'another world'. Fantasy worlds are often the settings for Josh's stories, nevertheless many elements of the real and recognizable are incorporated into those worlds.

The second kind of text authors draw upon to create an illusion of vraisemblance is cultural. Here the narrative assumes implicitly that there will be shared cultural knowledge between the reader and the text. In Josh's story such assumptions are present at the beginning where we are meant to understand that small boys who say 'bum' and 'go away' are 'very rude'. Other examples are the policemen who have the authority to ask questions, and the good father who provides children with breakfast, supper and a place to sleep. These behavioural codes are 'natural' only in terms of the norms of specific groups. Josh's story also refers to 'Notting Hill Gate' and to *Superman*, a place-name and a film which are not fictional, thus creating the illusion of a real setting.

The third kind of vraisemblance refers to conventions established within the institution of literature itself. Josh's story employs several literary conventions. 'Once upon a time' signals a children's fantasy story or fairy-tale and leads us to expect a journey or a quest, a struggle or a conflict, 'good' and 'bad' protagonists and a happy ending – all of which are present. The story is also conventional in other ways. In the long passage which suspends the action Josh uses the device of tripling, repeating everything three times, which is taken from folk-tales. More literary is the question posed by the text in T-Unit 20: 'And what was there?' Here both the narrator and the narratee are *implied*. There is no 'I' asking the question, no 'you' to whom it is addressed. This is the hidden, omniscient narrator of written fiction, rather than the direct, personal narrator of oral storytelling. Even the construction of a sequence of short main-clause T-Units in this passage, with no linking conjunctions as there would be in everyday speech, is suggestive of a degree of formality which is writing-like. This sequence creates a staccato rhythm, a punctuated series of actions whose formal arrangement signals danger and suspense. Another kind of convention is employed in the story dialogue: ' "There", said the police, "Now you can come home with me for tea" ' is a highly literary way of presenting speech.

Culler's fourth level of vraisemblance involves the denial that the text is indeed constructed as natural or real. Usually an external narrator vouches for the 'truth' of the story, or will even deliberately expose the operations of constructing the text, casting doubt on any sense of the real. But Culler points out that this is only another kind of narrative convention which attempts to create another reality (that of the narrator) while denying that of the story. This does not happen in Josh's story 17, but it is a frequent technique of Sundari's stories. Sundari usually invents a first-person narrator to tell her tales, and that narrator interpolates comments which imply that the story cannot be taken seriously. In Chapter 10 I have analysed these techniques of Sundari's very fully.

The final level of vraisemblance is the specific reference by the narrative discourse to other literary works. Culler discusses this exclusively as parody and irony, which are utterly dependent for their effect on the reader's knowledge of other texts. There are texts by Josh which parody news broadcasts and weather forecasts and these could certainly not be understood by a listener who had no familiarity with those forms. Parody has no part in story 17, but there are specific intertextualities in the borrowings from *Burglar Bill* and *Where the Wild Things Are*.

The analytic systems of Genette's *Narrative Discourse* and Barthes' *S/Z* uncover the layers of structuration outlined in Culler's levels of vraisemblance in enormous detail, yet the later analytic chapters of this book will show that this approach is capable of demonstrating literary/narrative competences which other story structure models do not make possible.

This chapter has examined several models of narrative analysis. I rejected story grammars for my own data because their systems are reductive, regarding narrative as primarily referential with the order of 'what happened' as the major focus. Psychoanalytic studies were also found to be of limited use, because their focus on story themes and content ignores the language which tells the tale. The more holistic analyses of Applebee and Sutton-Smith took greater account of narrative as a discursive form, but ultimately the focus of these practitioners on development, on the normative, also made their analyses too reductive for my purposes. Labov's narrative syntax opens the way to more inclusive analyses, since his category of Evaluation as the key to storytelling skill makes story style and language crucial. But though his categories are potentially applicable to literary narrative, they are developed only so far as oral stories of personal experience require them to be. Analyses that take account of plot, dialogues, the narrator's role, intertextualities, the social and cultural assumptions of the discourse and the larger metaphoric themes of stories are to be found in Genette and Barthes. The following chapters will show how I uncovered the children's knowledge of narrative as a discursive form. It is at the larger level of overall discourse rather than at the levels of words, sentence or surface intertextualities, that the extent of the influence of books on their oral narrating can be truly discovered.

NOTES

1. It is to Margaret Meek (*How Texts Teach What Readers Learn*) that I owe the underlying theory of this chapter, that children are taught structures which can be highly complex by the authors of well-crafted children's fiction. Meek fills a very obvious gap in theories of both narrative and literary competences by focusing on the primacy of narrative in literacy learning.
2. In his experiments Bartlett made considerable use of fictional material.
3. See Appendix A, pp. 200–3, for the series of retellings of *Hansel and Gretel* by Josh. Story 44 is recalled three months after Josh had heard the story and told his earlier versions of it. Compared to story 32 story 44 is very much less detailed, but shows better understanding of the total story.
4. The simplicity of Rumelhart's model of story means that dialogue sections containing the oral tradition formulae so loved and well-remembered by children are not included.
5. Of course, the distinction between the story and the discourse which narrates it is crucial in post-structuralist analyses of literary narrative, such as those of Genette and Barthes, which I use in chapters 8 to 11 of this book.
6. It would be useful to know whether children in the story grammar studies were able to construe story as part of *play*. Under such rigorous experimental conditions it seems unlikely that this could have been the case.
7. See Appendix B, p. 204, for transcripts of Robert's retellings of *The Three Little Pigs*.
8. In *Orality and Literacy* Ong gives a personal example of how his young niece would not allow his version of the 'I'll huff and I'll puff' formula, but insisted on the one she was familiar with. (Ong, 1982, p. 67).
9. The stories in Sutton-Smith's large-scale study (collected in *The Folk-Stories of Children*, 1981) are analysed using a variety of structural models. In Sutton-Smith and Botvin (1977) seven stages of story structure are identified, using a system derived from Propp. The levels

were found to be age-related. In Sutton-Smith, Botvin and Mahoney (1976) the focus is on children's socialization into public myth and legend. Different analytic models are demonstrated and contrasted. Analyses based on characters' interactions (derived from Maranda and Maranda, 1971) or on action sequences (derived from Propp, 1928) are considered to be more limited than a Piagetian analysis based on the idea of conservation in story structure. The authors argue that the Piaget analysis brings out levels of cognitive operations, whereas the other systems are too tied to content. The Piagetian analysis is similar in its aims and outcomes to Applebee's (1978) Vygotsky-based analysis of children's stories (see note 10 below).

   See also Sutton-Smith *et al.* (1975), in which there is an account of a Maranda and Maranda structural analysis. This paper, however, is interesting for its more general comments on fantasy storytelling. The authors find a relationship between children's willingness to narrate and their previous experience of stories, that children like to listen to themselves when the tape-recorder is used, and that some like to do a drawing before telling a story. These findings accord with my own study.

10. This is essential reading, not only for the student of narrative competences but also for the student of literary competences. The structural study is only a part of Applebee's book, but it is the part that deals with children's invented stories. In the rest of the book Applebee deals with children's developing sense of the difference between fact and fantasy and of critical reading. Applebee is one of the few practitioners to have called for case studies of the influence of literature on children's storytelling (Applebee, 1980).

11. The prosodic organization of young children's stories is a common feature of a wide range of studies, e.g. Weir (1962) in her account of pre-sleep monologues; Shirley Brice Heath (1983) in her account of the way Trackton children learn language through group storytelling. These studies, together with Sutton-Smith's and my own, can be put together with Ong's comments on the prosodic organization of oral literature (Ong, 1983).

12. Ong contrasts oral literature, where the bard plunges the listener *in media res*, stringing events together episodically, to early novels which were also episodic in structure and highly interpersonal with their first-person narrators. He argues that the pyramidal plot of modern detective fiction would be impossible in a pre-literate culture. While it seems to be the case that young children use prosody to organize their stories, and are not good at plot structures, I feel that Ong's view of literature is essentially plot-centred. Some very highly regarded modern novels have minimal plots and an extensive use of prosody, yet there is no doubt about the advanced literacy of their authors. One wonders why plots have to be regarded as more 'advanced' because they are a later development in literature.

13. For all the richness and multiple analyses involved in Sutton-Smith's structure studies, I consider it a weakness that he did not look at story language and style as such, though in the 1975 article (p. 94) he and his team do call for more research on individual differences in story style.

14. At the inception of my study, very few practitioners had suggested a direct connection between literate modes of narration and children's storytelling. Among them were Scollon and Scollon (1981), who contrast the literate features of their 2-year-old daughter's oral story to stories told by older, non-literate Athabaskan children at Fort Chipewyan in Alberta. These features include conventional framing of the story, explicit information structure, punning and verbal play, and the fictionalization of herself as author, narrator and character. Rachel actually 'wrote' her stories before 'reading' them in the manner of books, though at this stage she was pretend reading/writing. Here, prosodic features (punning and verbal play) *and* book-like features are part of Rachel's literary storytelling. The clear distinction drawn between orality and literacy by theorists like Ong does not take into account that many young children are immersed in literature from the time they learn to talk. In this view prosodic organization is seen as part of *both* literate and oral culture.

15. The material for this section, and for the analysis of Chapter 7 is taken from Labov and Weletsky (1967); Labov (1972) and Labov (1982).

16. Pratt shows that Labov's narrative categories can be applied to any work of literature. She casts doubt on structuralist claims that 'the language of literature is formally and functionally distinctive' (p. 66) and argues that differences in discourses are accounted for by

differences of situation, addressee, context and so on. I agree that the category of evaluation in Labov opens the gateway to stylistics and poetics, but I would have needed to create many new categories in addition to his to account for all the devices used in my data. Labov's categories, for example, do not account for dialogues between characters, first-person narrators who are not involved in the events narrated, intertextualities and the total metaphor created by a story. Rather than expand Labov's analysis to describe literature, I preferred to use systems directly arising from works of fiction – those of Genette and Barthes. However, while I can demonstrate that books have generated competences in my children, I could not be justified in describing their stories as either entirely literary or as entirely oral. The stories represent a transitional stage on the oral-literate continuum.

Chapter 7

The Children's Sense of Story Structure

Although I have argued in the last chapter that story grammars are inappropriate models for analysing the structure of my children's stories, I do accept that we must have a way of distinguishing narrative from other verbal forms. I have adopted Labov's criteria for defining narratives since they include both the plot structure (i.e. what happened: complicating actions and resolution), and any elaboration of the narrative events (i.e. setting information, and the narrator's own attitude to the story told).

Labov (1972) defines a minimal narrative as 'a sequence of two clauses which are temporally ordered'. In other words, two things must take place, one after the other. Although such minimal stories are analysable it is not likely that they would be reportable and worth listening to. His second major criterion concerns the ways in which narrators give colour and life to the narrative events by revealing their own attitudes. Labov insists that this is a central part of narrative structure and categorizes it as *evaluation*. The final essential component of narratives is some kind of setting information; without some *orientation* on who? where? when? how? and what sort? it is very difficult to make any sense of a narrative.

Labov includes two further elements: *abstracts*, which introduce stories by giving a general statement of their themes, and *codas*, which sum up the point of the story after it has been told. I have excluded these categories from my data since my children tell stories belonging to a different genre from Labov's narratives of personal experience. All five children tell invented fantasy stories, for which they use conventional openings and closures: 'Once' or 'Once upon a time', or 'One day' to start the story, and 'that's the end of the story' to finish it. The children use these conventions in almost all stories and there are virtually no abstracts and codas.

Setting information is often concentrated at the beginning of narratives but most competent storytellers continue to orient the listener to details of time, place and person throughout. Labov found that evaluation sections of his adolescents' narratives were typically placed just before the climax of the story, suspending the story events while the narrator built up his particular attitude towards them. However, Labov acknowledged that narrators can evaluate their narratives all the way through from beginning to end. Orientation and evaluation elements can appear anywhere in a story, then; they are free-floating parts of the story structure. In contrast, the story events (complicating actions, resolution) must happen in a temporal sequence and thus are fixed.

Perhaps the best way to demonstrate how these categories work is to apply them to a simple story. I have chosen a story by Justine, told when she was just over 4 years old. Beside the transcript are three columns: the first (A) in which to mark the complicating actions/resolutions, the second (B) to indicate orientations and the third (C) to show evaluations.

	Transcript of Justine story 2 (4:1)	A	B	C
1	(right-um) once upon a time there was two little dicky birds in a tree		✔	
2	(along came a- and Mammy said-) and Mammy one said 'Don't go out there'	✔	✔	✔
3	but the naughtiest was the little baby one		✔	✔
4	he went out 'cos he didn't listen to his mum	✔		✔
5	she said 'There's wolves out there and foxes and ugly lions (and-) (P) and other sort of things that will eat the birds (and-) (P) and crawling insects (P) and spiders and witches (P)		✔	✔
6	and he flyed out of the nest	✔	✔	
7	and (when) one of the tigers opened his mouth and (call-) gobbled him all up	✔	✔	✔
8	and the second little baby came to eat him up	✔	✔	✔
9	and that's the end of the story	CLOSURE		

DISCUSSION OF THE SIMPLE ANALYSIS OF JUSTINE'S STORY

If we extract from Justine's story the complicating actions and resolution (narrative clauses) we shall have the referential part of the story, the gist of 'what happened':

> Mammy one said 'Don't go out there'
> he went out
> and he flyed out
> and one of the tigers opened his
> mouth and gobbled him all up

These clauses are fixed in their temporal sequence. We cannot have the mother bird's warning at the end and the tiger eating the baby bird at the beginning. Labov found that the referential parts of narratives employed simple sentence structures – declarative sentences in the past tense. Any variations of this tend to be orientations or evaluations.

Orientations tell us about the who, what, where, why, how of stories, and introduce temporal, spatial and attributive descriptions. Evaluations answer the question *Why are you telling me this*? and are intended to ward off the response *So what*! They can be accomplished by very simple non-syntactic means, such as expressive phonology: changing the pitch and tone of voice to leave the listener in no doubt about how the narrator feels about that part of the narrative. But they can also involve the narrator in syntactically complex structures: modal verbs, negatives and questions, explicatives, and so on. Justine's list in T-Unit 5 is evaluative, and Labov would see her build-up of lexical items as a form of *intensifier*. She also uses a *negative* in 2, a *comparator* in 3, and an *explicative* in 4.

Justine orients the listener throughout; she identifies her characters explicitly: 'two little dicky birds'/ 'Mammy one'/'little baby one'/'one of the tigers'/'the second little baby'; she *places* her actions: 'in a tree'/'out there'/'out of the nest'; and though there are no temporal references beyond the conventional 'once upon a time' she manages the chronology of her story by changing tenses. Mammy bird speaks in the present tense while the actions happen in the past.

Although this story is simple and short, it fulfils all Labov's criteria for well-formed narratives: a) It contains a sequence of two actions and a proper causal resolution. b) It is explicitly oriented throughout. c) It is evaluated in simple and complex ways, and Justine's list in the Mammy's warning actually suspends the action in a way similar to that employed by Labov's adolescent narrators.

Justine was very young when she told this story and it is by no means her richest narrative, but it represents an example of a tendency I saw in most of the stories. *The children tend to take fairly simple sequences of actions and elaborate them extensively.* However, each child produces a variety of story structures, some considerably more complex than Justine's, and others which, for reasons I shall discuss, do not fit easily into structural models of any kind. What is clear is that one story cannot possibly give a fair account of a child's structural competence.

In all I selected a total of 24 stories to represent a typical but varied spread of narrative structures for each child. For each child I tried to find stories to represent five different criteria, as follows:

- a story from an early storytelling session;
- a story from a later storytelling session;
- a story showing an incomplete or problem structure;
- a story showing the most fully-formed structure the child was capable of;
- a retelling of a written story.

This selection does not produce an even number of stories from each child. Sundari and Jimmy do not retell written stories and Josh has no stories which could be said to be non-narrative in that they lack narrative clauses. It is not possible to show the analyses of each of the 24 stories here but I shall discuss my broad findings, taking Labov's major categories in turn, and quoting in full as many of the stories as space will allow.

ORIENTATION

Use of orientation

All five children use orientation very extensively. In 14 out of the 24 stories I analysed orientation elements predominate over Labov's other categories. In the remaining 10 orientation elements are only exceeded by evaluations. The use of the orientation category shows the children's concern to make specific references to time and place, and to identify characters. Their stories are elaborated with these references in order to make them explicit and credible.

Position of orientation in the narrative

Typically the children open their stories with a major orienting statement, confirming the findings of narratologists that stories need settings before there can be explicable narrative events. Opening orientation statements can be brief:

> one day there was a zoo (*Justine story 22 4:11*)

> Burglar Bill worked behind the police station   yes (*Robert story 22 4:0*)

Opening orientations of this minimal kind usually establish a vague past time (one day) and perhaps a place or a character's identity. Very few stories start without such an introduction. However, there are orientation sections which are more like paragraphs than single statements:

> there was a farm
> it had many horses in
> and it had many calves and sheeps
> now all the small pigs were in their barns
> it was a rainy day (*Josh story 4 5:0*)

In instances like this the child uses the orientation section of the story to set a scene rather than give minimal information. In other stories the orientation section is so extended that the storyteller simply continues to describe and fails to recount any narrative events:

> once there was a monster who liked eating [laughs] green bananas
> and once there was a monster who liked eating [unclear nonsense word]
> and once there was a monster who liked eating shalas and then a man who
> was too clever because he was a bit of Laurel and Hardy and a bit of Harold
> Lloyd and that's the end of the story (*Jimmy story 1 4:9*)

It is not the case that Jimmy's concept of a narrative consists only of setting information, since in other stories he includes complicating actions and resolutions. This story and several others were based on paintings Jimmy had just done. This seems to have pushed his story structure in the direction of pure description so that he forgot to have anything happen in it. In a later story his mother interrupts to remind him that something ought to happen in a story:

> once there was a cowboy fight
> (and the Indi-) and there was lots of dead cowboys and Indians
> and (once the-) once there was one with very long legs and once there was
> a Indian (with a funny s-) with a funny spear
> and once there was (one) a funny wizard
> and (P) once there was a big (P) boom from a barrel 'cos it had lots of
> dynamite

and once there was one that had red cheeks (P)
[Adult: Did they do anything? Did anything happen to them?]
and the one with red cheeks got killed (and he was a cowboy) but he
was a *COW-BOY* [shouted] and that's the end of the story (*Jimmy story
8 4:9*)

Here orientation clauses seem to be a formula that Jimmy enjoys recycling. Even when his mother tries to prompt some sort of plot Jimmy is clearly not interested in narrative events. Though these are good examples of play with a category of narrative structure, Jimmy does have a plot in all his other stories, and the inclusion of complicating actions and resolutions was clearly within his narrative competences.

Of all the five children Sundari has the greatest tendency to over-use orientation and to have nothing happen in her stories. It is worth quoting two of her stories in full. In the first she does not include any complicating actions at all:

once upon a time there was a little girl called Sarah   and she loved
dancing   she did all sorts of dancing   she did tap dancing ordinary dancing
Dutch dancing all *kinds* of dancing   I'll tell you all the ones if I
remember   she did (P) Swedish dancing (P)   and that is only the ones I can
tell you I'm afraid   I'm sorry I said all of them   well (um) she had a little boy
(P) the lady did   (um) and his name was (P) Joseph   and they had another
sister called Emma and a sister called Becky   and they were *all* the
Bucklers   there was Becky Buckler Joseph Buckler Emma Buckler and Sarah
Buckler and the last of all the lady   and the man was called Sona Buckler
(and-) (P) and (um) (P) (um-um-er-um) Jane Buckler   and they lived in a very
nice house   it had curtains at the windows net curtains a very nice pink
door   and inside there were some silver doors and gold doors   and there
was number one number two number three and the last   and there was
number one number two number three number four and number five and
number six and number nineteen   they're all the numbers on the doors one
on each door   nineteen was (P) Sarah Buckler's own door 'cos she was the
special special specialist one (P)   (um) and they *loved* their cottage cos it
was a cottage   I didn't tell you that   I forgot to   (um) and the lady and the
man and all the children were Buddhists   there's Buddhist children and Lady
Aman children   (um) I mean not children (um) Buddhists   and there was
Buddhas (P)   and the little girl Sarah's sisters loved dancing   they did
outside dancing   they did tap (tap) shoes   they was tapping (on the-) on the
concrete   and (P) they did somersault dances cartwheel dances head-over-
heel dances all sorts of dances   so did Sarah do outside ones   they did the
same as her as well   and the house was very nice   there was double beds
in *every room*   it was such a lovely time they had   they didn't waste any
time you see   they had a car which was white   they painted it all the while
until they painted it white again   they thought it was so lovely white   I can't
tell you anything more about the car   well they had lovely records lovely
shoes and all sorts of lovely things   they had lovely food as well   I can't tell
you everything I'm sorry to say (P)   there was nice trees fir trees Christmas
trees   anyway Christmas trees are the same as fir trees [chuckles] (P)   and
that is the end of the story (*Sundari story 5 5:5*)

Strictly speaking this story lacks the minimal two events linked temporally and sequentially which define minimal narratives. Actions do happen in several clauses, for the children dance, but nothing happens as a consequence of their dancing that would amount to a complicating action. Sundari's rondo-like movement back to the types of dancing and back to the lovely house suggest, like her interpolated narrator's comments, that she cannot think of anything that could happen in this story. In any case Sundari always prefers to describe a character or a scene than to fill her stories with actions. In most of her other stories, several of which are quoted in full throughout this book, she does manage to include one or two complicating actions, but it is clear that these are not of much interest to her, for they do not play an important role in the story. For Sundari elaborating characters, saying what they were like and how they spent their time, describing their clothes and their houses, creating an atmosphere, and, above all, interspersing the whole with narrator's comments that very often 'debunk' the story told, are all more important than what happened. What is more, Sundari elaborates her descriptions with clauses that fall into Labov's evaluation category. Sundari's concept of story structure, then, is to take minimal or uncomplicated narrative events, or even no narrative events, and to fill the story with elaboration, for the manner of telling seems to take priority over what is told.[1]

In some ways Sundari's stories challenge the Labov categories, since a large part of storytelling for her is the invention and celebration of a narrating voice. In contrast to her story 5 is story 7, told shortly afterwards and transformed from a book: *What Tina Can Do* by T.B. Jensen. There are actions, but the way the story closes is of greater interest:

I'm going to tell you another story about a boy this time a boy called Cletcher a very funny name   I made it up (P)   Cletcher was a good boy   his mother and father said he could go to the fair one day   he saw a clown at the fair   and the clown made these noises [sings a lot of nonsense syllables]   and he saw that   and he went on the fire engine that went round and round   and he kept ringing the bell like this — ding-ding-ding ting-ling-ling [sneezes]   I'm sorry I made a noise like that because I've got a bit of a cold [unclear word] (P)   and he had *girls'* things like talcum powder and perfume he loved to put it on   he had a sister who went to the fair as well because she was good   and they got a bottle (P)   and drank out of it like this   this is the noise it made [big slurping noises]   what they drank was called tonic water (P)   yes tonic water (P)   two bottles of nice fizzy tonic water lemonade   lemonade sort of tonic water   it was lovely   they drank it (P)   and also they went on some swings   they went as high and low and high and low and high and low [spoken with sing-song intonation] and the swing made a noise like this [creaking sounds]   (it was an) it needed oil   I'm sorry I said it needed oil (P)   we're gonna have a bit of a laugh now [loud laughing]   that's what they made (P)   when I said 'you can have a bit of a laugh now' the two children laughed (P)   you can laugh too when you have the tape on again (P)   you can go like this — ha-ha-ha-ha-ha-ha [affected adult laughter]   and one day they got a big fat green apple and a red apple   they were both big and fat (P)   and they did all sorts of things   I can't tell you all of them what they did at the fair   they swung round and round and round on

big wheels   they saw clowns and clowns and clowns and clowns   they
played music like this [imitates musical instrument] 'to-te-too-de-to-to' [at
some length]   that was a bagpipe sort of something (P)   and there was a
little bell they rang like this [sings] 'ting-aling-a-ling'   and they climbed
chimneys and climbed rooftops   they couldn't find the way back so they rang
the bell again   and it showed them the way [sings] 'ting-a-ling-aling-ling'   and
then they (sho-) shaked tambourines like this [sings] 'ding-ding-ding'   and
soon they were back home tucked in their safe little beds   they couldn't
do anything   not ring the bell   not play the bagpipes   not do the
tambourine   not see the clown clown clown   not go on the swings   not go
on the fire-engine   not pick apples   not see the pigs   not see the
horses   not swing swing   not see-saw see-saw   not watch telly like they did
at home (P)   not drink out of tonic water bottles   all they could do was snore
[snoring noises]   and in the morning they ate their breakfast   at dinner-time
they ate their dinner   at tea-time they ate their tea   and then they went to
bed again   and then they washed their face   and then they went like this
'rub-atub-tub rub-atub-tub rub-atub-tub-de-dub'   and they clapped their
hands   they clapped clapped clapped like this [claps]   and that is the end of
the story   I'll ring a little bell   tin-a-ling-ting (*Sundari story 7 5:6*)

The story contains actions but they are not complicated in any way by the difficulties
or problems we would expect to be part of even the simplest story. The nearest Sundari
gets to a complicating action is having the children lost, but there is no tension at all
in the way this problem is handled and in the very next sentence Sundari has it solved
by the device of the magic bell. We have to admit that the story fulfils Labov's criteria
for a minimal narrative, but that it takes very little of its interest from the events
recounted. Yet I would argue that this is very competent storytelling indeed. In making
her focus *not* the story events but *the way they are told* Sundari diverts our attention
from the minimal plot structure. The text of this story is filled with *intensifiers* in all
its repetitions, with *comparators*, not only in all the sound effects, but also in the long
list of *negatives* in the closing section of the story, which Sundari transformed from
a book, and with *correlatives* – the sections of the story where Sundari supplies
multiple adjectives. These are among Labov's most complex categories of *evaluation*
and he states that they are very rarely found in the BEV narratives of pre-adolescent
children. Not only does Sundari recount these rather minimal story events in the most
colourful (i.e. evaluated) way she can, but she also includes *the narrating itself* as a
source of comment on the story and of interest in its own right. At the same time as
she heavily evaluates the different sections of this story Sundari also orients her listener
with explicit setting information, giving us details of the children themselves, the
fairground rides, and attributes of both people and things. All of this is interspersed
with narrator's comments.

Types of orientation

In all I identified seven categories of orientation in the children's stories:

1. *Identification of character* (answers the question *who?*)

2. *Spatial* (answers the question *where*?)
3. *Temporal* (answers the question *when*?)
4. *Props* (answers the question *what*?)
5. *Attribute* (answers the question *what kind*?)
6. *Behaviour* (answers the question *what doing*?)
7. *Social* (answers the question *which group*?)

I found that categories 1 to 6 were used by all five children while the *social* category was used only occasionally by the two 5-year-olds. The children differed widely in their preference for different kinds of orientation, the bias being related to the sorts of themes they chose for their stories. For example, almost one third of Josh's orientation elements are *spatial*, a much higher proportion than in the other children's stories and this is explained by the fact that Josh tells stories about journeys over wide-ranging and varying terrains. Almost half of Sundari's orientation elements relate to *props* and *behaviour*, because she likes to tell stories about people and the things they like to do and play with. Jimmy, who likes to describe what his characters look like and sometimes bases the description on a drawing, uses *attributive* orientations more than the other children.

The category *identification of character* is well-used by all the children who tend to be strikingly explicit in their references to characters, preferring to name them rather than risk confusion by using pronouns, as in the following section from a story of Justine's:

and the next day it was *Timothy's* birthday
Mummy gave him her present
Nanny gave him her present
and then *the little girl Suzie* gave her present

Here Justine shows a control over noun/pronoun use which is typical of all the children. Temporality is usually indicated by the word 'then', though there are also adverbial clauses of time and other much more complex time references which I analyse very fully in Chapter 8. However, the children's frequent use of 'then'/'and then' indicates that their concept of narrative organization is moving from the additive (and) towards the temporal.

COMPLICATING ACTIONS, RESOLUTIONS AND RESULTS

Complicating actions are the sequence of story events. *Resolutions* and *Results* refer to the way the storyteller resolves the actions of the narrative. I have used the term resolution to mean a story ending which is achieved by some external agent, or by the device of saying that the characters went to bed, as Sundari does in story 7 above. I have used the term result to mean a story ending which is implicit in the earlier events of the narrative. Four kinds of plot structure emerge from the 24 stories I analysed:

1. Stories with no complicating actions
2. Stories with complicating actions but no resolutions
3. Stories with complicating actions and resolutions
4. Stories with complicating actions and results

These types of story structure are well distributed among the stories of each child. All the children but Josh tell at least one story with no complicating actions. All five children tell one or two stories with no resolutions. All five children tell between one and three stories with a resolution, and all the children but Jimmy manage a story with a result. For me the implication of this is that we do not necessarily get a true picture of children's competences for plot structure on the basis of one or two stories. Even on the same storytelling occasion a child's performance varies. What is true over the entire data, not merely the 24 stories I analysed for the Labov narrative syntax, is that *the stories with the most fully-formed plots and satisfying results are those which are either story retellings or highly intertextual inventions.* I shall briefly discuss each type of plot structure, and try to provide an illustration of each.

1. Stories with no complicating actions

I have already shown, using Jimmy's story 1 and Sundari's story 5, that stories with no actions sometimes occur as a result of over-use of orientation. The other major reason for stories with no actions is that the children are *playing* with story forms. Justine tells a story 'by' a baby:

> Once upon a time there were three bunny rabbits and that's the end of the story (*Justine story 8*)

This is announced as a 'baby's story' and clearly distinguished by Justine from her own stories. Robert does something similar when he tells his father a 'tiny' story:

> Sandy and Paul went to the beach and made a sandcastle then they went home (*Robert story 9*)

It is clear that these two children regard plots as the 'difficult' parts of story structure and that Justine sees them as beyond the competency of infants. She is in fact quite accurate. Pradl (1979) found that story beginnings were the first convention to be learned, followed by story endings.[2]

2. Stories with complicating actions but no resolutions

Of the 24 stories 7 have one or more complicating actions but no resolution. In some cases the child has an *implicit* resolution which is not actually stated. For example in story 23 Justine tells about a monster bird who consumes a succession of things, eventually culminating in the whole world. The end of the world must bring all stories to an end, but this is an implicit rather than a stated resolution to the narrative. In Josh's story 2, which I quoted at the opening of Chapter 1, Josh half resolves the story. When the father of the boy in the story says of the new torch 'We'll have that' it is intended to be understood that the father takes the torch away from the boy, for this part of the story is borrowed from *Burglar Bill* and these are the words Bill uses when he steals things. Josh leaves this implied and makes no explicit statement telling how the story ends. Sundari's story 9 is unresolved because she gets carried away with setting a long scene and fails to return to the action. This is a good example of a story with a few narrative events (in italic) but no perceivable outcome.

> Hello hello I'm going to tell you a story about a little girl and her mother and father well the little girl and her mother and father one day *took* the little girl to the seaside and the little girl liked the sea and the seagulls (P) the little girl *swam* in the sea (P) and they *went* on a little paddle boat called a dinghy (P) they *swam* to Decks Little Island not very far away from the sand and they *ate* their lunch . . .

Up to this point the story has some narrative actions but they can hardly be called 'complicating'. Hereafter Sundari gets carried away with some remarkable description and has very little else happen:

> the little girl always said 'please' and 'thank-you' (P) she was always being good she loved to play though she never fighted much she sometimes fighted at school though because people hurt her (P) not actually hurting though (P) they were being lovely and quiet all the time at the seaside the little girl had brought some of her friends one called (Claud-) Claudia one called (P) Natasha (P) one called Heidi and one called (P) Len [unclear] a little boy and it was Heidi's brother (P) and they loved to play at the seaside the paddle-boat wasn't as little as you think it was quite big enough for all her friends and her and her mummy and daddy they had brought a candle with them unless it- (the-) if it gets dark and starts raining they can put it up and if it's wasted if it blew out they had a torch (P) it was quite quiet by the sea the waves were going whoosh whoosh whoosh [swishing sounds] they only lived in a little tiny cottage really little but not as little as you think bigger than you think it was so quiet everywhere in their land 'cos it was a country they were so quiet in their land nobody was ever being noisy all the cars (we-) were put silencers on and nobody took them off it was so quiet you couldn't hear anything at all not even the cars it was so quiet it was as quiet as this [silence] I'm sorry there were a few noises because my place is quite a noisy place not near any (much-much-tch-) seasides the nearest one is called (P) [*Adult*: Winterton?]
> Winterton I've got a little rake and (I) next time I go to the seaside I'm going to bring it and play about in the sand raking lines I'm five did you know? well I've told you (an-) another story well this tape is a tape I'll tell you more about the story well the little girl was so quiet she didn't even snore one bit she did play a lot quietly I can't tell you all of them she ate very quietly she only made 'tit' sounds like this (faint tapping) wasn't it quite quiet? it was quiet sometimes when she slept she slept like this (little breathing noises) when she cried she went (soft sobs) and wiped her tears (P) she was never noisy not much talking just a bit not very much slow story she was always weared weary and weared and weared [pronounced as in 'weary'] (*Sundari story 9*)

This story moves on a little further towards a plot than Sundari's story 5, the one which was all orientation clauses. While there is no doubt about the complexity and skill of Sundari's descriptions of the quiet land and the quiet girl, it is clear that Sundari does not expect them to do anything or encounter any problems. It is also clear that Sundari regards this as a legitimate story, and at the end of it one feels one has experienced a narrative of what a girl and a place were *like* rather than what she did. Though this story certainly does not fulfil any criteria for well-formed plots, it is nonetheless a very skilled piece of narration, i.e. Sundari's well-developed storytelling skills are *narrative* skills.

3. Stories with complicating actions and resolutions

A resolution solves the problem of the narrative by means of an agency which is external to the preceding narrative events. We can see this in a simple story from Josh:

> there was a farm   it had many horses in   and it had many calves and
> sheeps   now all the small pigs were in their barns   it was a rainy day   all the
> animals came out   but the farmer told them to came in   except it was rainy
> and it was sunny so a rainbow came   but then the rain stopped   and the sun
> came out (and- and it was a little bit- er-er-er-) [*Adult*: A little bit . . . ?] and
> the farmer was a little bit mourning but not very   do you know
> why?   because just above the farm there was a fire   and the fireman came
> and put it out in the firecar   and that's the end   (*Josh story 4*)

Josh's story problem is added to the other events of the story. The fire is not related to anything that has previously happened, and it is resolved by an agency outside the rest of the story – the firemen. Perhaps Josh added the fire because he was aware that his rainbow did not amount to a plot. Jimmy does something similar in his story 5, introducing a story problem in his last four sentences and quickly resolving it:

> once upon a time I had a birthday   and someone gave me a magic box   and
> (when I) when I put some metal things in I heard 'ruckety-ruck ruckety-ruck'
> and out came real things   and once I put a plastics in it   and I heard 'Hey
> what am I doing?   Hey what am I doing?' [squeaky voice]   'Hey what am I
> doing?'   and one was Luke   and one was Yoda   (and-) and they went
> trample trample trample   (and they said-) and then I put one of my soldiers
> in   and I heard a English voice say 'Hey where am I?'   and then I put (a-) (P)
> Indian in   and I locked it   and I called it little Bill   (and that's the end of the-
> and that's the end of the- no-)   and then I made (a-) a cowboy   and they had
> fights   and the Indian won   and that's the end of the story (*Jimmy story 5*)

Jimmy has a schema for this story. Basically there is the repeating pattern of putting things into a magic box and having them come to life. This is a promising series of complicating actions, and Jimmy almost settles for ending his story with no resolution or result. Then he changes his mind, perhaps sensing an inadequate ending, adds the Indian and the cowboy who fight, and resolves things by having the Indian win. These final events, however, have little connection with the earlier story actions.

4. Stories with complicating actions and results

In these stories the outcome of the problem presented by the complicating actions is embedded in the narrative events from the beginning. These stories are strongly associated with book sources, for they are either retellings or very intertextual invented stories. There is no doubt that stories from books gave the children structural models which they could not easily invent by themselves. By retelling book stories they could practise handling more complicated plots whose outcomes were implicit from the beginning of the story. Robert, the youngest storyteller, at just over 3½ at the beginning of his story collection, provides the most striking illustration of the support that book texts gave the children. I regard the story retellings in the data as Vygotsky's 'zone of proximal development' in action; with the help of a known text the children can master structures they cannot invent for themselves.[3] At age 3:8 Robert gave a loose, summarized retelling of a *Topsy and Tim* story that he knew.[4] He does not attempt to use the words of the text in his retelling but simply gives the story events:

> (um-) Topsy and Tim were going out   and they never heard something a car
> coming around   and he was playing on his bike   'Top-Tim there's a car
> coming'   'No there isn't'   'There is'   and then he walked   and then (it
> caught-) it runned over him   and then he had to go to the hospital   and then
> that's the end of the story (*Robert story 5*)

Here the story problem is stated in the second sentence, the complicating action is that Tim ignores the warning, and the result is inevitable. Though this is a proper unforced result and this story could therefore be regarded as structurally more satisfying than the earlier stories I have quoted in this chapter, for me it raises questions about what we should value in narrative structure. All the important elements are in place; there is minimal setting information, there are complicating actions, there is suspension of the action before the result providing a degree of tension (Labov's evaluation), and there is a result. Yet Sundari's less complete narrative structures involve competences which are far more advanced, in complexities of chronology and narrating voice, and they require other analytic criteria than Labov's.

In the later chapters of this book I shall attempt to show what Sundari's narrative competences look like when Genette's categories of narrative discourse are applied to her stories. Plot structure is only a part of narrative skill. In contrast to Robert's minimal but accurate retelling of *Topsy and Tim* is one of two retellings he gave of *Burglar Bill*. Robert is now 4:0, a more experienced storyteller, and this time he tries to stay close to the original text.

> Burglar Bill worked behind the police station yes   he had stolen chips stolen
> beefburger and stolen cuppa tea for breakfast   and he goes off to
> work st-ea-l-ing things [said with great expression] (when he-no-no) when
> he comes to the second house he climbs through the bathroom window
> and 'That's a nice toothbrush and some beans—I'll have them'   so he puts
> them into his sack   and when he comes to the sixteenth house he stops
> there (on-on-) on the white step (was-) was a big big big brown box with
> little holes in it   'That's a nice box with little holes in it   I'll have that'
> when he came home there was a noise in the box   and it sounded like

one police car (sounds-and it came-) 'well it sounds like two police cars' so
he raises the lid 'Blow me down it's a ba-a-b-y' and he pats his hand and
he–'What was you doing in that box?' and the baby still cries 'I know
what you want- grub' so he gave him a apple to the baby *still the baby
cries* [said with emphasis] and he gave him a slice of marmalade and toast
to the baby but he still cries (and then he-and then he-) then he gives
(some- some-) some cuppa tea and [unclear] beans 'That's better I'll
have some beans meself' and he (er-) gives him (er-) a book a ball or
something he throws it at the cat he gives him a book to the baby and
the baby bites a hole in it the baby cries louder than ever and he falls
off the piano stool (stools-) [*Adult*: What's the baby say?] 'again again'
(and-) and he rubbed his nose (and) and he said 'I didn't want to do it the
first time' so (he-he-) the baby's (on his-) on his knee suddenly (he- um-
um) he heared a smell 'pooh' 'pooh' says the baby he changes the
nappy and he didn't have another one so he used a old bath towel
'That's better' take him round the park and he-(er-) 'Say "run for it" if you
see [unclear] 'Run for it' said the baby so he goes home and puts
him to bed and goes off hisself then he wakes up he hears a noise
downstairs someone climbing through the window carefully there with a
black mask over her face a woman lady 'I've got a baby' 'Hey blow me
down that's my baby' and he did the same (then he- that's him) and
then he gives him biscuits [*Adult*: Whát did Bill have] cup of coca-cola
(and he-and the-) and the baby starts to cry 'SSHH because they might
be after us' the baby starts crying 'I've been a *bad* man' 'I've been a *bad*
woman I've been a *terrible* woman' and so they give everything back
[*Adult*: Give what back?] the things- all the things and he (gets-) gets
married (and then-) and then 'Say "Burglar Bill" ' 'Burglar Bill' says the
baby he has the baby in his arms and that's the end of the story (*Robert
story 22*)

There is no doubt that this is a very competent performance for a child of only just
four. Robert has included every key action in the story in its chronological sequence.
All the orientation elements are in place, the story is heavily evaluated with humour
and the action is suspended at two vital points – Bill's discovery of the baby in the
box, and Burglar Betty climbing into Bill's house. Robert has learned all this from
Ahlberg's text, which, incidentally, is considerably pared down by Robert and
transformed in places to fit Robert's own language and experience ('widow lady'
becomes 'woman lady', and 'stolen chips' and 'stolen beefburger' replace Bill's more
conventional breakfast items).

EVALUATION

Labov (1972) lists four major types of evaluation which can be distributed throughout
a narrative. He noted that pre-adolescents used very few evaluations, yet I found that
all but two of his categories were present across 21 of the 24 stories I analysed – the
other three are two-line 'play' stories from Justine and Robert. Some evaluation

elements are non-syntactic – phonology and gestures, for example – but most represent syntactic departures from the grammar of ordinary, simple declarative clauses which characterize telling what happened in an unelaborated way. The categories in Labov are as follows:

Intensifiers
Gestures
Phonology
Quantifiers
Lexical items (e.g. lists)
Foregrounding
Repetition
Ritual (oral tradition formulae)
Wh-exclamations

Comparators
Imperatives
Questions
Negatives
Futures
Modal verbs
Or-clauses
Comparatives

Correlatives
Be . . . ing structures
Double ing structures
Double appositives
Double/treble attributives
Right participles
Left participles
Nominalizations

Explicatives
Simple qualifiers
Complex qualifiers
Compound qualifiers
Simple causal
Complex causal
Compound causal

Although I broke down the texts of the 24 selected stories into these categories I would need the space of several chapters to show the detailed analysis here. What I can do is show the most important findings, and illustrate some of the categories from the more complex parts of the children's stories.

1. Use of evaluation elements

I found that most of the children's narratives are very heavily evaluated indeed. This is the reverse of Labov's findings for pre-adolescents. My children's stories usually have a few straightforward declarative sentences saying what happened, and a great deal of elaboration which is either orientation or evaluation. I think there is a twofold explanation for this. One is that the model for the children's storytelling was very obviously literary; the authors of stories for children usually make them interesting and colourful by a large range of rhetorical devices. Secondly, the children here are using the genre of fantasy stories rather than narratives of personal experience. Fairy-tales and other fantasy forms probably lend themselves to a greater degree of elaboration than narrating a real-life experience. The former is concerned with the imaginative creation of a world, the latter with being true to the facts of what happened.

2. Types of evaluation in the children's stories

Do the children use the most simple types of evaluation most frequently – expressive phonology or repetitions, for example? I counted all the evaluation elements in each of

Table 7.1   *Types of evaluation in 24 stories by five children*

	Sundari	Josh	Justine	Jimmy	Robert
Intensifiers	61	21	29	12	43
Comparators	78	68	32	12	40
Correlatives	14	9	6	1	9
Explicatives	35	18	16	11	9
Total	188	116	83	36	101

the 24 stories, then quantified each of the four major evaluation categories for each child to show their distribution over the total (see Table 7.1).

These figures show that for Sundari, Josh and Justine, comparators are more frequently used than intensifiers, for Jimmy they are equally used, and for Robert there are only slightly fewer comparators than intensifiers. Explicatives are well established in the five children's competences, while correlatives, the rarest category in Labov, are still present for all five children.

Labov (1972, p. 383): Of comparators 'They are dealing with a level of expected and unrealised events which go beyond basic narrative sequence.' Comparators include not only direct comparisons, like similes, or grammatical comparatives and superlatives, but also modals, questions, negatives, futures and imperatives. For Labov all these forms compare what did occur to what did not. Comparators take us beyond the actual story events, and point towards what is implied, possible but as yet unrealized. For me this is an important insight, for it suggests that the generating centre of narrative (Labov's term) is about far more than 'what happened' and is linked to the multi-layered, metaphorical meanings of stories. Sundari's poetic passage about the quiet seaside in story 9 uses many comparators to create a series of images of silence, though she uses no similes or metaphors.

3. Passages showing complex evaluation

It is possible to illustrate how evaluation categories work from some brief passages taken from the stories quoted in this chapter. In story 7 (see p. 89) Sundari wants to tell her listeners about the delicious taste of the tonic water the two children drank:

> what they drank was called tonic water (P)   yes tonic water (P)   two bottles of nice fizzy tonic water   lemonade   lemonade sort of tonic water

This passage uses an *intensifier* (the repetition of 'tonic water'), an *explicative* (the simple qualifying clause 'what they drank'), a *correlative* (the triple appositive 'yes tonic . . . two bottles of . . . lemonade sort of'), a second *correlative* (the double attributive 'nice fizzy'), another *intensifier* (the quantifier 'two'), and a *comparator* (the comparative 'lemonade sort of'). This kind of passage is not very common, even in Sundari's stories. Story 7 more often uses intensifiers, in the form of repetition, rhythm and expressive phonology for its evaluative effects. A further example appears in story 9:

> it was so quiet you couldn't hear anything at all not even the cars

Here there are several *comparators* (the negative modal 'couldn't'; the two comparatives 'so quiet' and 'not even'), an *intensifier* (the quantifier 'anything at all'), and an *explicative* (the simple qualifying clause 'you couldn't hear anything at all').

4. The children's competences for overall narrative structure

I have tried to show in this chapter that the children's competences for elaboration in narrative (orientation and evaluation) were more highly developed than their competences for sequencing narrative actions with logical outcomes. Labov's categories of narrative syntax show what the children are best at doing, that is elaborating simple story events. I do not regard the children's descriptions and narrator's comments as empty verbiage, designed to conceal underdeveloped plots. It is true that if one adopts the story grammar, i.e. largely referential concept of narrative, then the narrative schemata of the children reveal competences at an early stage of development, *though this changes dramatically when they are retelling known stories from books*. But if one's concept of narrative is to regard it as a *discursive* form, as Labov does, then the children's competences are remarkably well-developed. When the children retell stories from books they are able to recall a great deal of the elaboration, as well as the story events. This should not be surprising at all, for the two are interlocked. Robert retells Burglar Betty's break-in to Bill's house in a highly evaluated way *because that is the most exciting and interesting narrative event in the story*. Robert remembers how it goes because of the emotional force it has. The same is true of Sundari's transformation of a story ending in her story 7, where she recounts, with astonishing accuracy for a spontaneously invented narrative, what the children could not do when they went to sleep. Sundari understands story closure as the death of all things, the negation of activity, the end of possibilities. This has enormous affective force which works through the *form* of all those negative clauses she strings out. It is not the case that stories have 'plots' which exist independently of the language which speaks them. In a competent storytelling form and content are interdependent. That the children perceive this, however unconsciously, is reflected in the fact that they do not merely recall the gist of the stories they retell but pick up all the communicative devices the authors employ to gain and hold their interest and attention.

I have quoted a few of the 24 stories in this chapter, but many others both from this selection and from the rest of the data are spread throughout this book. There readers will encounter some stories with plot structures and rhetorical devices which are well in advance of what I have analysed here. Two stories told by Josh at 5:9 are organized as chapters, with characters, themes, settings, complicating actions and outcomes contained within a unified structure that would probably tax a much older child. These are the particular focus of Chapter 11. Sundari, too, tells stories which are enormously complex in their control of time relationships and their awareness of narrating (as opposed to narrated). Labov's narrative syntax is not an appropriate analytic tool for revealing the most advanced competences of these two storytellers.

The different kinds of story time and narrating time in stories like Sundari's story 9 require a fine-grained analysis by themselves; the extended dialogues between Josh's characters in his later stories are not covered by Labov's categories; and the genre Labov was analysing did not take into account the invention in stories of first-person narrators like Sundari's nor of hidden, omniscient narrators like Josh's.

To do justice to the *temporality, dialogue* and *narrating* of the two 5-year-olds I have turned to Genette's categories of narrative discourse and in the following three chapters I shall show in detail how those categories uncover the more complex forms the children have learned from books. In Chapter 11 I have used Barthes' connotative codes to reveal the different kinds of social knowledge underlying Josh's long story in chapters.

NOTES

1.   I can only speculate on why Sundari's stories are low on plot content and high in description:
       a) There may be gender implications in Sundari's minimal story *actions*. It has often been observed in children's play that boys like to move around a lot and do things, whereas girls prefer to interact with people, often verbally. If such observations are true in general, perhaps girls are socialized to be less active and to observe behaviour more than boys.
       b) It is possible that Sundari finds it too difficult to invent plots. Her long pauses in the stories imply that something is being thought out. However, she does tell several stories with simple but satisfying plots: see story 4 (pp. 141–2), story 7 (pp. 89–90), story 12 (p. 51) and story 1 (p. 124).
       c) The inclusion of a first-person narrator in her stories, one who is not involved in the story she tells, makes Sundari's storytelling a more complex and difficult task. It is obvious that role-playing the narrator is as important to her as the story the narrator tells. However, Sundari's narrator's comments tend to divert attention from the story or even to despise and scorn it.
       d) Sundari may have been more impressed than the other children by descriptive passages in stories, poetic and prosodic effects, and states of mind and feeling, so that in her conception of story priority is given to these.
       Since one always feels that one has heard a story when listening to Sundari's tapes, her preferences raise the whole issue of whether stories ought to be defined at all by the requirement that they have a plot, however minimal. There is an interesting discussion of this in Mario Vargos Llosa's *The Perpetual Orgy* (pp. 38–41), in which he discusses a quotation from one of Flaubert's letters. In the letter Flaubert professes a desire to write a book (novel) 'about nothing' with 'almost no subject', a book which is entirely sustained by the internal force of its style.
2.   Pradl found that the majority of children started their stories with 'once upon a time' by the age of 5.
3.   See Vygotsky (1978). The 'zone of proximal development' is described by Vygotsky as the gap between knowledge which is completed and *potential* knowledge which can develop with the help of another. He says that two pupils may have the same completed knowledge, but that there may be great differences in what each can achieve with some help from another person. Thus, he argues, tests of completed knowledge do not tell us what children might achieve in the future.
4.   The Topsy and Tim stories are unlike most of the other book material the children drew on. They are not imaginative fantasies, but books which help to prepare children for real-life situations – going to school, going into hospital, and so on. They must be important as a genre to young children, since three of my five children retell them or make references to them.

Chapter 8

Time Relationships in the Stories

1 once upon a time there were three rabbits who lived in the trees
2 they were walking down
3 and the tree was in a very big forest
4 and one day they were hunting for foods
5 but they got their drinks from the streams
6 for the mother bear had a bedroom (on) in the tree
7 but the tree was a tree-house
8 and they all lived in it in a little grassy thing by the bridge
9 (now) now as you know there were some bears (who) who lived at the very edge of the forest
10 and they would hunt for rabbits
11 (so-so) so the rabbits couldn't have been eaten up
12 (but the daddy b- but the daddy bear) but the mother bear (er) had (he-s) her knives and forks
13 (so) so she wished to have them for dinner
14 but as you know who lived in the forest?
15 well shall I tell you?
16 well it was a big wicked grey wolf
17 (P) and (so-so) so how should they get away from this forest 'cos if he saw them he would surely swallow them up?
18 so one day they were walking down the street till they saw the bear a kind bear but not the horrible one that lives at the edge
19 but he said 'Good morning rabbits where are you off to?' (*Josh story 38 5:3*)

If the above passage were analysed using Labov's structural categories, we would have to mark 1 to 17 as *orientation*. We would observe that this is a strongly evaluated orientation section with its modal verbs ('would' in 10, 'couldn't have been' in 11, and 'should' and 'would' in 17), and we would note the implication of those modal verbs: that Josh is dealing not with what *did* happen but with what *might* or *could* happen in some unspecified time. In this passage Josh is in fact dealing with more than one kind of story time. There are the things that actually happened in a chronological sequence, the events of the story. Then there are the things which usually happened, or typically happened in another continuous past time which is beyond the actual events of the narrative. There is a third kind of time, too, for Josh's narrator's voice surfaces in this passage to address his listener directly in 'as you know' and 'now' and 'shall I tell you'. This is the time not of the *events narrated* but of the *narrating* of those events. The complexity of the movement of the narrative discourse between these different kinds of time is only implicit in the Labov categories; yet passages like this one demand an analysis of its chronology if we are to do justice to the competences of the storyteller. The different kinds of time relationship in the stories are the topic of this chapter.

How do young children who cannot read and write acquire the competence to differentiate time relationships in the way Josh does in story 38? It is my argument that such passages appear in the most intertextual stories, the stories which are closely modelled on books. We cannot state that the manipulation of complex chronologies in stories belongs exclusively to literature, but it is in literary studies that the kinds of analytic system required to describe such chronologies are to be found. Accordingly, the categories that I use in this and the ensuing two chapters come from Genette's *Narrative Discourse* (1972). The concern of structuralist poetics, as Culler (1975) describes it, was to reveal the network of relationships that narrative discourse sets up with readers in order to make readings of texts possible. To read a poem as a poem we need to have some familiarity with the conventions of poetry – our linguistic knowledge by itself would not be enough. Our previous experience of other poems would give us a set of expectations about how poems work, and indeed the same is true of all the other genres of literature.[1]

The idea that children learn from their early illustrated story-books subtle literary competences has been extensively developed by Meek (1988). Drawing on the work of post-structuralists such as Genette and Barthes, she shows that the authors of children's story-books demonstrate to children many possibilities of how texts can be read. She argues that the child who hears Burningham's *Come Away from the Water Shirley* experiences several kinds of story at once. In that book the only written text is a series of short, nagging statements from Shirley's mother, yet that mother's discourse is a metaphor for a whole story about Shirley's life with her ageing parents. Opposite each pastel picture of a 'real' beach setting is a vivid illustration of another story, the one going on in Shirley's head, which occupies another kind of story time and space. There are no words for this story, for the young reader learns that she must supply that text herself, make the story, as Shirley does, in her own head. The kinds of literary knowledge gained from such readings are implicit. That is why children's oral stories are a fruitful way for us to observe what has been learned, for in their storytelling such implicit competences have the chance to emerge without conscious forethought on the part of the child.

At a general level the interpretive conventions of literature are obvious enough to make it possible that even young children may begin to acquire literary competences. In this study they use conventional story openings and closures, for example. They also display considerable genre knowledge. In Chapter 5 I was able to show how a T-Unit analysis revealed different features of sentences in specific genres from Josh:

newsreadings, narratives, poems and conversations with his mother. The children invent genres too. Sundari refers to 'rubbish' stories, 'rhyming' stories, 'quick' stories ('you've got to quickly talk as quickly as possible') and 'nonsense' stories (based on Edward Lear). Robert talks about 'tiny' stories, 'little' stories, 'horrible' stories, 'joke' stories, and 'secret' stories. Justine has 'funny' stories and 'stories for babies'. Josh distinguishes between two types of poem 'sea' poems (lyrical and descriptive), and 'nonsense' poems (containing made-up words and rude bits). These categories cover several formal features of the texts: their *structure* (stories for babies and tiny stories), the *manner of narration* (quick stories), the *language* (nonsense stories and rhyming stories) and the *content* (horrible stories and joke stories). In a nonsense poem Josh actually makes explicit the difference between a poem and a story:

> mummy mummy did a dummy
> when she had done that ugly dummy
> mummy did a canny pummy
> when she had done that canny pummy
> mummy went to the shops
> and then when she was at the shops she got herself (for the tonight) for the tonight's meal
> *Oh no it was a poem*
> mummy mummy coming out mummy mummy mummy
> *(Josh poem/story 78 6:1)*

Genette proposes that readings are possible for narratives not because of the events the text refers to, but because of the network of structures comprising the discourse between readers and texts. He argues that the events recounted in a narrative cannot become the object of literary study because as fiction they have no reality outside the text. The act of narrating, too, is not to be confused with the act of writing, for the narrator is also fictional and can only be studied through the signs of his/her presence inside the text. It is therefore the text itself, the narrative discourse alone, which shows us how it is possible to read it. Genette's careful distinction between *narrative, story* and *narrating* calls attention to the act and functions of narrating, to complexities of the chronology of narrative time and story time and to variations in focalization and point of view. Since narratives must contain a sequence of actions, however minimal, Genette places the verb at the centre of his analytic system, using the major categories of *tense, mood* and *voice* to cover chronology, point of view and narrating respectively. The categories emerge from his reading of Proust's *A la recherche du temps perdu* and an enormous range of other fiction. Genette's interest in his analysis lies in uncovering what seems to break the bounds of 'narrative possibilities'. It may seem paradoxical to use a set of categories devised for the analysis of modernist texts on stories told on fairly traditional lines by very young children. However Genette always compares the complex and unusual to the relatively simple and regular,[2] which has the great advantage of offering the student of children's stories not only a structural taxonomy, but also a way of identifying those points of departure from the simple and traditional which establish unexpectedly complex modes of narration.

The stories told by the five children are often very long compared to narratives of personal experience such as those collected by Labov. The stories require the children to sustain the past time of the narrative events, while making them interesting and credible with description, comment and detail. Traditional genres allow for a more relaxed pace than the street stories of Labov's study, particularly when the story material is familiar. Knowing what is to come, the children can afford to savour the careful setting of a scene, or to report dialogue as it were verbatim. They can choose to accelerate the story events by leaving gaps in the story time or summarizing the actions, or they can suspend the story time by describing a setting.

In this chapter I shall show, using Genette's category of *tense*, how far advanced the children's competences were in the ways they varied the time relationships of their stories. In the two subsequent chapters I shall complete the analysis by considering Genette's other major categories of *mood* and *voice*. Tense includes three broad subcategories: *order, duration* and *frequency*. I shall discuss the children's narratives with reference to each of these in turn.

TENSE

Order

Typically the five children tell their stories in straightforward chronological sequence. Events follow one another, one by one, and reach a conclusion. They do not, like Graham Swift in *Waterland*, place some events from the middle of the story at the beginning, or give away the story's conclusion before the end, or look forward to events which will happen after the narrative is concluded. However, they do show the beginnings of these competences. Genette refers to flashback time and beyond-the-story time in narratives as *analepsis* and *prolepsis* respectively.

Analepsis

On the whole analepses occur rarely. When they do they tend to refer to earlier narrative events rather than take the form of flashbacks to events which pre-date this particular story. All the instances of their beginnings that I shall cite here are from stories strongly linked to a book source.

In *Hansel and Gretel* (version 2, see p. 201) the stepmother dies during the course of the children's encounter with the witch, but her death is only revealed at the end of the story, at a considerable temporal distance from its chronological occurrence. In a retelling of this version (story 32) Josh places the stepmother's death immediately after the witch's but before the children go home. A change of tense from past to pluperfect signals that an earlier time is being referred to:

> and they *took* them home   (but the) but of their stepmother she *had*
> *died*   but (the) for a hour they *came* to a river

In another retelling of *Hansel and Gretel* (story 34) he places the stepmother's death after the children have become lost and before they find the witch's cottage. Again he uses the pluperfect:

> and now Hansel and Gretel *were* in the woods but (their) their mother *had*
> *died*

In yet another version (story 44) he mentions the stepmother's death at the end of the story when the children arrive home and *they* would have learned of it:

and they *came* back (a- and-their) and the old stepmother *had died*

Interestingly, each time Josh makes this analepsis he stumbles on his words. As far as the story is concerned it is an important analepsis. If it comes after the witch has been killed it strengthens the possibility of an identification between the witch and the stepmother – a reading favoured by Bettelheim (1976).[3] Even though the step-mother's death is out of chronological sequence and mention of it involves a change of tense, Josh always includes this analepsis. Other details of the Williams-Ellis version of *Hansel and Gretel*, on which Josh based these retellings, are omitted, but the consis-tent inclusion of this one shows that it is important to Josh's understanding of the story. This is a good example of the way in which a narrative technique can be absorbed from hearing a story with a strong and powerful meaning read aloud.

A more complex form of analepsis occurs in Josh's story 65, an intertextual, lengthy, invented narrative. At the beginning the story tells of a journey over the world from one place to another on different kinds of transport, a schema borrowed from a favourite picture story-book called *How Far Does a Rubber Band Stretch*? (Thaler, 1976). In this opening journey there is no deviation from chronological sequence. The second episode tells how the group of boys, who are the story's protagonists, get into a big box to go to sleep. While they sleep a skeleton takes the box away, with the five boys in it and locks it into a room. The boys escape by converting the box into a ladder to help them get back down the mountain. Then they rebuild the box, leave it and discover the skeleton in it when they return. They eventually encounter the skeleton in a museum in the form of a mummy, but when they unwind his mummy's bandages, find their friend Paul beneath them. This explanatory passage follows:

and under there was Paul he said 'how on earth did you get there?' 'Well'
he asked 'When you were doing the ladder I got in and the skeleton didn't
know I was just behind him and he was squashing me up but I gently
quietly went in (and then- and then-) and then I did it earlier before that I
cut down the box' 'Ah how did you get out?' 'I jumped after (you'd) you'd
done it (you were) while you were making it' 'Oh' (P) (so) so the skeleton
was no longer seen . . . (*Josh story 65*)

This is not a completely successful narrative scene. The actions are over complicated and there is some confusion about who is speaking to whom, but the gist is clear. Paul is relating an embedded narrative telling what happened to him *during* the previous narrative events. This is a sustained analepsis which is difficult for Josh to accomplish, for he needs to have instant simultaneous recall of everything he has narrated so far while he is inventing the embedded narrative. However, making the attempt involves him in a whole array of *time* clauses: *when you were doing the ladder*, I did it *earlier before that, after you'd done it while you were making it*, and *no longer seen*. Josh has to use three forms of the past tense, the imperfect, perfect and pluperfect, to get some sequence of order into the present reporting of parallel sets of past events. His difficulty is to confirm that the embedded narrative ran alongside the primary nar-rative. Doing this also involves a change in point of view; having so far heard the boys' side of things we now hear another story from the point of view of one who was not present. In an impromptu invented oral story this is difficult to accomplish if you are only 5 years old. Yet there is quite an advanced understanding here that stories can contain parallel sets of events that intersect with one another.[4]

Sundari has similar problems in story 14, which concerns Harriet, the usual sensitive Sundari heroine, who dies at T-Unit 14 of a broken heart. Subsequently the narrator tells us that two sisters and one brother were born into Harriet's family. Then Harriet is re-born:

> their other sister who had been born was born again and she said 'once
> I was born to this mother a long time ago   and then I died when I was still a
> little girl   and I didn't know I would have a sister   two sisters and one brother
> now there's four of us but I'm still little (*Sundari story 14*)

Harriet's embedded narrative is full of time references: *once, a long time ago, when I was still a little girl, now* and *still*. The tenses of the verbs are more complex than those in the preceding extract from Josh's story 65, for she uses the past and pluperfect, projects a future time from past time ('I would have') and returns to the present of the speaking at the end. Birth and rebirth are themes that tend to appear in the children's stories. This theme is not only a matter of using convenient magic to overcome difficulties of plotting the story. There are deeper meanings: protecting characters from the consequences of death by not making it final is one, but here Sundari seems to be using the story to solve an existential problem: how can a young child understand that there was a time when her older siblings were in the world and she was not? How can she be simultaneously the oldest and the youngest child in the family? The narrative competences which are emerging and developing in passages like these are important for later writing and reading. But even more important are the implications for children's thinking and problem-solving. Making impossible and magical events believable in terms of the story, or fictional truth, involves children in explanatory language, language which pushes storying in the direction of hypothesis and argument.[5]

I shall return to this theme in the final chapter of this book, but it is important, in discussing the implications of narrative competences as they are revealed by Genette's categories, to establish that it is not a mere bag of narrative tricks which is being analysed here, but complex ways of thinking about time, about what could conceivably be possible, about what can be accomplished by language. At points like these in the children's stories, complicated thoughts, complicated narrative techniques and complicated syntax all come together, and at the same time are tied into the children's deeper meanings and feelings.

Neither Josh's analepsis in story 65 nor Sundari's in story 14 is credible. Their storyworld implicitly accepts the impossible and magical, where characters are born and re-born, appear and disappear. However, it is part of storytelling competence to explain events in such a way that they appear possible and believable. Writers of fiction suspend our disbelief in these ways all the time; we have only to consider a fantasy like *Sir Gawain* or an apparently *realist* text like Robert Cormier's *Fade* to realize that appearing and disappearing are well-established conventions of stories. Though these examples are clearly alterations to the strict chronology of the narrative events, and in that respect could be seen as analepses, there are no instances in the children's stories of real flashbacks to a time before the primary narrative began.

Prolepsis

Genette's category of prolepsis looks forward to events which lie ahead of the chronological sequence in the present story. In the children's stories it does not occur at all, for the good reason that it requires prior knowledge of the narrative events and the end of the story. In Josh's retellings of known stories, however, there are the beginnings of prolepses; future events are anticipated rather than revealed. The listener is warned of what *might* occur rather than told what will:

> when their dad learnt (um-what) they were deep in the forest he scolded his wife and he said that they in great danger of the wicked old witch in the forest (*Josh story 29*)

This passage has been taken almost verbatim by Josh from another version of *Hansel and Gretel*, this time not the Williams-Ellis version but one he would listen to on a gramophone record.[6] At this point of the story the witch is mentioned for the first time even though the children do not encounter her until 16 more sentences have passed. In story 34 Josh puts his warning into the story's opening:

> once upon a time Hansel and Gretel were safe at their cottage but they knew that there was a little house covered with sweets in the wood that had a big pine trees with wooden faces now they knew that that was the house of a very bad woman   she was the wicked old witch

The cottage and the pine trees owe something to the gramophone version of the story heard by Josh, but the rest of the passage is his own. Having used the children's thoughts to anticipate events Josh then returns to the orientation section of his narrative. In a later retelling, three months after Josh had heard or told either of the versions of *Hansel and Gretel* familiar to him, he places his warning passage further into the narrative, at the point where the witch invites the children into the cottage:

> (and the) and then who was very pretending in being very kind (who was) who put Hansel off to bed   (she was) she cackled to herself   (she was no mo-) she was no mother but (a wicked) a wickedest witch in the forest   this witch was the worst (*Josh story 44*)

This passage does not refer directly to some future event of the narrative time, but it does help the listener to anticipate future events. Though this passage owes something to the Williams-Ellis original text, these are very much Josh's own words. Warning or hinting of future events is again a long-established literary convention – we need only think about the opening scene of *Macbeth* – but it is probably the beginning of placing future narrative events out of their chronological sequence in a story. Indeed, I shall show at the end of this chapter that by the time he was 12 Josh knew how to do this in composing a written story.

In Josh's retelling of *Ferreyo and Debbo-Engal the Witch* (Arnott, 1962), an African *Hansel and Gretel*, there is an analepsis at the beginning of the story which has the effect of a prolepsis. Saying what has occurred in the past acts as a warning of what is to come:

> and once they decided to go to a hut where there were ten beautiful girls (I

mean ten boys and girls)   and they went there one night   but their mother
said *'Don't go there' she begged them 'cos lots of men have gone there and
never returned'*

After this the story proper begins and we do not arrive at the hut referred to until
the 38th sentence of the narrative.

To summarize, although it is difficult to find examples of alterations to chronological order in stories, Josh and Sundari sometimes refer to events which occurred
before the present events of the story and, more rarely, anticipate future events of the
story. These are the beginnings of competences in analepsis and prolepsis, and *they
occur when the stories are strongly influenced by books.*

Duration

Genette's category of story *duration* concerns the rhythm and speed of narrative
discourse. A simple, chronologically sequenced narrative will move from event to event
regularly without changes of pace. This is typical for children's 'and then . . .' narratives,
where there tends to be no dwelling on a particular scene, slowing down the telling of the
story, nor any omissions of actions or speedily summarized events, making the story go
faster. Examples of such regular duration are difficult to find in my data, surprisingly
enough, but story 7 from Josh is untypically simple in this (and other) respects:

> once upon a time (P) (there was- er-er) there was (an)
> a little (er) girl called Julie
> and she was walking down the street with David
> (she) David fell on his head
> (er -er) and (he) he fell over (the) and fell on the
> spikes of the fence
> (and he) and he got cut through
> (and he) and he was took off to hospital
> and that's the end

No doubt Labov would see this as a referential story likely to elicit from a listener
the response 'So what?'. Skilled storytellers will be able to highlight the interesting parts
of the story, even show us some 'scenes' verbatim as though in a play, and quickly
summarize essential but rather boring parts. The point of this section then is to
discover the extent of the children's competences in varying the pace of their stories.

There are four major categories of Duration in Genette:

Ellipsis (fast): a period of story time, possibly lasting years, is completely omitted. The
passing of time is a gap in the text and is not referred to explicitly in phrases like 'weeks
passed'.
Summary (fast): a period of story time is dealt with in a summary of events, without
elaboration
Scene (slow): the time of narrating and the time of the story are more or less equal. In
dialogue passages they are exactly equal.
Pause (slow): the story time comes to a stop while a description is given

Since variation in the duration of storytelling depends on the interaction of these four
categories, I shall consider them together.

In simple narrative, like Labov's narratives of vicarious (not personal) experience, or the 'folk' tales of the story grammars, the omission of *scene* and descriptive *pause* is almost the defining characteristic of the story structure. Such stories usually *only* summarize events. Certainly I would expect, and the data confirm my expectation, that summaries are well within the competences of all five children. They coincide very often with one of the categories of long T-Units I referred to in Chapter 5. There I had found that some T-Units of 12 + words were long because they consisted of a series of co-ordinated clauses. Such T-Units are often employed in Josh's stories when he wants to finish off the closing actions of the story:

> and flash   they flew up into the air but Spiderman just stayed there (and) and got the Incredible Hulk into his rubber sack (and) and took him along (to) to the police station and that's the end (*Josh story 37*)
> and (so) so they threw all her magic things cut her arms off and (er) threw them in the fire and put her in the fire till she burnt and the wicked old witch was die (then-then) then he drove them home   and that's the end (*Josh story 28*)

Sundari's story 12 (see Appendix to Chapter 10, pp. 163–7, for the full text of this story together with an analysis using all the major Genette categories) is a very slow-moving, lyrical story about a little girl who would rather play with her dolls on the beach than go to school. It is strongly influenced by Joan Aitken's *A Necklace of Raindrops*. In stories like this, summary is a useful way of changing the scene and moving the story on:

> she went home to play with her dollies and whistled again (P)
> but then she got bored went to bed
> next morning she ate her breakfast but didn't go to school

In this section Sundari relates briskly actions that cover an evening, a night, and the following morning. Then she slows the pace:

> she played and played in the seaside playing with her dolls   making little roads and houses for them to go in   little sandpies for them to eat and little cool rivers for them to wash and drink cups full of the drink from the little river –   for the dolls that really could drink 'cos most of them –   but the other dolls could really eat   so could the ones who could (ea) really drink and to dolls that could really eat and drink (what all of them – and) (PP) all little things could fit down their little (little) mouths   and when they (w) wanted to wee (P) they went to the toilet which was really a little potty made out of paper and they got on it   and a drink came out (P) by holding their clothes

This passage starts with a narrative action ('she played') and ends with two ('they got on it' and 'a drink came out'), but in between we have a mixture of description and explanation; Sundari wishes to linger over this scene and therefore fills it with detail. The present continuous tense for the verbs 'playing' and 'making' helps to establish a sense of time drawn out, in contrast to the summarized past tense verbs which she uses to close this section of the story:

> (P) and she clapped her hands danced about then she went to bed (*Sundari story 12*)

Summary seems the most basic and simple of the categories of duration, for narrative is more selective than memory (which is also selective) foregrounding the scenes the narrator considers most important in the story; the rest can be sketched/inferred by the listener/reader. Many stories for adults, of course, omit summaries altogether, and leave the gaps between scenes entirely to the reader's inference. Until the end of the 19th century, according to Genette, the pattern of scene/summary was the most usual one for the novel, providing a basic rhythm for the story duration. Summaries most commonly occur when there is a change of scene. Josh's story 75a is a very good example of this pattern; the story is structured as a series of scenes which are linked by highly summarized narrative actions. The story is a retelling of Kathleen Arnott's *Ferreyal and Debbo-Engal the Witch*. Josh had heard this story read aloud two or three times, and retold it several days later. He had no book with him, and in any case a book would not have helped him since this was a story without pictures. He had started to tell *Hansel and Gretel* again, but broke off and began telling the African story instead, a change which was not arbitrary, since the themes of the two stories have much in common.

The first part of the story consists of three repeating episodes, in which Ferreyal, the magic 'midget' youngest brother of a family of brothers, attempts to persuade his siblings to accept him as one of them so that he can protect them from the witch, Debbo-Engal. Each scene uses dialogue and is complete in itself, with narrative time and story time more or less equivalent. Josh links the scenes with elliptical statements (given below in italic) which have the function of moving the action into the next scene, so that in these summaries the narrative time moves faster than the story time. Since this is a very competent story retelling it is worth quoting from it at length, starting with the first of the story's incidents:

(they they) a little man catched up with them   'I'm Ferreyal your youngest brother'   (and) and then one of them said 'Who are you?'   'I'm Ferreyal your youngest (brother) brother'   and then they started beating him   and (er) when they'd done that they left him lying on the ground   and they said 'That (raggy) that dirty little scoundrel'

and then they walked on

and then one of them found a piece of cloth   and he said 'What luck it is   look what I've found' (P)   they walked up a little road   and then he found it heavier on his shoulder   and then he (passed it) passed it on to the other brother and (th) then passed it on and passed on until it got (um) to the biggest brother   and (when it) when it was at the biggest brother (he said) he shaked the cloth   (and) and Ferreyal's voice came out   'It's Ferreyal your youngest brother'   and then they started to beat him again

and then (when he had-when) when they'd gone a little while

one of the brothers kicked their foot on a piece of metal   and then he (P) looked down to look what it was   and then it was a ring   and he put it on his finger   and then it grew heavier and heavier   and he passed it on and passed it on until it got to the oldest brother   and he said 'There's something odd about this ring'   and then he shaked it   and out fell Ferreyal   and then the boys was just gonna beat him when the youngest (the-P) [*Adult*: The oldest] the oldest brother said 'Don't beat him he's willing to come' so they didn't (beat him) beat him

and then they let him (came) come

and when they got there she said 'Hello I'm delighted to have some guests' so then she (ga) let them dance (with their sis-) with the maidens and after that for a while (um) gave them palm food and drinks and lovely food and danced until she said 'Don't go through the bush it is very dark and there is lots of wild animals and snakes at this time of the season' (so-so they) so they agreed

and then they (slep) sleeped

There are several other 'tripled' incidents in the story, in the manner of the oral tradition, and later in the story Josh only tells one of the 3 incidents in the set apologizing for omitting the other two. The repeating structure of many folk-tales, written down in story-books for children, surely helps them to perceive the pattern of regular scene–summary–scene because it is so mnemonic. Josh's most successful invented story (number 62; see Chapter 11, pp. 187–8), influenced by three or four books, in fact uses this story structure in a very original way, producing one of the most complex plots of the whole story collection.

Between the fast speed of summary and the time-standing-still duration of descriptive pauses is the *scene*. We have observed scenes alternating with summaries in the extract quoted above, and little more needs to be said about them. They remain constant in time and place, and when they include dialogue they are intended to give the illusion of the exact duration of that section of the narrative. Scenes deal in more detailed movements than summaries, and are interesting in their variation with summaries, pauses and ellipses. A competently handled scene and scene change occurs in Josh's story 30 where there is virtually no interlinking summary:

as soon (as the) as the afternoon came they went in and the man said 'Here's your ticket' '(ca-ca) Can we go?' they said 'Yes go to the main entrance' so they went to the main entrance and they paid their tickets and they went up to their seats a dark hole and they saw the screen and everybody was there   (and all) and then the picture came

At this point Josh switches the story back to the hospital from which the boys have escaped in order to go to the pictures:

(and-and- and they) and the nurse saw in the beds that they weren't there

This is the nearest any story in the study comes to an ellipsis, though it cannot be said that very much story time has been 'lost' in the ellipsis.

Descriptive *pauses* mark story time at its slowest, for during them nothing happens and time seems to stand still. Modern readers who are used to fast-moving thriller genres but lack experience of reading literature from the past often complain about descriptive pauses in 19th-century fiction and tend to skip them to get back to the action. Of the five children Sundari includes more, and more extensive, descriptive pauses than the other children. Here are some examples:

> well she had the high-heeled shoes for herself white high-heeled shoes with
> a pretty pattern across (P) and (P) across the – it wasn't at the top (or the)
> or the middle it was at the bottom but not the proper bottom 'cos there was
> a little place for her shoes to go – her feet I mean – her little toes (*Sundari
> story 6*)
> she looked so nice with a shining crown shining little bracelets all nice
> shining things a shining wand shining rings they were all shining (*Sundari
> story 10*)
> what they drank was called tonic water (P) yes tonic water (P) two bottles
> of nice fizzy tonic water   lemonade lemonade sort of tonic water (*Sundari
> story 7*)
> and one day (P) which was when she woke up there was a dreadful sound
> going what the sea was making going 'swisshh swisshh swisshh' 'Tinkle
> tinkle' went the bells 'Oh oh' went the dolls   and her necklace
> rustled   everything was awake (*Sundari story 12*)

Descriptive passages of this kind, brief as they obviously are compared to the sort
of thing found in adult fiction, are nevertheless very rare in children's oral stories;
Labov found them very infrequent in his narratives of adolescent personal experience.
Labov's analysis places them as part of the orientation categories since they add setting
information to the events of the story. In the Labov syntax temporality is only one
aspect of orientation.[7] Genette on the other hand gives time relationships a more
central role in narrative structure; the categories of duration show how deeply
embedded in the overall story organization the pacing of the narration lies.

Summaries, scenes and descriptive pauses, then, are well within Josh's and Sundari's
narrative competences. According to Genette a *temporal ellipsis* consists of a silence
in the text; even though years of story time may have passed we proceed from one
scene to another with no mention of the gap. This kind of intentional ellipsis is rare
in stories written for children. It leaves the reader much work to do for his/her
imagination must recognize the gap as a convention of narrative structure and fill in
what has been passed over by inference. Though the children do gloss over long periods
of story time (summary) they do not deliberately omit all reference to it. In Sundari's
story 14, for example, a little girl dies and then her siblings are born (see p. 106 above).
This process must take years of story time, but in fact Sundari does minimally mark
the arrival of each sibling by using the phrase 'one day' to introduce each clause. In
story 12 Sundari approaches a real ellipsis when she abruptly changes scene from the
girl at the beach to the girl in school, but again the phrase 'one day' is used to move
the listener to a new phase of story time:

> now she was playing a little soft tune to her baby dolls like this [whistles a
> tune]   like that   and she had loads of things she had to do at school   one
> day a girl called Meg said 'Why can't I wear that necklace?' (*Sundari story
> 12*)

In fact the story time of the second sentence here is the same as that of the first, since
the second only gives us more information about the girl. The shift of story time comes
at the beginning of the third sentence. If as Meek (1984) has suggested,[8] children use
stories to sort out their concepts of temporality, then it is unlikely that an ellipsis of

the Proustian kind would be present, for to leave unmarked gaps in narrative temporality requires complete prior conceptualization of the time relationships of the story – it must be planned in advance.

The analysis of story 12 at the end of Chapter 10 shows how complex the pattern of scene, summary and pause can be in a 5-year-old's story.

Frequency

The question which concerns us here is, do the children narrate each event once, as it happened in the story (*singulative frequency*), or do they make single statements about events which happened more than once, events which perhaps usually or often or sometimes happened (*iterative frequency*)? At this point of the discussion of narrative time and story time we are perhaps beginning to perceive the pattern of simple stories; their order is chronological, their duration consists of summary or summary/scene, and their frequency is singulative. Singulative narration is more usual in the data than iterative, but the latter is more firmly established in the children's competences than the anachronies of story order. When he is defining frequency Genette (1977, p. 115) makes a rare reference to children's literature, pointing out that the repeating narrative, the story where each event, however repetitive, is narrated in turn, is a characteristic of stories for children. From an adult point of view it is these repetitions which can make children's stories monotonous; they are too predictable. Folk-tales model the repeating narrative for children, and modern children's writers, such as Allan Ahlberg and John Burningham, borrow the technique. We have encountered tripling in Josh's story 17 and in his retelling of *Ferreyal and Debbo-Engal the Witch* (story 75a). A very familiar example can be taken from his retelling of *Goldilocks and the Three Bears* (story 31):

> (and) and the father said 'Who's been eating my porridge?'   and the mummy said 'Who's been eating my porridge?'   and 'Who's been eating my porridge?' [squeaky voice]

Children always remember these repetitive passages, and where they are retelling known stories they always include them. In contrast to this highly predictable singulative frequency there are some sustained iterative passages in the data from Josh and Sundari. I have quoted one of them at the beginning of this chapter (p. 101), a story opening from a rather loose retelling of *Snow-White and Rose-Red* by Josh. Here, in the orientation section of his story, Josh is giving us some essential background information before the narrative proper begins. Hunting for rabbits (10), being ready to eat the rabbits (12/13), and getting away from the wolf (17), are actions which do not belong to the time of the story. They belong to a time further back than the story, a continuous past time where such things typically, or usually, or habitually happened – that is *iterative* time where one set of actions happened more than once. Iterative time is often marked by modal verbs: '*couldn't* have been eaten up' (the latter a complex passive/negative/modal/pluperfect structure!), '*would* hunt for rabbits', 'so how *should* they get away from this forest 'cos if he saw them he *would surely* swallow them up?'. The last example here is in fact one of those 'warnings' of events which may take place in a future time which I have described above as the beginnings of prolepsis. The use of the iterative 'would' is unusual in spoken language and probably in oral storytelling, but it is common in the rather archaic language of fairy-tales. It is typical of the Williams-Ellis style on which Josh based his retellings of fairy-tales. It makes an appearance in story 32, a retelling of *Hansel and Gretel*: 'and their stepmother *would* go out to the forest'.

The first version of *Hansel and Gretel* Josh heard, on a gramophone record, is really a dramatic musical version of the story. The lengthy story opening is told in the present tense, a technique which can be used for iterative passages in a past tense story when the author wishes to establish a set of actions which were customary.[9] Josh starts his retelling in the past tense and *only* uses the present for the iterative passage, which he recalls very clearly:

> once upon a time there were two fireworks boxes who had faces   they lived
> in a big big tree among branches   and there was (a) some children in the
> forest by the name of Hansel and Gretel   and this little cottage was the
> house of Hansel and Gretel   now they weren't (a) of a very rich family

Up to this point the past tense narration is established. But now Josh changes to the present:

> (da) dad gets up early in the morning and starts his long walk to the village
> where he sells brooms   the mother does some of the chores around the
> house   and Hansel and Gretel have their jobs too   but children would much
> rather like to play   but they make brooms (P) and do the chores

Having established what was usual in the present tense Josh then takes up the story again in the past:

> (till they were) and they were playing
> and when the mother saw them playing (um-um) and laughing she was furious
> . . . (*Josh story 29*)

It is more usual for iterative passages to be signalled by the continuous past tense than the present, as in Josh's story 28, told at the beginning of the *Hansel and Gretel* period:

> 19 (and th-) and then they *were walking* down the street *just looking*
> 20 their hair *was just looking* outspreaded
> 21 (a-a) and they had to have it brushed
> 22 then it *became* night
> 23 (er-th-) their mother *was looking* all over the place
> 24 and *now* they *ran* round the corner 'cos the wicked witch *was coming*
> 25 she *was trying* to get them

Here there are two kinds of narrative time operating: what *was happening* is not tied to any specific moment of narrative time, and what *did happen* was that night came and the boys ran round the corner. In 20–21 there is a descriptive pause, broken at 22 with the use of *then* and the past tense to move the narrative on; *now* in 24 signals a return to the story time and the recounting of the narrative events.

Sundari's stories, as I have noted, often have very few narrative actions in them. Her manner of narration is measured, and the duration of her stories is considerably slower than the other children's for she includes many scenes and descriptive pauses. Iterative frequency is very well established in her stories. She often signals it by using the terms *sometimes*, *always* and *never*, rather than by using a continuous past tense:

> and her sister and brother *always* let her wear the bestest dressing-up clothes
> even her other sister did (*Sundari story 14*)
> she was so sad she told a nearly
> crying story nearly nearly nearly
> she *would never* stop talking about the rock (*Sundari story 10*)
> the little girl *always* said please and thank-you
> she was *always being* good
> she loved to play though
> she *never fighted* much
> she *sometimes fighted* at school though because people hurt her (P) not actually hurting though
> they *were being* lovely and quiet *all the time* at the seaside (*Sundari story 9*)

Sundari's interest in character generates this iterative frequency; she wants to tell us what her characters were usually and typically like. The five children in general have only a simple grasp of character in storytelling, usually having stereotypical characters with fairly fixed and predictable roles – the witch, the soldier, the friends. Sundari is exceptional in her lengthy *telling* of the thoughts and feelings of her characters; Josh has some very consistent characterization in his later stories, but he tends to *show* through dialogue and actions rather than tell. In the passages above Sundari shows that she can use a varied mixture of adverbs of time (sometimes, always, never), the iterative 'would', and the continuous past tense (were being) to signal a time other than the time of the events of the story.

The most sustained, poetic and frequent iterative passages in the entire data collection come into Sundari's story 12, which is analysed in full (pp. 163–7) using all the Genette categories. Story 12 is a true narrative; it tells a story about a little girl who would rather play with her dolls on the beach than go to school. Most of the story gives lengthy descriptions of the girl on the beach, though there is a scene change in the middle of the story, where she goes to school and has her necklace stolen by another girl who is jealous. Story 12 is strongly influenced by two stories from books, Joan Aitken's *A Necklace of Raindrops* and a story about a little girl playing with her dolls called *Ukelele* (I have been unable to trace the author). In this passage Sundari tells *once* what her heroine, Laura, did *often* on unspecified 'sunny days':

6 (P) she liked *doing* things (P) *playing* about at the beach on sunny days (P) when cool wind *was blowing making* sandcastles *playing* with her little necklace with people on it and some little raindrops *falling* from the people and bags on it what the teddy-bears were in what the people *were holding* (P)
7 and she had little teddy-bear earrings (P)
8 she had lots of things
9 and she *usually* played with her dolls made sandcastles for them and little beach houses (P)

Here Sundari achieves a strongly poetic effect by her repetition of present participle verbs, and in 6 there are eight dependent clauses. Always in the children's stories complex syntax occurs when there is complex thinking, and one kind of complex thought lies in the time relationships of the stories. In other words, the narrative techniques that the children have absorbed from their experiences of hearing written language have implications for cognitive and linguistic advances. On reading the whole transcript of story 12 the reader will see that there are further complexities of time relationships in the narrative, for Sundari always invents a narrator whose narrating is in the present tense, so that all her stories weave in and out of the time of the narrating and the time of the story.

Iterative passages are more numerous than analepses/prolepses in Josh's and Sundari's stories. They are always elaborative, detached as they are from the time of the actual story events. They characterize stories which are descriptive and slow-moving, especially in Sundari's case. Such sustained descriptions may occur in oral 'literature' (the Homeric poems are full of them) but they are not common in oral stories from children and adolescents. I was able to find only two short iterative passages in Sutton-Smith's (1981) collection of invented narratives from 5-year-olds, and on closer inspection the children turned out to be 7-plus at the time of narrating them. I am confident that the source for sustained iterative frequency for my children is written literature. Authors like Amabel Williams-Ellis and Joan Aitken teach children how to do this, and it is taken in by the children as implicit knowledge.

To summarize what the data reveal about the chronology of the stories, we see that the children's concepts of narrative time are more complex than Labov's temporal orientation category reveals. Josh and Sundari at 5 years old are able to move well beyond the simple, basic form of telling a story – each event in its chronological order, each event summarized without acceleration or deceleration, and each event that happened once told once. They are beginning to use narrative anachronies occasionally as analepsis, and sometimes as a kind of primitive prolepsis. They are in command of variations of narrative duration using scenes, summaries and pauses, but real ellipses are beyond their competences. They are not confined to singulative frequency, but have several means of signalling iterative time. All of these competences, which may seem surprising in the oral stories of such young children, can be closely identified with written sources.

Chapters 9 and 10 will use Genette's categories of mood and voice to show further complexities of point of view and narrating voice in the children's stories, but as a footnote to this chapter I would like briefly to discuss some of Josh's later written stories. The National Curriculum for England and Wales (DES, 1990) makes a clear demarcation between chronological and non-chronological order in the development of narrative and non-narrative genres of children's writing. It does not consider other variations in time relationships in children's texts, though as independent literacy develops, competences like Josh's and Sundari's can only be expected to increase. As children come to read silently longer and more complex stories, so their writing will reflect aspects of those literary models. There is no doubt that a gap of many years can open up between oral stories like those of this study and the stories children are able to write down for themselves. By age $7\frac{1}{2}$ Josh was writing narratives which were not unduly restricted by lack of secretarial or handwriting abilities. Meek (1984) discusses how literature models for young readers 'shifters' in the time relationships of stories. She illustrates how children, by shifting from one narrative time which is 'realistic' to another narrative time which is fantasy and takes place in other worlds, can break free from the straitjacket of representing time in everyday orders of minutes, hours, days and nights, following one another in succession. Instead, like John Burningham's Shirley, they can conceive of story time as happening on another imaginative plane, and can move about in their narrating between these two planes of story time. Josh has several stories in his oral story data which do this. Typically two children meet in everyday 'real' settings of time and place, but then take off into other fantasy worlds with a quite different chronological scale. Meek connects Josh's competence in this sort of shifter at age 5 to a story opening written at age 8, showing that his grasp of time relationships in storytelling has remained complex.

When he was 13 Josh experimented with writing several very short stories told in the first person, with a present time of the narrating and a past time of the narrated. In the most highly developed of these stories he manages not only to balance these present and past times, but also to project forwards towards a story that is never told but only implied. It is worth quoting this story in full.

> I am a builder by trade, but I'm locally known as an exorcist but not a priest. There are no religious strings attached, purely my own methods. There is a large gap in the market for this sort of thing. You see, if you can get the punter to believe that you can give them a better service than the normal priest, you are in for a great deal of money, mainly because most of the call-outs are senile old people and all of the call-outs are false alarms (of course the punter does not know this). Having said that, I am not a con-man. Once I have been to their house and done my stuff I set their minds at ease. In fact, I feel quite sorry for them, but we all have to make a living one way or another.
>
> Anyway, enough of that, let's take a look at today's bookings. Aha, old Mr Dempster, Oh and after that Mrs Turnbull. Christ this takes me back to the last time I visited Mr Dempster's house. It was my closest encounter with a ghost, and here's me thinking that ghosts are the biggest load of bull ever invented (well they are really).
>
> Anyway, as soon as I got in I felt a presence. I tried my usual trick to find out if there was any spiritual presence. What you do is get twelve candles and place them in a circle round a table and light them. If there is a spirit a candle will go out. I usually daub the wicks in flammable fluid to give them staying power through draughts and gusts like that. Almost straight away one went out. I went into a cold sweat. I lied to Mr Dempster that as long as some of the candles (or one) went out the house was immune, which puts me in a rather awkward position today. I was shaken for days, until a close examination of the candle involved showed that it was never soaked in meths. (*Josh written story for school, 13/10/88, Age 13*)

This story has several forms of iterative frequency, has a sustained analepsis in the last paragraph, and is at least hinting at a real prolepsis (what will happen when I get to Mr Dempster's house today?). It is in fact one narrative scene, which includes summaries and pauses. Although there are subtleties of point of view and characterization here (does the protagonist really believe in ghosts or not?) and a very competent use of brackets to raise questions in the reader's mind, what interests me about this in the context of my discussion of Genette's chronologies is that this is a written version of an oral narrative in which Josh varies the narrative time and the story time in ways that he was beginning to do at age 5. A major difference between the oral narratives and this written one is that at 13 Josh had a more conscious control of this kind of storytelling, so that he was able to manipulate the chronology to suit his characterization of a con-man. No doubt literature had continued to play its part in the development of these more explicit kinds of competence, just as it had in the stories he told much earlier in his development. An awareness of Genette-like categories of story time would help teachers to develop their pupils' narrative writing well beyond the simple National Curriculum category for all narrative *chronological writing*.[10] It would help them to move away from considerations of words and themes only in stories and towards the techniques of writing. And of course the time relationships of a story or novel are important in extending children's reading, so that they learn to tolerate stories whose endings are told at the beginning or which start not at the beginning but *in media res*.

NOTES

1. There are a few studies of young children's literary competences, for example Gardner and Gardner (1971). In a story-retelling activity a few 6-year-olds were found to be sensitive to literary style. But test stories were devised for the experiment, so the children may have been unable to reveal the competences which can emerge from long-term familiarity with a favourite story. Green (1982) used texts from books normally read in kindergarten and asked the children to identify authors as the same or different. Like Gardner she found that a few children were able to discriminate literary styles.
2. The simpler categories in Genette are taken from adult fiction; he rarely mentions children.
3. While I agree with Bettelheim's identification of the witch/stepmother, on the whole I find his ego-psychology interpretation of the fairy-tales limited, though I accept his general comments on their emotional power.
4. Story grammarians stress that embedding of sub-narratives is an advanced competency. I noticed that in the development of his *written* stories the word 'Meanwhile' was used by Josh to open an episode at 8 years old. It does not appear at all in the present story data from any of the children.
5. I have looked elsewhere at the stories in terms of developing competences for argument (Fox, 1989a and 1990).
6. *Hansel and Gretel*, version I, narrated by Jean Aubrey with music by Humperdink (Walt Disney Productions, 1967). Disneyland Record DQ 1253. This was the version of the story Josh knew first. He would listen to it several times a day for several weeks. However, it was striking that when I introduced him to version 2, another recording of Claire Bloom reading the Amabel Williams-Ellis text, this more powerful version took over from the first and much more familiar one.
7. The use of modal verbs and other tense variations in verbs in Labov's analysis are considered to belong to the *evaluation* category.
8. Using a story by Josh from these data Meek shows how Josh creates two kinds of story time in one narrative, a *realistic* story time which frames events that happen in *fantasy* story time when Josh's two characters fly off to another world in a magic bin. Meek shows exactly how the authors of children's books give their readers lessons in aspects of chronology which go well beyond straightforward sequencing of events.
9. The change from past to present is Josh's own. The original story is narrated entirely in the present.
10. *National Curriculum for England and Wales: English in the National Curriculum*, Dept. of Education & Science and the Welsh Office (HMSO, 1990). See Attainment Target 3: Writing. In the Statements of Attainment pupils should 'shape' their chronological writing at Level 3, and 'write stories which have an opening, a setting, characters, a series of events and a resolution and which engage the interest of the reader' (see pp. 12–13). This is an extraordinarily prescriptive, and potentially limiting, model of narrative structure.

Chapter 9

Whose Point of View?

1 once upon a time in the night (P) (um) the Incredible Hulk was walking down by midnight punching houses down
2 he saw the police coming after h–
3 but he punched their car down
4 but Batman and Robin flew up to him (and) and said 'We'll take you to Spiderman
5 and he'll put you in his sack [attempts American accent]
6 so they did
7 now (as they took) as they took (Spi- um) the Incredible Hulk to the car they put him in that rubber sack put it on the hook
8 then Spiderman drove off
9 now there glowed a little light up in the sky
   [*Adult*: There glowed?]
10 and then (it) down came Superman
11 and he said that Batman wasn't feeling well
12 (so) so 'Well' said Spiderman 'What shall we do then if Batman isn't well?
13 Robin's got a chest ache
14 and Batman's got flu
15 Well what shall we do now? (um – we haven't [unclear])
16 Now what shall we do?
17 We never can get help'
18 'I don't know'
19 (but again – but that) but that stupid Spiderman fell in the river again
20 so they have to (go) pull him out more
21 well the only one who could do it wasn't Batman
22 it wasn't Robin
23 it wasn't Spiderman (er – I mean – I mean it wasn't –)
24 and it was Superman who done it
25 he pulled him out of that disgusting water
26 but they saw a cave

27 (P) but the Incredible Hulk that was his house
28 so they ran away
29 they could hear big steps coming out of the cave punching and clumping
30 and out came the Incredible Hulk bashing them down
31 they fell
32 but not any sound could they hear (till) till the rescue helicopter came down
33 'Look down there
34 Look a big monster
35 Come on
36 Let's go
37 Look he's punching two (er – things) people down
38 Come on
39 Let's go down there'
40 so the helicopter went down
41 (and it –) and it park-ed [2 syllables] on the airport
42 and there they (lay) lay sleeping
43 (P) they thought it (was) might have fell dead
   [*Adult*: They thought it was what? *Child*: they thought it was – they thought it
   was dead]
44 but then they thought feel his heart beating
45 'Look at that big monster over there
46 Don't go near him
47 He'll eat you up'
48 (P) 'Right come on
49 Come on
50 Let's put them in the rescue helicopter
51 Oh he don't have a heart'
52 'Why?'
53 'Cos (he's) they're Superfriends da-da-da-da [sung as fanfare]
54 (and when) and when the others came back (they) all the other rescue
   helicopters came
55 (it was –) how surprised they were
56 (now they –) now the superfriends waked up
57 and flash! they flew up into the air
58 but Spiderman just stayed there (and) and got the
   Incredible Hulk into his rubber sack (and) and took him along (to) to the
   police station
59 and that's the end (*Josh story 37 5:2*)

Piaget's view of symbolic play and storytelling in young children was dominated by his theory of childhood egocentricity. He saw such play as primarily affective and oriented to present pleasures and satisfactions. Its character is assimilative and it is egocentric in its prime purpose of assimilating reality to the ego. Piaget asserted that children aged 4 to 6 cannot 'tell a story verbally in the right order or reconstruct at will a sequence of events' (1951, p. 136)[1]. The idea of point of view in early storytelling is contradicted by the notion of egocentricity whose central premise is that young children's mental operations are limited by an inability to see things the way somebody else might see them. Imaginative activities, like role-play and storytelling, must seriously challenge Piaget's theory since they require players and storytellers to invent characters who have their own views of the world. Unlike Vygotsky, Piaget would not accept that young children are capable of imagination, but thought that in fantasy play the child merely 'reproduces what he has lived through' (1951, p. 131). In this chapter I want to challenge Piaget's view by showing that the children in my study were sometimes able to vary point of view in their narratives, especially when their stories were closely modelled on known stories from books, and especially when they included passages of dialogue in the storytelling.

Genette's second major category of narrative analysis is *mood*. Mood deals not only with questions of point of view in a narrative but also with distance/nearness to the events narrated and with what is brought into focus and what is not. Perhaps we can liken this to a photographer taking a picture. Let us say I am photographing my mother standing outside the Colosseum in Rome. I must decide the angle of the shot: shall I stand on a wall and take the shot from above, or crouch near the ground so that I have an impression of walls rearing up? How about the length of the shot? Should Mum be a dot against the huge building which I shall try to photograph from a distance of 50 or 100 feet, or shall I stand 10 feet in front of her with only a part of the building in the background? That decision in turn will depend on what I want to emphasize – my mother or the Colosseum, and I will want to be sure that the main subject is in focus for the shot. Similar sorts of decision are implicated in Josh's telling of story 37 at the head of this chapter (though those decisions were probably largely unconscious ones). Sometimes things are told by an omniscient hidden narrator who seems to be situated equidistantly from the characters and the events of the story. Sometimes we see or hear things as the characters would have heard and seen them at that moment, so that there is a one-sided focus. And at other times, when characters speak to one another, we are involved in an exchange of point of view along with the turns of the dialogue. Genette (1972, pp. 161–2) explains the concept of mood clearly and precisely:

> one can tell *more* or tell *less* what one tells, and can tell it *according to one point of view or another*, and this capacity, and the modalities of its use, are precisely what our category of narrative *mood* aims at.

Questions of focalization and distance are strongly implicated in the dialogue sections of a narrative. A dialogue in a story needs to have the resonances of real speech, perhaps with the colloquialisms and phatic markers of everyday conversation or perhaps with more stylized characteristics to reflect a character's power or status or personal characteristics. In Josh's story 62, various characters visit Heaven and speak to God and St Peter. Frankenstein, who obviously is very familiar with God, addresses him 'Hey-God!' whereas a 'kind dragon', who has never met God before, begins 'What is your command?'. Sometimes dialogues will be elliptical, leaving the reader to make up what is not said. Sometimes characters in dialogues will pose the vital questions which the story has to answer – there are several examples of this in story 37. When characters speak the point of view of each is represented in turn. Skilful narrators can show the feelings and responses of characters in dialogue, thereby demonstrating 'live' their individual qualities and characteristics. Children have the models of real-life conversations to help them in this, and are often well-practised in role-play by the time they are 5, but by themselves these experiences will not help them in presenting dialogue as it is written in books. In books dialogue needs to be presented in varied ways, and can never be truly mimetic of actual speech – the hesitations, gestures, false starts of everyday speech would have more limited functions as part of a story to be read. There are also dialogues of the mind, telling us what characters thought, or remembered, or decided. We may expect that young children will find the representation of inner speech difficult in storytelling. All these aspects of talk in stories are analysed by Genette under the category of mood. I shall take each of Genette's subcategories of mood in turn, and show where the children seem to be developing competences which are more complex than the most simple forms.

UNFOCALIZED NARRATIVE

This, Genette's first category of focalization, is the most basic mode of storytelling, in which events are reported in an equally distanced way, usually by a hidden, all-knowing, third-person narrator.

Perhaps at this point Genette's distinction between the two major categories of mood and voice ought to be made clear. The extent to which the narrating voice, hidden or not, influences a narrative is an aspect of the category voice. Voice deals with questions of who is telling the story rather than with questions of which characters' points of view are implicit in the narrative discourse. Mood is about what is narrated. Justine tells a simple story (story 23) which is entirely unfocalized, yet which includes a narrating voice:

1   once upon a time there was a little fox and some poppies
2   he wore them every day and every day and every day
3   but then a bird went and eated them all up
4   and he ate all the people up 'cos it was a monster
5   *do you know what?*
6   he ate all the houses up too the concrete and all the books and all the curtains and all the glass and all the tinsel (and all–and–and–) and all the teachers and all the schoolchildren
7   and he ate their school
8   he ate islands and water sea and starfish and fish like that (and) and everything even the whole world
9   and God made us [unclear word] in his tummy and then . . . [story trails off here and ends]

In this story every event is told from an equal distance to the actions narrated. We never come close to the monster bird's point of view nor to those of his victims. Thus there is no focalization. This is just a simple report of what happened. However, there is a narrating voice which we can hear in sentence 5; 'Do you know what?'. This implicitly assumes a teller and a listener, but it does not allow us to see the events narrated from a particular viewpoint. Though it is quite usual in the data for passages of unfocalized reporting of this kind to appear, it is rare to find whole narratives which do not at some point present events from the eyes or ears or feelings or words of one of the characters. Focalization is essentially a way of *showing* events rather than telling them, and in this sense it is close to a dramatic presentation, especially when characters speak to one another as in a play. If a passage of a story is unfocalized it does not mean the storyteller is unable to paint a portrait of a character; on the contrary she can do this, but she *tells* rather than *shows* what the character is like.

Here is an example of a vivid characterization from Sundari, which is nevertheless *told* by the narrator in a distanced way:

38 well the little girl was so quiet she didn't even snore one bit
39 she did play a lot quietly
40 I can't tell you all of them
41 she ate very quietly
42 she only made 'tit' sounds like this [faint tapping noises])
43 wasn't it quite quiet?
44 it was quiet (P)
45 sometimes when she slept she slept like this [little breathing sobbing noises]
46 when she cried she went [soft sobs] and wiped her tears (P)
47 she was never noisy not much talking just a bit not very much slow story
   (*Sundari story 9*)

There is no question that this passage is unfocalized even though it dwells on character to an unusual extent in the children's stories. The narrative discourse stands *outside* the little girl character, looks at how she typically behaved (the passage is iterative in terms of chronology), and illustrates each kind of noise she made. If a character's point of view is coming through at all it is Sundari's first-person narrator's. Narrating, in all its functions, is analysed by Genette under the category of *Voice*. This passage is fairly typical of Sundari's stories. She very often narrates by telling us what happened rather than by showing in a dramatic presentation of a scene. She keeps some distance between herself as narrator and the events narrated, thus allowing herself to frequently break off from recounting the story events to comment on them in some way.

The great advantage of the story with the omniscient, hidden narrator is that that narrator can always know more than the characters know. This is a technique that children have the opportunity to learn in hearing stories from books, and Josh replicates it in his retellings of *Hansel and Gretel*. Josh tells the story in a mixture of focalized and unfocalized narration, as the following passage shows:

45 she pulled out a bone
46 (and she) and in dismay she thought it was his finger
   [Adult: In dismay?]
47 so then 'First we can bake however'
48 what she really meant was push (Han) Hansel and Gretel in the oven as well
   as Hansel (*Josh story 32*)

Here 46 and 47 are strongly focalized, since Josh renders the witch's *thoughts* and her speech, but in 48 the narrator confides in us what the real intentions of the witch were. The opening of Sundari's first story uses this narrator's knowledge as a tripling device to set out the problem of the story:

1   once upon a time there was a little girl
2   and her name was Mandolin
3   (she liked) she said to her mother 'Mumma Mumma I would like to (P) have a picnic'
4   and what she took was a paper bag which her mummy had wrapped up (P) with some (P) stones in painted like raisins round stones (P)
5   and she took them and put them in her bag
6   and next her mummy gave her some (P) biscuits
7   what they really were were flat round stones painted brown like biscuits
8   and then she took those and put them in her bag
9   and next she gave her some eggs really round stones (P)
10   and she painted them white white eggs
11   and she banged them in half
12   (and then) and it was (yellow) yellow and (P) white inside which we had painted
13   and (ga-) she gave her some egg sandwiches which were really the stones and which the bread sandwiches were really (P) what (P) little (P) flat round stones made like a little biscuit which she put colours in brown as well
14   and then she took them all (*Sundari story 1*)

In this passage there is a little focalization in 3, where the girl speaks directly. Otherwise we are told what the mother and girl did in a neutral and unfocused way. This is relieved of course by the narrator's omniscient 'inside' information, so that we know the little girl is being deceived. Skilful as Josh and Sundari are in using narrator's knowledge, that is not the same thing as *showing* a character's point of view.

The use of narrator's inside knowledge to tell what was happening out of sight of the main characters in a story is probably the first move towards setting up a sub-plot. Josh complicates a story about a group of boys by using the omniscient narrator to tell us what happened to the boys while they were asleep in a box:

23   and then in the night-time they were fast asleep
24   they didn't know [to adult: Get my skeleton out] – a little skeleton picking the box up
    [conversation with adult here]
25   and then he gently picked the box up and took it away to a big cave in the mountains
26   and there he took it away and went into another cave that you couldn't see the four hide from
27   and then they went through the passageway more the whole lot of 'em
28   and then the skeleton carried the box into a little room
29   and he locked the box in there
30   and then they woke up they did
31   *and they saw they 're in a room* (*Josh story 65*)

In this extract 23–30 is a summary, narrated at some distance from the events described, using the narrator's special ability to see what his characters cannot see. The voice of the 'hidden' narrator actually surfaces in line 26. But line 31, strongly focalizing views in the vision of the boys (literally since Josh uses the verb 'to see'), brings us back to the point of view of the main characters and begins a strongly focalized subsequent episode.

There are many passages of unfocalized narrative in the data, particularly in simple stories that the narrator did not seem to become much involved in. In discussing some of these passages I have tried to show the ways in which the children were able to leaven the flatness of this straightforward 'telling' by using narrating techniques. It is clear that they can tell stories in a reporting fashion. Are they also able to relate events as it were through the eyes and ears of one character?

FOCALIZED NARRATIVE

Genette has three sub-categories of internal focalization:

Fixed: Everything is related from the point of view of a single character.
Variable: Focalization changes from character to character.
Multiple: The same events are related from several points of view as in epistolary novels.

Genette makes it clear that different kinds of focalization are likely to be present on one work; it is rarer to find a work consistently focalized from beginning to end. This is the case with my story data; where there are focalizations they are variable. There are no examples, either, of stories told from several points of view. This is not surprising, for here we are dealing with unplanned, spontaneous oral narratives, whereas the story which narrates the same events from more than one point of view needs to be particularly well thought-out beforehand. I have just finished reading such a novel, *The Spider's House* by Paul Bowles. The first third of this narrative is told from the point of view of an uneducated Moroccan adolescent, the second third recounts the same events from the point of view of an American writer resident in Morocco, and the final third takes off from the end of the first two parts, bringing both characters together for the climax of the story. To structure a story in such a way requires prior planning of the whole. So in this section I shall discuss consistent focalizations and variable focalizations.

Fixed focalization

Fixed focalization may be the natural way for a young child to tell an invented story. Although we cannot make the mistake of confusing the child storyteller with the character she invents, nevertheless the least complex way to tell the story would be from the point of view of the hero or heroine. This is sometimes the case with the five children, though several circumstances move them from fixed to variable focalization. For example, there is more likely to be varied focalization if there is more than one strong character in the story, if there is some dialogue in the story, and if the story is re-told from a known text. Stories which are consistently focalized are likely to be told in the first person, as in the story written by Josh at the age of 13, quoted at the end of the last chapter. The five children tell virtually all their stories in the third person, a fundamental story convention. This means that sections of stories are reported by the narrator in an unfocalized way, while others are shown through the viewpoint of one or more of the characters. However, even though none of the narratives are in the first person, there are some stories which certainly have the feeling of consistently focalized points of view. Several of Sundari's stories are about one little girl heroine, to whom things may or may not happen. Some of the narration in these stories is unfocalized, but nevertheless we are left with the feeling of having encountered only one way of looking at things. I quoted one of these stories at the end of Chapter 2 (pp. 22–3), and another in Chapter 3 (p. 29). Sundari's capacity to dwell inside the head of one of her heroines is exemplified by story 12, a long, lyrical story which is so impressive in its range of narrative techniques (at least for a pre-literate 5-year-old) that I have given a complete analysis of it, using all the major Genette categories (Chapter 10, pp. 163–7). In this story, as in several others by Sundari, we get the feeling that we know what the little girl is like from the inside.

Variable focalization

Variable focalization is most naturally achieved with the turn-taking of dialogue sections of a story, but before I discuss these I shall present some examples of non-dialogue variations in focalization. We get an impression of point of view in the narrative discourse when the storyteller presents events through one pair of ears or eyes, from one standpoint rather than another:

19 so they went to the main entrance
20 they paid their tickets
21 and they went up to their seats
22 *a dark hole and they saw the screen*

In 19–21 events are told in a distanced way, but in 22 the impact of the elliptical 'a dark hole' brings us into the cinema as the two boys go in – *we see what they would have seen*. The story continues:

23 and everybody was there
24 (and all) and then the picture came
25 (and-and-and they-) and *the nurse saw in the beds that they weren't there*
26 and she went to the cinema
27 and *she saw them just sitting there watching the film*

At 25 there is an abrupt change of focus to the nurse in the hospital who realizes, at the sight of the empty beds, that the two boys have escaped. This is strengthened in 27, where we see the boys sitting in the cinema as the nurse sees them. This kind of focalization appears at certain points in Josh's story 37, quoted in full at the opening of this chapter:

 9 now *there glowed a little light in the sky*
10 and then (it) *down came Superman*

Superman's arrival is reported as Spiderman would have seen it from the ground. There follows some dialogue where the point of view follows the exchanges of the conversation, then again the narrative action is focalized from the point of view of the Incredible Hulk's opponents:

26 but *they saw a cave*
27 (P) but the Incredible Hulk that was his house
28 so they ran away
29 *they could hear big steps coming out of the cave punching and clumping*
30 and *out came* the Incredible Hulk bashing them down
31 they fell
32 but *not any sound could they hear* (till) till the rescue helicopter came down

Here the point of view is achieved in lines 26, 29, 30 and 32 by the narrator's making use of what his characters could see and hear. Josh uses a similar technique several times in the next story he told, story 38:

36 but what a dream (in the night) *in the night they heard big steps coming along*
37 *they looked out of the window*
38 *they saw the big bad grey wolf*

and later in the same tale:

56 and well (as y-) as you know do you know what they had?
57 what a dream *they heard big big bumps coming along*
58 and *they looked out the window*
59 (um) *what did they see?*
60 *a big big fat tall heavy giant*
61 but *he wasn't looking at them*
62 so they hid (on) under the bed *so he wouldn't see them*

and a little further on:

66 soon they went to bed
67 *downstairs there was a noise*
68 *it is a noise that they have heard before*
69 (it's) it's of the big wolf carefully stepping in

Focalizing part of a story is not simply a matter of stating what the characters saw or heard, but of stating it in such a way that the listener/reader feels the impact of what happens just as the characters would have. The focalizations above use very expressive language: 'punching and clumping', 'bashing them down', 'big steps', 'big bad grey wolf', 'big big bumps', 'big big fat tall heavy giant'. In his analysis of narrative structure Labov calls phrases like these correlatives, and sees them as among the more complex evaluative devices, for, of course, these *are* evaluation sections of Josh's stories; they suspend the action, and tell us something about the narrator's stance to the events narrated. The point of this kind of focalization is that we feel the fear that the characters felt. To relate it all from the point of view of the Incredible Hulk or the wolf would require different language. In this sense, such techniques are designed to manipulate a response, a theme I shall return to in the discussion of the children's use of Barthes' hermeneutic code in Chapter 11.

The powerful parts of strong stories which were very meaningful to the children are the parts they best remembered – a clear illustration of Bartlett's idea that the affective is implicated in our remembering.[3] In their own storytelling they have an opportunity to re-live these moments as often as they like by simply transporting those sections to new contexts and actions. In this way the children's competency in narrative discourse can be natural and spontaneous and effortless. In story 38 Josh replays the suspense scene in the middle of the night three times, as the tripling in narratives like *Burglar Bill* has taught him to do. Lines 66–9 from story 38 (above) are in fact lifted from *Burglar Bill*.[2] The following extract from a retelling of *Hansel and Gretel* shows clearly that this text, too, has taught Josh how to focalize at key points in the story:

19 and they started to eat some of it (and suddenly) *until they heard a 'tip-tap tip-tap who's that knocking at my door?'*
20 *and then the door of the cottage opened*
21 *Hansel and Gretel were very frightened*
22 *they had to drop their pieces of cake* before the witch came out (*Josh story 44*)

Here, by keeping quite close to the Williams-Ellis original text, Josh helps us to experience what the children experienced by ordering the events in a suspenseful way – first what they heard, then the door opening, then dropping the pieces of cake from fear and finally the appearance of the witch. The focalizations I have quoted so far are strongly associated with the *dangerous, threatening, fearful* parts of narratives; often making use of the narrating voice as well as characters' points of view, they invite the listener to question what is coming next, and prepare us for the climax of the story. In Chapter 11 I shall return to these suspense sections and show that all five children had developed considerable competency in presenting them. For the moment I shall leave them and turn to the children's competences in reporting speech and representing points of view through what characters say or think.

Still staying with Genette's category of *variable focalization* I want to show how the children were able to accomplish this through the inclusion of conversations in their stories. I think this is a simple preference or tendency of the storyteller. Josh includes more dialogue in his stories than the other children do, and sustains his story dialogues for longer. Sundari's stories are very dialogic, too, but in a different way, for she sets up dialogues between her narrator and her imagined audience.

In some ways the reported utterances of a character must always present that character's point of view, and in this respect any dialogue is focalized. But dialogue appears in stories for different purposes. Sometimes its purpose is not so much to present any strong viewpoint as to move the action on or to announce that something has happened:

69 'If we can do something to catch those people (that's right) . . . [trails off here]
70 'If we can try something to catch one of those skeletons (P) (um) I'm going to tell the mayor about that'
71 so they (went to) walked up the stairs to the Mayor
72 and they said 'There's a skeleton
73 and we've only killed the leader

74 we haven't killed them
75 but (we – we –) he was dressed up in the museum as a mummy
76 and we pulled the string
77 he came whizzing out
78 and then he was just to bits
79 he wasn't to bits
80 he was just in a piece of string and a piece of that flat rope that they are tied up in'
81 (and then) and then he said 'If you can catch (all the rest) all the rest of those I'll give you my gold chain' (*Josh story 65*)

The function here is to decide on a plan of action. This moves the story on to the next episode, in which the boy characters catch some skeletons and claim the mayor's gold chain from him. To have some actions planned, recalled, or announced in this way makes the narration more dramatic and immediate and provides variation from the narrator's stating what happened. There are many examples of such exchanges in the data, and generally they are weak in terms of viewpoint because that is not their prime function.

Another kind of exchange that appears is the rather ritualistic or formulaic one in which characters speak in customary ways to signal their status in relation to other characters:

50 and then the king said (what) 'What is your command?'
51 and she said 'How dare you come near me'

This exchange between a king and a witch reflects the difference between a formal approach and an impolite repelling one, confirming what we already know in the story about the two characters and only representing point of view in the most basic of ways. In a retelling of *The Wizard of Oz* formulaic expressions like these appear at the appropriate moments: 'Make your best wish as you will be granted and this is what will happen' and 'follow the yellow brick road'.

In Josh's retellings of *Hansel and Gretel* one version was based on a gramophone record which presented many of the scenes in the story dramatically using different voices; thus Josh has a model for presenting dialogue without any surrounding narrative ('he said'/'she said', and so on) Genette regards this as the least distanced way of representing speech, since it has the 'live' immediacy of lines in a play.

40 W: 'Ahahahaha'
41 H: 'Get off me'
42 H: 'Who are you?'
43 G: 'You leave my brother alone'
44 W: 'Now is that any way to talk to a friend?'
45 G: 'A friend doesn't tie someone up with a rope'
46 W: 'I'm just getting you ready for (a) a big supper. Ahahahaha'
47 W: '(the) a step and you'll become a tree'
48 W: 'Izzard gizzard a step and you won't feel so well'
49 W: 'I'll put her in
50 W: 'and she'll be done for tea' (P)
51   just then she quietly slipped around Hansel and put him in a cage

52 H: 'You let me out of here'
53 G: 'You leave my brother alone'
54 H: 'Who are you you stupid crow?'
55 W: 'Just put your head in like this'
56 H: 'Push her' (*Josh story 29*)

In this passage there is a distinct feeling of words being uttered while a lot of action is taking place, in fact the actions implicit in the dialogue make it possible to identify the speaker even though Josh never indicates directly who is speaking. There is no doubt about point of view which, in each utterance, is clearly that of either the good or the bad character.

In another version of *Hansel and Gretel* Josh, by contrast, presents the dialogue more as it would be written down in a book. A comparison of the two versions will show that point of view becomes less clear when the narrator's voice can be heard presenting the speech of the characters.

37 and she said in a loud in a grumbling voice 'I'm going to get that boy
38 I'm going to leave that boy in that cage (to-when he-) till he's fat
39 and when he's fat I'm going to eat him'
40 (so) so she (a cook) a kill cook her and eat them
41 'and first we will bake' the witch cried
42 (they need) 'they need fattening'
43 and she called in a grumbling voice 'Gretel let me feel that your hands are
       getting fat'
44 (and) and then she did
45 she pulled out a bone
46 and in dismay she thought it was his finger
       [Adult: In dismay?]
47 so then 'first we can bake however'
48 what she really meant was push (Han-) Hansel and Gretel in the oven as well
       as Hansel
49 (but) but' put your head in just like me
50 I can even get in myself' (*Josh story 32*)

It is difficult to decide whether this passage is focalized from the point of view of the children watching and listening to the witch, or whether we are consistently seeing things as the witch sees them. Josh is careful to show how unpleasant the witch's voice is ('in a loud in a grumbling voice', 'cried', 'called in a grumbling voice') and, in fact, changes his tone for the witch's words on the tape, using a thin, cackling old lady's voice. These phrases seem to be focalized from the children's point of view, since the witch would hardly perceive herself in this way; on the other hand, though we know the children are there, we are given none of their responses to this scene, so that there is considerable focalization from the witch's point of view. Line 46, 'in dismay she thought it was his finger', seems strongly focalized because of the phrase 'in dismay'. The source for this phrase is not the original text of *Hansel and Gretel* (much of this scene is Josh's own with one or two phrases borrowed from the text) but its source is undoubtedly literary, reflecting the rather archaic language used in fairy-tales told for children. What Josh is doing here is *telling* us, through the narrator, what the witch's thoughts were, rather than leaving the dialogue to *show* us, on its own, as it did in version 1. Josh's skill in version 2 is to balance telling and showing, using his narrator and the witch herself to vary the focalization.

Genette uses the term 'narratized' to describe the kind of speech or thinking which is *reported* by the narrator rather than simply shown by the direct quotation of the character's words. Inner speech, that is the thoughts, intentions, memories etc. of characters, is often reported by the narrator, since in real life we do not often say our thoughts aloud. In the following brief passage from an invented story Josh moves from distantly focalized narration (lines 59–61) to direct focalization through the eyes of his two main characters. (lines 62–6).

59 they stopped and looked and listened
60 they didn't know something little ran behind them
61 it run up behind them
62 David said 'run'
63 'Why?'
64 (I'm not-er-er-) but (um) he looked back
65 and Joshua looked behind
66 he said 'yes let's run' (*Josh story 55*)

About three-quarters of the way through his storytelling year Josh told a long story organized into three successive chapters: stories 62, 63 and 64. In many ways these stories are quite remarkable. They are the culmination of a whole series of narratives about a group of boys, the fictionalized Josh and a group of his friends, who leave home and have adventures together in a world of mountains, caves and underground tunnels. Josh gradually introduces an imaginary world, and the inclusion in them of characters who are called 'Mumby' 'the witch of the East', and so on, indicates that he was using Baum's stories *The Wizard of Oz* and *The Land of Oz* as a kind of inspiration.[4] By the time he gets to story 62 Josh seems to have found a setting, some themes and some characters that he is able to maintain with great consistency. The setting is Heaven, albeit a Heaven which is based on both the Hades of *Theseus and the Minotaur* (Serraillier, 1965) and the Emerald City of Baum's Oz stories, which I was reading aloud to Josh, a chapter at a time, every night during this period. Baum's stories are much longer than children's picture story-books, and there are few illustrations in them. The child listening to them would need to create the scenes and events in his/her imagination depending solely on words to create the meanings. At the beginning of this series of 3 stories Josh starts from the end of *The Wizard of Oz* when Dorothy's dog, Toto, is left behind in the Emerald City. In Josh's story God and St Peter find a little puppy in Heaven who does not belong there and must somehow be returned to his owners on earth. As his narrative grows Josh replays the motif of unsuitable visitors to Heaven, including in the cast of characters baddies like Frankenstein and Dracula.[5] Throughout the chapters God and St Peter talk together, arguing over the problems each of these characters presents. Stories 62 and 63 are saturated with dialogue, dialogue which is used simultaneously to establish consistent characteristics for the dramatis personae and to advance the plot. Here I want to look at five, strongly focalized dialogues from story 63, where, because problems are discussed and solutions found for them, points of view are presented alternately as they are in an argument. The ability to present both sides of a rational argument is precisely what Piaget thought egocentricity would prevent in young children, yet stories in books teach children, even at this age, to hear the voices of different characters in their imagination and to turn those voices into storying.

As story 63 begins St Peter is walking around the passageways of Heaven, looking at all the diamonds and pearls God has placed on the walls:

4 and suddenly he got a fright because (God-God) God (was) was walking along the passageway
5 'Oh sorry' said God
6 'It's alright' said St Peter
7 'What you doing here?'
8 'I'm just looking at the diamonds and pearls on the walls'
9 (so then) so then he said 'Where did you get them from?' said St Peter
10 'Oh I got them from some (from some) (mountains) mountain clouds'
11 'Oh I thought clouds were just ordinary clouds that you could just fall through'
12 'Oh but sometimes I make em magic and turn into rocks
13 and then I get all the pearls'
14 'Oh you greedy thing'

Here Josh gives us just enough narrative surrounding the speech to let us know who is speaking, though as the exchanges continue less of this is required and the speeches stand alone, as in a play. The point of view varies from St Peter to God with each turn, yet the dialogue as a whole is more strongly focalized from St Peter's point of view than from God's. This is because St Peter is asking questions and requires more information from God than God does from him, and because St Peter expresses more attitudes than God does. Throughout these stories Josh sustains distinct characterizations for God and St Peter. God is more powerful (having 'magic' powers), detached and fun-loving; St Peter has less power but more conscience. In the extract above the difference between God's magical powers to create diamonds and pearls out of clouds, and St Peter's puzzlement that this can be so is presented dramatically in the exchange of speech rather than through the narrator's telling. The turns of speech are made more lifelike by Josh's inclusion of the phatic markers of everyday conversation ('Oh sorry'), which also, since they are responsive, contribute to point of view.

In the next extract St Peter and God have met their old enemy Dracula disguised as a spaceman:

26 one spaceman was disguising
27 it was just Dracula
28 and it came through the window and caught God
29 (but God) but God (um -got his hands-um) got his axe-[tape ends, new cassette put in] and chopped his head off
30 *then* the head came back on
31 Dracula was magic just like any other person
32 St Peter said to God 'There's no way to get this evil man'
33 'Well the only thing we *can do* is *really* try hard to chop him up in *little tiny bits*'

34 'But he might come alive again'
35 'We'll never get him'
36 'We'll just have to take care of him'
37 'I know what — Dracula!'
38 'What?'
39 'You want to be on our side?'
40 'Yes I'll be pleased to'
41 'Right then he's our friend' said God to St Peter

Dracula's point of view is not presented here at all, for God and St Peter mostly discuss him as though he were not present. In only two places, 32 and 41, does the narrator indicate who is speaking to whom. In 33 and 34 Josh opens the speeches with the cohesive markers 'Well' and 'But', each of which indicates a change of turn in the conversation, while 35 and 36 could be uttered by either character. In 37 God does not make an argument in reply to St Peter but enacts an idea he has had. This is a completely dramatic technique for moving the action forward, not distanced in any way by the narrating voice.

In the third extract the focalization stays with God in a surprisingly subtle *showing* of God's ability to think 'on his feet'. Here God has offered Dracula one of the diamonds studded in the wall, and while Dracula is choosing God is whispering to St Peter:

47 so God whispered to St Peter (Dracula's) 'Dracula's just walking about
48 and know what he's doing?
49 he's looking at (the) those lovely diamonds'
50 'Why shouldn't [unclear] I?'
51 'I was just talking to him to tell you what you were doing (because-
   because-um- I just wanna tell him what you were doing) — because he
   wasn't looking
52 he was just looking on the floor to see (the) if there are any mices to chase
53 we *should* have a cat because I just saw a mousehole'
54 'Oh no we need a cat'

In this passage there is very sharp focalization from God's point of view even though St Peter and Dracula are both present. The garble in 51 probably arises for two reasons; it is difficult for young children to cope with any extended indirect speech, but here the indirect speech is embedded inside God's direct speech and this causes Josh to muddle his pronouns; Josh also needs to do some quick thinking here. God is whispering to St Peter behind Dracula's back, and has to think of a feasible explanation for his rudeness and a diversionary ploy to distract Dracula's attention – the idea of the mousehole. The story is narrated breathlessly by Josh, as though he has such a rush of ideas that his words cannot keep up with them. There was no time for advanced planning of the mousehole ruse, yet Josh comes up with it at the right moment and is subsequently able to use it to move the story on. The only explanation for such strong centredness on the point of view of one character is that Josh was 'living' the parts as he was telling them. It is the ability to create a world of characters, and to dwell in it imaginatively with the characters, that enables Josh to make these conversations convincing. This is precisely what Piaget thought young children were incapable of doing.

The next extract from this story continues directly from the last one; Josh simply keeps the voices going, but now the focalization shifts between God and Dracula with the turns of the conversation:

55 'Yes but I'll get him' said Dracula
56 'Where's my teeth?'
57 'Oh I don't know
58 I think I dropped em
59 when I pulled em out I dropped them
60 Oh I can remember where they are'
61 'Where?'
62 'Back on my throne they were under my throne'
63 'Oh there they are
64 they're under your throne'
65 'yeah thank-you I'll put them in
66 and if I see any mouses I'll just *bite* em
67 and then they'll fall in half'
68 'Oh great' said God' That's a good help
69 we love you very much now'
70 'So do I' said Dracula

This dialogue changes point of view with each speaker. It is not necessary for Josh to supply more markers of the speaker than he does, for he can rely on the implicit speaker markers of the conversation itself, i.e. a question receives an answer, a request is granted, and so on. It would be an easy matter to turn the dialogue sections of story 63 into a play by placing each character's name beside each turn. Genette sees this kind of speech in narrative as most mimetic of life, most immediate and 'live' in its effect. In such passages the time of the story and the time of the narrating come together so that we are *at* the scene of events. In the first 'chapter' (Josh's term) of this story, story 62, God dispenses with Dracula by taking out Dracula's fangs and stabbing him with them. The problem of the story is that Dracula keeps coming back to life, and God and St Peter must obtain his friendship rather than kill him. Dracula's teeth are then brought out in the second chapter to deal with the mouse problem and Dracula is able to prove himself an ally at last.

Josh ends this chapter with more dialogue, though this time it is slightly distanced, since the narrator takes a larger part in it than in the sections of the story quoted above. After a general celebration of Dracula's friendship the story moves into its final episode, which again calls back to events which happened in the first chapter when Frankenstein paid God a visit and introduced to him a 'kind' dragon:

81 (and then − and then they −) and then (they − God) God got the big bed
    out which he had never done before
82 and they all slept in it
83 in the night they went right u-under the blankets for if there was any danger
    for the big dragon *he* (was) was (in−) *in* the bed somewhere
84 but God forgotten where he was
85 he was right down the bed
86 God (c) − could (f) − feel his little ear with his toe

87 (and then −) and then God said 'DRAGON! [shouted] *Where*'s the dragon?'
88 (said) 'I'm getting out of here' said one of the servants
89 (and then) and then they said '*Don't* get out of here'
90 (it's a good − it's a good −) it's a good one'
91 (so-so then they-) so then it crept out and said (to the servant) to the servant who was frightened 'I'm not a bad one
92 I'm a good one'
93 'Oh I'm not running away
94 one's already run away
95 and all the rest has not running away
96 Hey! Come back'
97 so the other servant came back and said 'It's alright
98 he's a good one'
99 and (God) God said 'Look here servants (this one was −) Frankenstein gave (th −) this one to us for any dangers
100 (and) and Dracula wanted to be on our side for dangers so there's two people (who will −) who will save *all* our lives'
101 'Yes well I'll tell you the life that I had on earth once
102 once somebody tried to get me
103 they couldn't get me
104 I didn't suck anybody's blood
105 I'm a good (Dracula −) Dracula'
106 (um-um) 'We were sorry to chop your head off and all the rest of the things'
107 'Oh it's alright for that'
108 (um) so then he said ''Why don't we have a climb up the mountains?
109 'Why don't we make a house in the mountains?'
110 'Yes'
111 so they *all* made a house in the mountains − the mountains' rocks
112 and then they slept in it with all their things
113 (and then) and then they lived happily ever after
114 and that's the end (*Josh story 63*)

Again there are some very sharp focalizations here, accomplished through a combination of the narrator's voice and the speech of the characters. The fact that the dragon is down the bed somewhere is given as a piece of omniscient narrator's knowledge which builds us up towards the dramatic presentation of the encounter between the dragon's ear and God's toe. The 'indwelling' in the character of God is particularly impressive here, for, having felt something in the bed he asks where the dragon is rather than immediately concluding that the dragon is there. The panic of the servant running away is offset by the narrator's use of the term 'crept' for the dragon's emergence from the bed, a timid verb to choose, reinforcing the fact that this is a harmless dragon. There is a great sense of everything coming together and being resolved by kindness at the end of this story. In the final episode Josh manages to bring back the dragon from the first chapter, and then, in his speech to the servants, God also reminds us that Frankenstein was present in the earlier chapter too. Dracula confirms his goodness by changing the story about himself and God apologizes for his former violence. The point of view goes from God, to the servants, to the dragon, to God, to Dracula, and finally back to God. In this scene Josh's narrator indicates who is speaking to whom more explicitly than he does in earlier parts of the story, probably because more characters than usual are brought together. This explicitness is strengthened *inside* the speeches by phatic touches like 'look here servants'.

The important cognitive implication of focalization in narrative is not that the young child is capable of achieving it at all, but that the child is able to make it change while maintaining unity of characterization, plot and setting. To do this, the child must have conceptualized that events can be seen and felt from the point of view of all the actors in them. Storytelling experience must contribute greatly to such an understanding, helping children to free themselves from the one-sidedness that infantile egocentricity may impose upon their thinking.

VARIATIONS IN FOCAL LENGTH

Any direct speech in a story will provide focalization but Genette also differentiates between the focal lengths of various ways of reporting speech. Speech reported as in a play is the most immediate and close-up; other reporting methods create a greater distance between the listener/reader and characters' utterances.

Reported speech: Most near. Character's words given as they were supposedly uttered.
Transposed speech: More distanced. The gist of the character's words is given.
Narratized speech: Most distanced. No attempt to represent character's words.

One might expect children who have heard thousands of story readings to be aware of both close-up and distanced ways of representing characters' words and thoughts. For the final section of this chapter I want to look at the means of presenting speech at the children's disposal, using as a template Genette's three categories of distance/ nearness in the focalization of dialogue.

Reported speech

Here the character's speech 'is fictively reported as it supposedly was uttered' (Genette 1972, p. 170). The majority of speech representation in the data comes into this category, as the examples above from story 63 have shown. The children had plenty of experience of real-life conversation and role-play, and the mimetic quality of Josh's dialogues reflects this, especially in his use of polite conversational 'markers', such as 'Oh', 'I'm sorry to tell you but . . .', 'great', 'thank-you', 'well', and so on. The children use their voices expressively during dialogues, but otherwise show that they realize dialogue in stories must rely more heavily on words alone to carry the meaning than in real speech in life, where we are helped by a host of paralinguistic cues – gestures, facial expression and other kinds of body language. In stories speeches must be more 'to-the-point' than in real life. In Josh's dialogues in story 63 there seem to be a limited number of clear functions for the speech:

- to help to tell the story and advance the plot
- to establish the personality and feelings of the characters
- to establish and maintain relationships between the characters

The more distanced and literary way to present reported speech, one much employed by the children, is within the framework of surrounding narrative. At its most basic this involves using: 'and x said'. To tag the speech with *subsequent* narrative, especially in the form of 'said x' or 'said y' is more common in writing than in oral language. In the extracts I have quoted from story 63 above, there are 15 speeches where Josh adds some surrounding narrative. On 8 occasions he places the narrative in the subsequent position ('Oh sorry' *said God*; 'It's alright' *said St Peter*) and on the other 7 introduces the speech with the narrative, often including the addressee (*St Peter said to God* 'there's no way to get this evil man'). A less usual variant on tagging the speech with subsequent narrative is to place the dialogue on either side of the tag, (Oh great', *said God*, 'that's a good help'). In the children's stories there are surprisingly few variations on the term 'said', though we have in the extracts above 'cried' and 'called' from Josh's retelling of *Hansel and Gretel*, and 'whispered' in story 63. Presenting dialogue mimetically, as Josh does in story 63, makes the story duration fast and the focalization close, giving a strong feeling of 'living' the scene; presenting the dialogue with some tagged narrative slows the duration and slightly distances the discourse from the events narrated. The competent storyteller moves from one to the other, at times letting the turns of conversation speak for themselves, at times taking control through the narrating voice. Josh shows himself skilled at combining these techniques.

Transposed speech

Transposed speech is Genette's term for indirect speech with the gist of the words reported. It is necessarily more distanced and less mimetic than reported speech, for it is essentially the narrative discourse telling rather than showing. There are some examples of it in the data, in spite of the fact that it requires some syntactic adjustments that the children occasionally find difficult. Here are some examples.

15 when their dad learnt (um – what) they were deep in the forest he scolded his wife
16 (a –) and *he said that they in great danger of the wicked old witch of the forest (Josh story 29)*
4   his mother and father *said he could go to the fair one day (Sundari story 7)*
7   but *the farmer told them to came in (Josh story 4)*
11 and *he said that Batman wasn't feeling well (Josh story 37)*
70 but *God said it was* (alright –) alright (um – St Peter –)
71 *God said it wasn't alright*
72 (he –) *he had to* (um –) *keep an eye on as well as God in the night (Josh story 62)*

Josh's syntactic problems are obvious here; he omits the verb 'were' in the transposed speech of story 29, unnecessarily transforms the verb infinitive 'to come' into the past tense 'came' in story 4, and confuses his pronouns in the more extended transposed speech in story 62. The fact that most of these extracts come from Josh's stories is probably a reflection of his interest in using dialogue in stories in all its forms. I am not at all surprised that the children stumble on the syntax of transposed speech. As a former secondary school teacher of English I found that many much older children had great difficulty in putting speech into writing in this form.

Narratized speech

This is the most distanced category of reporting speech for there is no attempt at mimesis: 'the discourse is treated like one event among others and taken as such by the narrator himself' (Genette, 1972, p. 170). In this form the speech is so highly summarized by the narrator that the original words completely vanish:

75 and then he told all the other people *what the two boys did (Josh story 55)*
37 Hansel got on her back and told his sister *to come on the back (Josh story 34)*
 6 and when they came to God's palace they told him *to help* because a wicked witch (was just-) was just down on earth *(Josh story 56)*
30 and then he told her *to get the guard of God's palace (Josh story 56)*

In contrast to the examples of transposed speech from Josh, these narratized forms are attached to the verb 'to tell' rather than the verb 'to say'. Perhaps the most highly narratized example of all comes at the end of a story about a rescue at sea when, at the end of the story, there is a storytelling:

23 and then at home when they got home he (told-) told him (er) *of all the deaths of seamen there is (Josh story 71)*

A more difficult form of narratized speech occurs when it is embedded in dialogue; one character reports what another character has said to a third character. We have had one example of this in Josh's story 63:

51 'I was just talking to him to tell you [sic] what you were doing . . .'

Another example occurs two stories on, indicating that Josh was just beginning to experiment with this competency:

64 'and there's (two) a hundred and ninety-nine left
65 (and- and-) and *that's how many the skeleton told me* because *I heard him say that* from the prison' *(Josh story 65)*

Genette distinguishes between narratized speech and narratized *inner* speech, the latter occurring when the *thoughts* of a character are summarized by the narrator. The presence of verbs of cognition in the data (knowing, remembering, realizing, thinking and so on) are of interest since they reflect the children's explicit awareness of cognitive processes and the role that these play in story events. Knowing that characters think things, understand things, have ideas and intentions, must be part of realizing that characters do not just behave in one way or another in stories *but have motivations*. Narratized inner speech is closely related to point of view. Although there are still more frequent examples from Josh's stories, some narratized inner speech appears from all the children:

8 and they cooked something for us
9 and *we thought it was magic*
10 and the teddy-bears *told us*
11 and *we told Mummy (Jimmy story 9)*

In this example narratized inner speech in sentence 9 is followed by two examples of external narratized speech in 10 and 11. Several examples in Josh's stories come from his retellings of *Hansel and Gretel*:

46 and *in dismay she thought it was his finger (Josh story 32)*
2 but *they knew that there was a little house covered with sweets (Josh story 34)*

Others come from stories with strong written models:

96 but he *remembered he had to go out in the snow to guard his treasure (Josh story 38)*

An interesting example of this kind of cogitation occurs in:

67 'yeah let's try and get out of here again'
68 (P) (um-) and then there was silence for a moment
69 (P) and *after that they found a new way*
70 there was silence 'cos they were thinking *(Josh story 66)*

Examples of transposed and narratized speech are harder to find in the story data than direct speech, and I am convinced that direct speech is the natural mode for inexperienced storytellers. Very often the children use direct speech even when it seems rather obvious or forced to do so. Characters tend to say things aloud even to themselves, as in the following example from Sundari:

3 and she took some things to make a scarecrow
4 she was very pleased about them
5 but then she said 'They're girls' things
6 I'll make a girl scarecrow'
7 so she did *(Sundari story 6)*

Even when there is no addressee for the speech Sundari gives us spoken words to represent her heroine's thoughts. Sometimes Josh quotes the uttered words of a group of characters, rather than an individual:

25 and then they got the keys and went in and looked inside
26 and then *they said* 'Why don't we put the engine on?'
27 so (we-) they started the engine *(Josh story 55)*
71 so they (went to-) walked up the stairs to the Mayor
72 and *they said* 'There's a skeleton . . . *(Josh story 65)*

This is not realistic since it is hardly likely that a group would speak in unison, but it is certainly easier for the children to handle and pleasurable for them to vary the narration with some speech.

SUMMARY

Genette's category of *mood*, then, deals with the modalities of representation in narrative discourse: telling or showing, from one point of view, many points of view or no point of view, in a distanced or a focalized way, using a range of techniques for presenting the speech and thoughts of characters. From the examples I have quoted in this chapter it is clear that the two 5-year-olds, but particularly Josh, were by no means limited to the most simple ways of telling, or the most direct ways of showing, what their characters said. Josh's dialogues are presented in such a way that the speech and the surrounding narrative have varying duration, focalization and distance. Josh and Sundari are developing an awareness of characters as having inner thoughts and motives as well as outer words and actions, so that their stories show an emergent psychological aspect. Passages like those in story 63, where Josh is able to change strong focalizations, imply that he is not limited to one view of things but, identifying with the viewpoints of his characters, can see several ways around a story problem. Sundari's stories are less developed in terms of mood because they are very highly developed in Genette's third major category of narrative discourse, *voice*.

NOTES

1. Although Piaget seems to have underestimated young children's storytelling ability, his account of play sometimes accords with the other theories I discussed in earlier chapters. He gives a central place to affects and regards some kinds of play as similar to Lacan's mirror-stage. For example, he proposes that the imaginary companions children invent for themselves 'provide a sympathetic audience or a mirror for the ego' (p. 131).
2. Chapter 2, p. 11, note 1.
3. Bartlett (1932). See Chapter 6.
4. Sale (1978) sees Baum's stories as frontier tales which are metaphors for the exploration of the American West in the 19th century. It is very striking that Josh picks up the *terrain* from these fairy tales, and transforms them into explorations by children like himself. The theme of leaving one's parents and living independently is fundamental in most of the stories Josh retold or transformed.
5. Frankenstein and Dracula certainly come from comics and TV cartoons. Josh had never seen any full-length feature films in this genre.

Chapter 10

The Voice of the Narrator

1 there was a witch yes a witch
2 and her *name* was Porridge
3 she was called Porridge because she ate porridge
4 and her maidens were called Double, Bubble, Toil, and Trouble (P)
5 *and* what she ate in her porridge was frogs' legs dogs' tongues (P) and (P)
  tch-tch-tch- hedgehogs' prickles and
6 (P) it was *horrid* porridge
7 and they ate *people's* hair and people's legs (P) so dirty and horrid (P) the
  porridge was
8 and they had a notice up on their door
9 and they had two little babies the first one called Mmmmmubble and the
  second one called Trrruggle
10 they're silly names aren't they?
11 did you say yes?
12 well if you did I'm pleased
13 if you didn't I'm still pleased
14 *and* (P) the witch had two daughters the first one called Santi second one
  called Sundari which is *my* name
15 and (P) they had a big big girl about nineteen
16 and the two little daughters were about five and seven
17 (P) and the mummy was about (P) thirteen
18 (P) one day when her birthday was about (it) she would be thirty-one
19 (P-No) *and* they one day said 'We are going to collect a seven year-old to
  cut its tongue off (P) *stick* it in our *stew*
20 so they did
21 and they got a seven-year-old one day
22 it was *really really* seven
23 and they cut off its tongue (P) and put it in their stew then ate it
24 and they put buckles [unclear] the heads of flowers in the stew and made it
  look all *yucky*

25   and the tongue was sticking up like that at the witch looking *so silly* which it
     would do
26   and the witch went 'Ah-ah-ah-ah'
27   and that was what it did
28   they had also a little dog
29   as you know what 'also' means
30   and the little dog's name was Dougall
31   it was a furry white dog with lots of furs on
32   ding-a-ling-a-ling (*Sundari story 4*, with narrator's emphases)

In the last chapter I argued that the relationships of mood in the children's stories
showed that they were sometimes capable of seeing things from more than one point
of view, and that, at least in the context of imaginative storytelling, they do not seem
to have been restricted by Piagetian egocentricity. The same can be said of the
narrating *voice* in the stories, a voice which is often heard addressing us directly in
Sundari's stories. In her story 4, above, for example, there is an 'I' narrator and a 'you'
presumed listener. Sundari sometimes told her stories alone with the tape-recorder, and
at other times with her mother present. Whatever the case, though, it is clear that the
'you' Sundari is addressing exists in her imagination rather than in reality. She would
hardly need to ask her mother 'Did you say yes?' if her mother was there in front of
her; the question is obviously addressed to an unknown audience, whom Sundari
knows will not have the benefit of the storyteller's physical presence, when s/he listens
to the tape. To be able to imagine an audience, an addressee, in the absence of any
physical reality, is another way of seeing things from somebody else's point of view.
It is an ability which writers need, an ability to foresee the effects of the writing on
the reader and to anticipate the reader's responses. Storytelling is not only an act of
communication in the sense that characters are sketched for us and their personalities
and actions relayed to us through the narrative discourse. It is also an act of
communication between a *narrator* and a *narratee*. If Sundari is required by the
situation of tape-recording an oral story to invent an unknown audience for herself,
she is also required in some ways to re-invent herself as a storyteller – to take on the
role of storyteller for the duration. Of all the five children, Sundari makes this role
most explicit, though it is present in a more hidden, implicit way in the stories of the
other four children. Genette's categories of voice classify for us the different ways in
which narrator's and narrating voices play a part in narrative discourse, and the
distinctions he makes have been very useful for discovering further layers of
complexity in the children's story structures.

TYPES OF NARRATING

Genette's classification of different kinds of narrating returns us to questions of tense,
but this time we are dealing not with *the time of the story that is narrated* but with
the time of the narrating that is telling the story. This distinction can be very clearly
seen in Sundari's story 4 above. The *narrated* story, about the witch and her daughters,
is told in the past tense and the third person, the most traditional and primary story
mode. However, the *narrating* of the story is told in the present tense and the first

person; Sundari's narrator is telling *now* with the 'I' of the narrator placed inside her text. Throughout her narrative Sundari has to maintain these two kinds of time, narrating time and story time, alongside one another, a necessity she has imposed upon herself by inventing not just a story but a storyteller as well. Of course I have chosen to illustrate this crucial distinction of Genette's through one of Sundari's stories because she makes the narrator's voice so explicit, but this does not mean that there is no narrator for stories told by Josh and the other children entirely in the third person and past tense. There is a narrator in those stories but its voice is kept hidden. It manages to tell us things without surfacing in the narrative discourse too often, yet it does surface from time to time, robbing us of the illusion that this story is somehow 'natural'. The narrating voice of Josh's stories revealed itself explicitly several times in the passages I quoted in Chapter 9, becoming a presence in such phrases as 'as you know', 'what a dream', 'what she really meant was' . . . , and in the places where the text asks a question of itself: 'so how should they get away from this forest . . .?'. Such questions are being asked by somebody: the narrator who, for most of the time, Josh keeps well out of hearing.

Genette offers four major types of narrating:

Subsequent: the past tense narrative. The narrating *follows* the events narrated.
Prior: the future tense narrative. The narrating comes *before* the events narrated.
Simultaneous: the present tense narrative. The narrating is *contemporaneous* with the events narrated.
Interpolated: the narrating occurs *between* the events narrated.

He is very clear about the relative simplicity/complexity of these narrating types, declaring that, to date, *subsequent* narrating has dominated the novel, that *simultaneous* narrating is the simplest form and that *interpolated* narrating is 'a priori the most complex since it involves a narrating with several instances, and since the story and the narrating can become entangled in such a way that the latter has an effect on the former' (1972, p. 217).

Though it is possible to agree with Genette in theory that simultaneous narrating is the most simple, the evidence that we have from young children belies this. We know that by age 5 children tell stories in the past tense and the third person, so subsequent narrating is where children start (Pradl, 1979). The stories I have quoted throughout confirm that subsequent narrating is the dominant form for Josh, Jimmy, Justine and Robert. Sundari is a rather different case. Robert was the youngest child in the study, and his data include a retelling of *Burglar Bill*. Unusually in stories for young children this is told in the present tense (simultaneous narrating). Though Robert adheres quite closely to the text he has difficulty in keeping the story in the present, moving between present and past. An extract will show what I mean:

12 when he came home there was a noise in the box (*past*)
13 and it sounded like one police car (*past*)
14 (sounds- and it came-) well it sounds like two police cars (*present*)
15 so he raises the lid (*present*)
16 'Blow me down it's a baby' (*present*)
17 and he pats his hand (*present*)
18 and he —'What was you doing in that box?' (*present*)

19 and the baby still cries (*present*)
20 'I know what you want – grub' (*present*)
21 so he gave him a apple to the baby (*past*)
22 still the baby cries (*present*)
23 and he gave him a slice of marmalade and toast to the baby (*past*)
24 but he still cries (*present*) (*Robert story 22*)

There is a more successful example of simultaneous narrating in this book, in the written story by Josh at age 13 quoted at the end of Chapter 8 (p. 117). The difficulties Josh experienced with changing to first person/present tense writing of stories at round about this age convinced me that it is a later development, at least in writing. It may well be that writing is the crucial variable here, for I have heard many oral narrators using vernacular English tell stories in the present tense, both children and adults.

There is an interesting example from Robert, at age 3:9, of a story started in the future tense (Genette's *prior* narrating) and the first person (plural):

I want to tell a story about (when-wh-wh-) where we're going on holiday
[*Adult*: Alright. Have you finished that other story? *Robert*: Yeah.]
1   one day (l-a-we) we are going on holiday (to the- to the-) to the – (um)
2   we're going to see grandma
3   we're going on holidays to see grandma
4   and we didn't know we go on holiday
5   and we did not know anything
6   we don't know something
7   but we do –
I finished that one (*Robert story 13*)

Robert's opening and closing remarks show that he intends to tell a story. However, having started in the future his job is to get into the past or present so that a story can be told. This temporal switch is too much for him. The story itself can only be a matter of speculation, but my guess is that he wants to tell about the surprise he had when he found out that he was going on holiday to see Grandma. The remaining category, interpolated narrating, is consistently used by Sundari.

In the 19 stories from Sundari there is a total of 799 sentences (T-Units), and of these 143 (17.7 per cent) contain, or consist of, some kind of direct narrator's comment. Most of these narrator's interpolations are sandwiched between the events of the story. In the witch story at the start of this chapter the narrator intrudes on the narrative in T-Units 10, 11, 12, 13, 14, 25 and 29, and she is lurking in other places too, for example in the opening line 'there was a witch *yes a witch* – that 'yes' is very much the narrator's emphasis. There is even one place in story 7 where Sundari's interpolated narrating becomes entangled in the story she tells, a characteristic, Genette tells us, of the Proustian narrative:

21 and the swing made a noise like this [creaking sounds]
22 (it was an-) it needed oil
23 I'm sorry I said it needed oil
24 (P) we're gonna have a bit of a laugh now [loud laughter]
25 that's what they made

26 (P) when I said "you can have a bit of a laugh now" the two children laughed
27 you can laugh too when you have the tape on again (P)
28 you can go like this 'ha-ha-ha-ha-ha-ha-ha-ha'
29 and one day they got a big fat green apple and a red apple

Here Sundari has collapsed the distance between her first-person narrator and the story she tells. The effect is of what Genette calls a 'narrative impossibility'; we know very well that nobody laughed in the narrative discourse when the narrator said 'we're gonna have a bit of a laugh now', but the effect is that we presume somehow this could have happened, that somehow the story has a reality outside the discourse which tells it. By such means storytellers try to convince us that the narrative is not an illusion spun from words but is 'natural'. What Sundari is concealing here is the impossibility of a narrating event and a narrated event happening at the same time. Sundari's stories are full of interpolated comments and distractions of this kind.

Another interesting feature of story 4 is that it clearly shows Sundari's fictionalization of herself as a character and the distinction between that character, who just happens to be the same age and have the same name as Sundari herself, and Sundari the narrator:

14 and the witch had two daughters the first one called Santi second one called Sundari *which is my name*

The implication is that it may be my name but it isn't necessarily me. The fact that Sundari can stand back from the narrative and see a character who is ostensibly modelled on herself in a distanced way, as a fiction which she herself has invented, is an aspect of what Genette calls the *narrating stance*.

NARRATING STANCE

By stance Genette means the position of the narrator in relation to the narrative s/he tells. Is the narrator involved in the narrative, telling his/her own story from the inside? Or does s/he tell a story about other people in which s/he has no part? Such questions can be very complex in adult novels. *Wuthering Heights*, for example, has two narrators; Mr Lockwood begins the story in the first person and is also involved in the narrative events at the beginning. He then encounters the second narrator, Nellie Dean, who tells the rest of the story, in some of which she was involved as a minor character, but for most of which she was merely an observer. Here one narrator passes on the narrating to another, who, at certain points in the story, tells it as she heard it from the characters. We can be quite surprised at the sudden reappearance of Mr Lockwood in this novel, and even of Mrs Dean, for the two narrators are really devices to tell a past-tense third person narrative.

When considering narrating stance we might compare Sundari's narrator to Josh's. Josh's narrator is the hidden, omniscient third-person narrator, who occasionally surfaces with a reference to 'I' or 'you', reminding us that somebody is telling this story. Josh's narrator is no way a 'character'; beyond that hint from time to time that he is there, directing the narrative, we know nothing at all about him. Josh's narrator does not tell stories about himself, but often invents a character called Joshua: ('one sunny morning little Joshua was awake'). The fictionalized Joshua is treated as a character in the story, just as the Incredible Hulk and God and St Peter are. The narrator does not comment on events nor does he come outside the narrative to divert us from what is happening in the story; he is rather sewn securely into the narrative discourse so that when he asks the listener a question he asks it in an entirely impersonal way:

85 and now (he looked) he looked through his kaleidoscope
86 and what did he see (but the) but the English riding away in his boat? (*Josh story 39*)

Sometimes Josh's narrator does become unravelled from the narrative but quickly disappears again into the impersonal form of addressing the reader:

14 but as you know who lived in the forest?
15 well shall I tell you?
16 well it was a big wicked grey wolf

Here the narrating persona shows in 'you', 'I' and 'well' but it is immediately swallowed up again in the past tense/third person:

17 and (so-so) so how should they get away from this forest 'cos if he saw them he would surely swallow them up? (*Josh story 38*)

Sundari's narrator, by contrast, is not woven into the fabric of the story she tells. She is detached from it, at times condemning it or dismissing it. She also tells her listener quite a lot about herself, so we have to regard the narrator, too, as a character, albeit not one who is involved in the events narrated. Can Sundari's first-person narrator truly be regarded as a fiction?

This question is complicated by the fact that Sundari's narrator is announced as Sundari herself, the author/inventor of the story:

13 and one day I'll be nineteen (P) because I am *five*
14 (P) I tell stories
15 that's why I'm on this tape
16 she tells a few stories as well on the tape (P)
17 and the *girl* told lots of stories on the tape (*Sundari story 6*)

Here Sundari is talking autobiographically about her real non-fictional self when she refers to 'I' who is clearly contrasted to the 'she' of lines 16 and 17. In what respect can Sundari's narrator be fictive, then, as I would argue she is? Sundari's consciousness of narrating as a fictional *role* in storytelling is revealed by the fact that she sometimes introduces a second narrator, an obviously fictional one called Angeli who sings songs but does not have any narrating role as such. Angeli of course is Sundari herself. Sundari the narrator, the 'I' of lines 13–15, is a fiction to the extent that she is the real Sundari reinvented as a storyteller, playing a role that causes her to address imagined listeners in a special way that the role calls for. Sundari's real everyday life is of no importance for this role and beyond telling us her name and her age she offers us no information about it. She only asks her physically present mother one question in the course of 19 long stories, and is obviously very concerned to present a storytelling autonomously, to deny the reality of the room where she is sitting and the fact that her mother and sister were sometimes there. In this respect, although this is very much an *oral* monologue, full of sound effects and narrator's references to the tape-recorder, Sundari's narrator is like the first-person narrator in a work of *written* fiction. The narrator in *The Mill on the Floss*, for example, surfaces from time to time to tell her readers directly what she thinks of her characters' actions or the society in which they are based. We see her as the narrator *and* the author – both are George Eliot of course, yet as narrator her life outside the narrative discourse is of no importance, either to the story or to the narrating of it. Eliot's narrator is distanced from the story she tells, and so is Sundari's.

I did not realize until well after the tape-recording was over that Sundari had made some adjustments to her speaking voice for telling stories. I don't want to exaggerate it; she did not 'put on' a very posh voice, but she certainly shifted her standard English speech in the direction of RP (received pronunciation), with a style resonant of the carefully pronounced, scripted speech of radio broadcasters, and even at times adopting the slightly superior, adult-to-child mannerisms of some broadcasters for young children; that style is scarcely with us any more, but Sundari made her tapes in 1980, well before the demise of the BBC's 'Listen With Mother'. Radio is of course an oral medium, yet for all that it is dependent on spoken language, that language is very often scripted. Sundari's understanding of the oral qualities of tape-recording a story are therefore not at odds with the writing-like quality of her language.

The tape-recorder as a medium had a great effect on the explicitness of all the children's stories. Josh was the only child I *saw* making recordings, and occasionally he would make a gesture or a deictic reference, but these are unusual lapses; he, and the other children, had no difficulty in understanding that their words, however expressively spoken, must carry the meaning by themselves. Indeed, I believe this understanding is partly responsible for the colourfulness and inventiveness of the words that I discussed in Chapter 3. Sundari's stories are full of sound effects, supplied by her first-person narrator, and this does distinguish her texts from those to be found in books – though younger children's stories in books often attempt onomatopoeia: 'quack-quack', 'puff-puff' and so on. One has the feeling, when listening to Sundari's tapes, that she is telling stories either to children younger than herself or (more often) that she is reinventing herself as a narrator *older than herself*. For all these reasons I regard Sundari's narrator as a role she has created for herself, rather than as a persona indistinguishable from the everyday Sundari. Genette sees the narrator as a fiction even when, as in the case of George Eliot, the author and narrator appear to be the same person:

> the role of the narrator is itself fictive, even if assumed directly by the author, and where the supposed narrating situation can be very different from the act of writing (or of dictating) which refers to it. (Genette, 1972, pp. 13–14)

Perhaps what Genette means here is that the narrator has no more reality outside the narrative discourse than the characters in the story the narrator tells.

What then is Sundari's narrating stance? Although Sundari's main characters are very often 5-year-old girls (sometimes called Sundari), Sundari's narrator herself is *not* telling a story she has any part in, but is absent from the events narrated. Sundari's narrator observes her characters' actions, and, indeed, her own performance as narrator. This has the effect of placing a great distance between the narrating and the narrated, even to the extent of destroying the listener's belief in what is going on or of his/her ability to take the story events seriously. Sundari plays with her listener's responses, as though she is saying that all this is far-fetched and silly, but it's fun to do it because I'm in charge. There is an example of something similar from Justine whose story is worth quoting in full:

1   (one day-P) one day there was a zoo
2   it had grew
3   and (it had) (P) it had clip-clopped *'cos this is a funny story* (P)
4   *so there you are*
5   one day I bought Rita some flowers
6   *and you know what happened*
7   *now my little girl she was a naughty little girl*
8   (and sh-) and her mother said 'Don't pick those flowers away'
9   but she said 'yes'
10 and she did
11 *she's a naughty girl you know*
12 *(P) and that is the end of the story*
13 *but it's not really because I'm telling you it*
14 and there was a book once once upon a time
15 *it's still the same day*
16 *I know I said it's the end of the story*
17 *but I don't mean it's the end of the story*
18 once there was two flowers
19 and one said 'poppity poody' to the other flower called Poppity
20 'Poppity will you please come for a journey with me?'
21 and he said 'yes'
22 so they went off
23 and then they grew in another place
24 it was somewhere where the flowers grew
25 and they lived happily ever after
26 *and that is the end of the (for-) story*
(*Justine story 22 4:11*)

In many ways the narrator's intrusion into this story is similar to Sundari's narrating stance. Justine has a strong sense of controlling the narrative, of making it do anything she wants it to. She could have broken off from her first narrative (1–4), which she herself announces as a 'funny story' and which does not really get anywhere. But instead she uses her first-person narrator to license other stories, continuing on 'the same day' from the first one (15–17). This act of the narrator casts doubt on the possibility of any story reality at all, something I believe all the children seemed to become aware of in the process of tape-recording invented stories. They *know* they are spinning words, that characters can be given silly names and that the whole story world can be nonsensical. Sundari, too, experiments with nonsense words and forms (see Chapter 3, pp. 29–30), and is just as concerned as Justine's narrator that we, the listeners, should not take any of this too seriously. This is really meta-narrating – letting us know that they are only too aware of the narrator's role in storytelling, far too aware to take some of their own narrations seriously by *believing* in them in any way. In must be added that both children also tell stories in an intense *believing* way too. However, it seems that the inclusion of a distanced narrator in a story, who is free to comment and even cast doubt on the story, puts in jeopardy any sense of involvement in the narrative events. This is in stark contrast to Josh's stance, whose narrator is certainly present but always exists to involve us more deeply in the story events. These very different narrating stances affect the *pace* of the telling. Sundari's narratives are punctuated by very long pauses and her voice speaks slowly and proceeds at a very leisurely rate, while Josh's words tumble out with very few pauses indeed and far more syntactic garbles as he sorts out his sentences aloud.

The witch story at the opening of this chapter never really takes itself seriously, though the list of ingredients for the witch's stew are unpleasant enough and the plan to 'collect' a 7-year-old is narrated very expressively indeed. In spite of this Sundari's narrator is always ready to debunk the whole thing. The tongue which sticks up out of the witch's stew is a horrifying image which Josh would certainly have made a lot of had he been telling this story, but Sundari's narrator withdraws from any feeling of horror by commenting that the tongue was 'looking so silly which it would do'. Sundari's very first story starts off seriously enough. It's the one about the mother who deceives her little girl by giving her egg sandwiches made from stones; for the first fifteen sentences it's as credible as a children's fantasy story can be, especially as Sundari takes great care to explain in detail how the deception was accomplished. At the 18th sentence in comes the narrator:

15 and the little girl's name just vanished off her door
16 it was painted on her door (P)
17 and so she didn't have a name
18 *there's all people called her was Rubbish 'cos this is really a rubbish story*
19 and she was very angry and annoyed
20 *now you know what annoyed means* (P)
21 and she met a bird *(Sundari story 1)*

In Sundari's narratives the balance between narrating and narrated is sometimes tipped entirely towards narrating, as though what she found interesting about stories was doing experimental things with the *telling* rather than with the *told*. In story 8, below, she seems to be mocking what she tells at the same time as finding out what happens when you tell a story very quickly. Always an opportunist about story material Sundari happens to have a pair of roller skates by her as she narrates so she makes use of them to start herself off. Her concern, though, is less to have anything at all happen than to tell the story in a certain manner. In spite of her claim that this is a 'fast' story she still cannot avoid some of her usual long pauses:

Hello my name is Sundari the little tinkling noises are me rolling my feet on the roller skates (P) (um-) I'm going to tell a story today (P) I thought it would be about some roller skates

1 (spoken rapidly) once upon a time a person had some roller skates (laughs)
2 *I thought it was very funny when I said it quickly*
3 I think I'll tell all of the story quickly
4 the person was called [untranscribable nonsense name]
5 *that's what it was called*

6 (they had) they had a white car (very fast pace) which was (P) an Austin Allegro
7 (P) and the piles of roller skates was in some quickly quickly time [? unclear]
8 the door-bell rang and went ding-aling-ling like this (P)
9 there were two purses one purple round and one orange round (P)
10 there was a little black rabbit in the garden (P) a pear tree an apple tree an orange tree (P) all sorts of fruit trees
11 there was a toilet tree
12 (P) *oh it was so quick this story*
13 *I'll tell you when it's at the end* (no-)
14 *so I'll quickly hurry on with the story*
15 they had a *silly* carpet which had bears and teddy bears and all sorts of *silly* things on it (P)
16 and the roller skates that the little girl had rolled all about the house (P)
17 and there was (P) a fruit tree growing in the middle of the house (P)
18 it had all sorts of fruit hanging on it
19 they picked and picked and picked
20 and as long as they picked more and more and more and more and pick and pick and pick and more and more and pick pick pick more more more (ooh-) mo-mo-mo-mo-more pick pick pick pick pick pick
21 and they had such a lot of time
22 *I can't tell you all but* [child is heard shouting in the distance] (P)
23 *you quickly have to tell it the story*
24 a little Bo Peep story was a long time ago told by a little girl
25 *You quickly (P) turn off the tape when it's the end*
26 *so you've got to quickly talk as quickly as possible*
27 (P) the roller skates were rolling about the floor as fast as possible
28 and they were making a quick noise like this [rapid noises] quick-quick-quick [repeated a dozen times] (*Sundari story 8*)

There are 12 long pauses during this narration, in spite of Sundari's intention to tell a 'quick' story. There is no real narrative and nothing happens other than the movement between the remarks of Sundari's narrator and the list she narrates, an increasingly nonsensical list which culminates in the 'pick-pick' sentence.

Sundari's second narrator, Angeli, is a singer of songs. She never comments on the stories, and her only remarks are to introduce herself and her songs. The songs in Sundari's stories are not necessarily related to the rest of the story material. They are additional attractions, musical interludes, like the nursery rhymes in young children's radio programmes (BBC's 'Listen With Mother' again comes to mind as a possible model). Though the songs are usually 'variety turns' which happen in the middle of a story, Sundari sometimes sings an entire story through. Telling a story and singing one are not separate activities for her and she has a much greater prosodic/poetic emphasis than the other children, by which I mean that for her rhythms and sounds can be more meaningful than 'making sense'. It is tempting to align this with Sutton-Smith's 'verse-stories' – stories with very undeveloped plots but whose coherence was one of sound pattern and rhythm. Sutton-Smith found such verse-stories so prevalent in the data he collected from pre-school children that he regarded them as the first, pre-literate stage of oral storytelling (Sutton-Smith, 1981). Is Sundari still in this early 'verse' phase? I think this is too simplistic. Firstly she is capable of telling stories with plots. She uses the most complex syntactic structures in the study, her stories show many traces from books and her style is often remarkably explicit, writing-like and literary. Sundari is much more interested in describing things and role-playing the narrator than she is in talking about events and actions. In stories like story 8 above, I feel her rebelling against dominant story forms and using her narrator to have fun by subverting them. If story 8 fails to have a coherent plot, that does not mean there is no interest to be had in exploring the means by which a narrator can narrate at speed. The story which opens this chapter, story 4 and story 12 which closes it, both have 'well-formed' plots but both are full of the narrator's interpolated comments, not allowing us to forget that this is all being made up by a little girl.

I think the distinction Barthes (1970) makes between 'readerly' and 'writerly' texts helps us to understand better what Sundari is doing. The readerly text, according to Barthes, is the classic 19th-century novel, which creates the illusion of the 'real' by concealing all the 'codes' or 'voices' which make up that illusion. Barthes explodes the myth of the readerly text in order to subvert the power relations traditionally implicit between readers and writers; when we 're-live' a readerly text we consume it and are at its mercy; we want to find out what happens next, to suspend disbelief and so on. To uncover the structures in such a text is, on the contrary, to produce it, to take charge, in a sense to 'write' it. Sundari controls both her narrative and the listener's response to it by limiting the degree of possible involvement in her story; she always reminds us that this story is a mere illusion. Josh, on the contrary, uses everything in his power to keep the listener 'inside' the story, wanting to know what happens next. This major difference in narrating stance probably accounts for the very different storytelling styles of the two children; Josh tells his stories at speed, usually has a central story problem to be resolved, and presents 'live' scenes by employing dramatic dialogue; he has a very firm sense of plot structure, is concerned for the vraisemblance of the story details, and, in many sentences, takes two or three runs at them before delivering the complete sentence, resulting in a high number of syntactic garbles. Sundari tells her stories very slowly indeed with some very long pauses, sometimes omits a central story problem altogether, and uses very little dramatic dialogue; she has a weak sense of plot structure, but a very strong narrating voice, whose effect is subversive and upsets the vraisemblance; her sentences are delivered as complete syntactic units with no garbles.

Josh has woven his narrator below the surface of the story he tells, hiding his part in the production of the narrative discourse, but allowing him to surface from time to time in order to manipulate the listener into a feeling of suspense or fear. Sundari's narrator plays a major role in the narrative discourse, is not woven into the narrative at all but set at some distance from it, making it possible to adopt a subversive stance in regard to the narrative events.

Sundari's narrating stance involves her narrator in making assumptions about the (imaginary) audience. Such assumptions add to the feeling that Sundari is narrating to somebody younger than herself, and that she, the narrator, possesses knowledge that the listener cannot possible have:

15 (P) they loved to play at the seaside
16 the paddle boat wasn't *as little as you think*
17 it was quite big enough for all her friends and her and her mummy and
daddy . . .
23 they only lived in a little tiny cottage really little but not *as little as you think
bigger than you think* (*Sundari story 9*)

What is going on here is not that Sundari's narrator really assumes that she knows
what is in the listener's thoughts, but that she is operating a convention of narrating
which is able to use such assumptions about the imaginary listener to clarify a description; in this way Sundari co-opts her imagined listener to a role in the creation
of the story. This convention openly tells the listener that s/he must use his/her
imagination to visualize what Sundari is describing, and its use reflects Sundari's
conceptualization of story as something which happens inside our heads, something
which has no reality 'out there' beyond what our minds are able to conjure. If Josh's
narrating brings us into what stories *are*, Sundari's tends to deny that stories *are* at
all but to stand outside her stories to tell us how stories *get told*. The fact that Sundari
is also able to paint verbal scenes that are convincing in their detail and *do* allow us
to get nearer to the story that is being told, means that she is constantly moving not
only between the time of the narrating and the time of the story, but also between
the distanced, ironical stance of her narrator to the close-up dwelling-in-the-scene that
she accomplishes in the presentation of the narrative she tells. In other words, by
inventing a narrator and allowing the narrator a superior view of the story and the
story characters Sundari can have it both ways, moving in and out of the story at will.
This requires a great degree of control over language, for Sundari must balance present
and past times and first and third person narrating. The cognitive implications are
enormous. What Sundari accomplishes is the point of view of an entirely invented alter
ego (her narrator) as well as the points of view of her characters; nothing could be
further from Piagetian egocentricity.

NARRATING FUNCTIONS

Genette classifies a number of uses of the voice in narrative discourse:

Narrative: to tell the story
Directing: to give 'stage directions' on the narrative discourse, regulating how it should
proceed
Communicative: to maintain contact with the listener/reader
Testimonial: to bear witness to the truthfulness of the events narrated, vouch for own
feelings, show an affective attitude to the story
Ideological: to give an authorized commentary on the action from an ideological
position (as in satire, parodying, etc.)

I shall take each of these functions in turn, and show the range of the children's competences and the extent of their departure from the most simple and basic forms. Like
all functional analyses of language, Genette's categories will have considerable over-

lapping. It is quite possible for an interpolated narrating comment to simultaneously direct the narrative, communicate with the listener and provide some testimonial evidence.

The narrative function

In the narrative function the narrator tells directly what happened or what a character or scene was like rather than *shows* through the actions/dialogues of the events narrated. In traditional, fictional, third-person narratives there will inevitably be a fair amount of straightforward telling about events and characters, even if the inventor of the fiction is capable of showing what happens through demonstrating characters' behaviour, actions and speech. Telling what happened must be the most basic function of the narrator, hidden or not. At this stage of considering Genette's categories a clear picture of the simple narrative appears: it is told in chronological order, with summarized duration, and singulative frequency; it has little sense of point of view, few dialogue exchanges and its narrating stance may well be concealed, for the narrator's function is to tell the story events. Of course the story genre may well affect some of these categories. Oral stories of personal experience, like the ones told by adolescent boys in Labov's study (1972), will have different narrating stances and functions from oral fantasy tales for children like the ones in my study. Long sections of all the stories from my five children consist of the distanced and hidden third-person narration of the information needed to get the story told:

1 one day two rabbits woke up
2 they got their guns out
3 (and they put-) and they put their soldier helmets on
4 (a-) and they put their uniforms on
5 and they got all the soldiers to come
6 and they marched along the street
7 (P) and then (they-they) they all tried to kill all the penguins in the world
8 no — they didn't kill the penguins
9 all the people they killed
10 (P) none people were left only the soldiers
11 and there was one boy that was in the forest that wasn't dead
12 he was just a little boy with his daddy who lived in a small tree
13 and it had a (spa-) spiral staircase
    [*To adult*: You know owls? They live in trees. *Adult* Yes.]
14 (and) and h-h-how to go up you see
15 (they have-they) there's stairs in the tree (for the little) for the little things to get up
16 but the upstairs is for them to hide
17 (P) the downstairs (w-) must be the living-room
18 and the kitchen must be down there and the bedroom (P)
    (*Adult*: Has your story finished yet? Josh: No.)
19 (and the-and) and they went (uh) all over the world fighting people
20 and they had a fight all around the world (and)

21 and they killed
22 and they killed
23 and they killed the little boy who lived in the forest
24 no they didn't kill (hi-) him
25 (he) he began to be a soldier
26 and that's the end (uh-uh-uh) [in tones of hee-hee-hee] (*Josh story 20*)

In this story the narrator is largely hidden, only surfacing to correct his own errors
in the story information he has given in lines 8 and 24 and in the 'you see' in line 14.
I use the word 'information' because the details other than the story actions are to do
with the setting. Even the narrator's speculations on the tree-house have the function
of telling us what something was like. We have a feeling that although there is a
narrator telling this story he is not quite sure of what he is telling and is not sufficiently
involved in the story events to do anything other than relate them. For a story to be
interesting the narrator needs to give the impression of knowing far more about the
characters and actions than Josh does in story 20. Contrast this with Sundari's story
19 in which the narrator does some *showing* what happened through dialogue but
mostly *tells*:

> Today I'm going to tell a story about the hot country lane   and it goes like
> this
1   one day there was a lane
2   it was boiling that day
3   and I'll tell you where the lane (P) led to

This interpolated narration at 3 performs several functions: it is *communicative*
because it introduces an 'I' and a 'you'; it is *testimonial* because it implies that the
narrator has knowledge which will be revealed shortly; and it is *directing* because the
narrator is announcing what is coming next. As the story continues we can be in no
doubt that the narrator has very detailed knowledge of the setting:

4   it led to a lovely little cottage
5   and this cottage was decorated with flowers and (P) silver bits of chain

and of the characters:

6 (P) and this house had two little girls in just like –
7   but one had just a skirt on
8   and the other had a bikini and a skirt
9   and the other had just a skirt and flowers round its head
10 and the other had bikini skirt and some flowers holding them

Having given us a description of the girls the narrator moves onto the story problem:

11 and they lived in the teeniest bit because their mother was *rotten* (P)
12 and she *whipped* them

Now the narrator begins to show as well as tell:

13 she said one day because they were being naughty 'You must *go*
14 You must *go*
15 You're horrible you children'

16 so they crept into that tiny bit and made loud noises like this –

In 16 the narrator has intruded again; not only is she showing us what happened but also telling us that she knows what it was like:

17 [shouting] 'My mum is stupid
18 My mum is stupid'
19 and she *cried*
20 she went 'You naughty children you haven't left yet'
21 she was so angry she went all over the house but could not find them

In 20 and 21 the narrator places us with the mother's view of things; now she tells us what the mother did not know, before shifting to the children's point of view:

22 they were in the littlest *teeni*est bit (P)
23 (very soft voice) they had to watch everything in the house
24 what they had with them was a *teeny* mouse (P) and a loaf of bread some jelly and some milk and two cups
25 and they have nicked everything 'cos that was their house

At 24 and 25 we are given some omniscient narrator's information and an explanation for the things the girls had with them. The narrator then tells us in summarized form what the mother's response was:

26 their mum was so cross she cried and cried and moved

and this is followed by the narrator's still telling what the outcome was for the children but in a far more elaborated way:

27 so they just lived there all their lives in that very pretty corner 'cos that was the pretty bit in the house with paper chains and silver for Christmas cakes and things to eat (P) and a little tune-bird which was a nightingale

Sundari's story continues with another short episode.

   Although both Josh in his story 20 and Sundari in story 19 largely use narrator's information to tell the story events, it is clear that there are more and less elaborated ways to make use of the narrative function of narrating in which Genette's other categories of tense and mood are implicated. In order to reveal the children's particular storytelling competences I have examined each of the Genette categories in turn while at the same time realizing that for a full appreciation of what the children can do the different skills need to be put together. For that reason I have placed a full analysis of Sundari's story 12 at the end of this chapter.

   It is clear that the children can scarcely avoid the narrative function of narrating and that their awareness of the contribution the narrating voice can make to a story will be better revealed by their use of the other four functions.

The directing function

Genette comments that the directing function is metalinguistic since it focuses not on the events narrated but on the narrative discourse itself. Narrating in the directing function happens when the narrator comments on his/her way of telling the story; it is language used about language, and therefore is very revealing of the children's conscious awareness of what they were engaged in. There are far more examples from Sundari than from the other children, although it is possible to find a few from all of them. Obviously if a storyteller invents a first-person narrator as Sundari does then the narrator is more likely to interpolate comments on the discourse itself into the storytelling. I have already quoted Justine's story 22, in which her first-person narrator actually denies the ending of the story she has just told in order to continue with the storytelling. For the three boys in the study the narrator is usually hidden and any metalinguistic awareness in the discourse is shown in explanations of what words mean, such as the following from Josh:

95 and then (he-um) (P) Fereyal nearly got his life cut off
   cut off – that's another word for getting his life cut down (*Josh story 75*)

In contrast to the few examples of this sort in the data from the other four children, Sundari's narrating makes very extensive use of the directing function. She comments on her own narrating in several ways. She often apologizes for it.

22 (it was an-) it needed oil
   I'm sorry I said it needed oil (*Sundari story 7*)

22 (um) and they loved their cottage 'cos it was a cottage
23 *I didn't tell you that*
24 *I forgot to* (*Sundari story 5*)

 7 she did maypole dancing (um-) all kinds
 8 *and that is only the ones I can tell you I'm afraid*
 9 *I'm sorry I said all of them* (*Sundari story 5*)

It is Sundari's self-consciousness of her narrating role and her ability to formalize her apologies, incorporating them into the narrative discourse, that make these inter- polations interesting. Of course by bringing the 'mistakes' in the discourse to the surface like this and making the narrator give a formal apology for them she conceals their accidental nature. Sundari often uses the directing function to announce the end of the story:

64 they bought her presents
65 *and it's nearly nearly the end of the story* (P)
66 she had jelly-babies and crisps (*Sundari story 14*)

20 *it's nearly the end of this story* 'cos it's not a long story
21 it's a quick story not talking fast though talking slowly and wearily along
   (*Sundari story 10*)

12 (P) oh it was so quick this story
13 *I'll tell you when it's the end* (no)
14 so I'll quickly hurry on with the story (P) (*Sundari story 8*)

In the examples from stories 8 and 10 Sundari is using the directing function to comment on her style of narrating as well as to announce the end. She also does this when she is telling stories with invented words and rhyming stories:

3   so the little mouse went over the hills again
4   *you know well this is a rhyming story*
5   he saw some very nice cans (*Sundari story 13*)

Sundari has other uses for the directing function: commenting on the words she uses, the story as a whole and her ability to invent names. Most of these comments tend to debunk the whole narrative:

9   and they had two little babies the first one called Mmmmubble and the second one called Trrrruggle
10 *they're silly names aren't they?* (*Sundari story 4*)

17 and so she didn't have a name
18 there's all people called her was Rubbish *'cos this is really a rubbish story* (*Sundari story 1*)

1   (P) I'm going to tell you(a st-) another story about a boy this time a boy called Cletcher *a very funny name*
2   *I made it up* (P) (*Sundari story 7*)

The communicative function

There is a sense in which all the examples I have given of Sundari's narrator's comments are communicative because they are all addressed to the narratee. However, some comments are more personal than others, having the function of telling the listener who the narrator is, what she is like, and so on, or of co-opting the listener's participation in responding to the story. This kind of thing does sometimes happen in books for young children, though it can seem rather patronizing to adult readers. To invite audience participation is of course a much stronger feature of the oral narrative tradition, though it must be remembered in Sundari's case that her audience is imagined. The other four children also co-opt the audience into the story by addressing them in some way, usually by having the hidden narrator ask a question such as 'Do you know what?'. This is a very fundamental way of communicating with an addressee in any kind of storytelling, even in the most casual and informal circumstances. Children and adults alike will try to gain the listener's attention by such openings as 'Do you know what happened to me . . .?', 'Guess what!', 'You'll never guess what happened', and so on. Such phrases are intended not only to gain the listener's attention but also to provoke some kind of suspense. The most usual form for such questions to take is the direct, narrator-to-listener first-person form, a form that we use in everyday telling of personal experiences as well as in more formal kinds of storytelling.

The more literary way is to embed the question in the third-person narrating so that the discourse appears to question itself in an impersonal way. Josh uses both the first-person and the third-person technique in his narrating:

28 *and do you know what?*
29 they all had supper
30 but a strange thing happened

31 (a-) *in the morning do you know what (the-) the boy had?*
32 the mother (borned-er) borned a sister for him (*Josh story 38*)

85 and now (he looked-) he looked through his kaleidoscope
86 *and what did he see (but the-) but the English riding away in his boat?* (*Josh story 39*)

Very occasionally Sundari draws attention to herself as a storyteller sitting at home with the tape-recorder narrating this story:

29 it was so quiet it was as quiet as this (silence for a few seconds)
30 I'm sorry there were a few noises *because my place is quite a noisy place not near any (much-much-) seasides*
31 *the nearest one is called* (P)
    [Adult: Winterton.]
    Winterton
32 *I've got a little rake*
33 *and (I) next time I go to the seaside I'm going to bring it and play about in the sand raking lines*
34 *I'm five did you know*
35 *well I've told you (an) another story* (P)
36 *well this tape is a tape*
37 *I'll tell you more about the story*
38 well the little girl was so quiet she didn't even snore one bit (*Sundari story 9*)

Here, after giving us more autobiographical information than is usual in her storytelling, Sundari moves from the communicative function of lines 30–35 to the directing function in 36–7. Sundari is well aware of her own (i.e. her narrator's) age, and will often mention it to distinguish herself as narrator from a character in the story:

12 and (P) she loved her number her best number she had ever had which was nineteen
13 *and one day I'll be nineteen* (P) *because I am five* (*Sundari story 6*)

Sundari sometimes confirms that she is also the narrator of other stories on the tapes:

10 and she did lots of things (P) loads of things
11 I can't tell you all of them *like I've told on most stories* (*Sundari story 12*)

Occasionally Sundari's narrator assumes shared knowledge with the listener in phrases like 'as you know what also means' and 'as you know what annoyed means'. 'As you know' is a communicative tag frequently used in traditional fairy-tales, and Josh too includes it sometimes in his narrations. A variation on it is:

4   *you know well this is a rhyming story* (*Sundari story 13*)

Sundari's narrator refers the listener to herself as a contrast with a character or a feature of the discourse:

31 (P) and their houses – *I might have told you them but I think I've forgotten* – were called coggly woggly wogs

32 *(P) as I've got two names if I've told you*
33 *if I haven't* (P) *they have got two names* (*Sundari story 15*)

and in the same story:

14 (P) *and they have houses shaped a diamond* (P) *with* (P) *triangle windows
   and square doors not oblong ones like you do have* square ones (P)

Earlier in this chapter I quoted a passage from Sundari's story 7 (see p. 144) where
she collapses the time of the narrating and the time of the story by inviting the listener
to laugh with her: '*We're gonna have a bit of a laugh now.*' She does this sort of thing
in other stories where she assumes a response from her listeners:

17 *and one day there was a silver coin just under the door*
18 *can you guess (wh-) who it was from?*
19 *Santa Claus yes*
20 *it was (Santa Clause-) Santa Claus's very best day* (*Sundari story 18*)

The '*yes*' in line 19 assumes that the listener actually made a response to Sundari's
question, rather than assumed it to be merely rhetorical. This is not just a well-worn
technique of oral storytelling; some children's books do it in rather a condescending
way, which Josh imitates when he retells a *non-fiction* information book for young
children called *Vikings*:

11 *you can try making a Viking boat*
12 *cut a cardboard out and stick it together*
13 *and that's the end* (*Josh story 23*)

In an earlier narration, which was not a retelling of *Vikings* but a transformation of
it, Josh also includes some direct communicative narrating:

18 *and then he took (the three th- poor things on-on) the three poor things
   home*
19 *do you know why they were poor?*
20 *because they had no money*
21 *do you know why?*
22 *because they're so poor the Vikings came and stole their money* (*Josh story
   19*)

The testimonial function

Genette describes the testimonial function as the narrator's bearing witness to the veracity
of the events narrated. In an oral story of personal experience like those quoted by Labov
it is a common, almost essential part of the narrative structure that the narrator seeks to
convince his listener of the truthfulness of events, or to impress on him the danger or
terror or excitement of events by saying how he felt at that moment. We all do this when
we are telling stories to one another, using phrases like 'It was so terrifying that I began
to pray', or 'I thought: it's now or never'. Even if we are telling of rather ordinary events
we tend to say things like 'honestly' or 'I mean it' or 'I swear'. Because the five children
are on the whole narrating traditional fantasy stories which do not involve the narrator
as a character they have to present an *illusion* that the narrator can vouch for what went

on or what a character was like. Sundari, for example, uses a large number of sound effects in her narrating, constantly making a sound and telling us it was 'like this' or 'like that'. *as though she were there and she knew.*

28 he had to hobble over the walking bridges *like this* (P) [makes a tapping noise]
29 *that's what his wooden leg made Sundari story 3)*

7 she sang little songs so sweet
8 *I'll tell you one*
9 *it goes like this (Sundari story 2)*

The extract from story 2 is followed by Sundari's narrator singing the song that the heroine in the story sang, concealing the fact that the author/narrator Sundari is actually making the whole thing up on the spot; *she is providing (illusory) evidence that a song was sung.* At a later point in the story Sundari repeats this effect but this time passes the job of demonstrating the song over to the second narrator, the singer 'Angeli':

39 *here is a story she sang in her sleep from Angeli*
40 *it goes like this*
41 'A poor little girl she was so sad to see . . . [sings] *(Sundari story 2)*

The testimonial function can give an extra precision to the use of certain terms. Here it is used to confirm the child's understanding that there is a difference between a live bird and a gold and silver ornament:

2 he had a gold bird *but not really not a real one* with diamond eyes and a silver mouth *(Sundari story 3)*

It can be used to give an extra emphasis to a description or a fact:

26 and there was the little girl crying like this [sobbing noises]
27 *she had real tears (Sundari story 6)*

21 and they got a seven year-old one day
22 *it was really really seven (Sundari story 4)*

Sundari tries to create the illusion that she is 'remembering' the details of her story, implying that the story refers to a body of 'fact' that only needs to be recalled.

4 she did tap dancing ordinary dancing Dutch dancing all kinds of dancing
5 I'll tell you all the ones *if I remember (Sundari story 5)*

39 they had a car which was white
40 they painted it all the while until they painted it white again
41 *I can't tell you anything more about the car (Sundari story 5)*

The ideological function

Strictly speaking it is difficult to claim that there is any evidence that the children have acquired conscious ideological positions that they are capable of relaying through their narratives, though it is true to say that they have some idea of values, notions like good and evil (as opposed to goodies and baddies) which they use stories to explore. Josh's God and St Peter stories are full of enactments of good and bad behaviour which provide the central story problems: how to return the live puppy to earth where he belongs, how to welcome the kind dragon without being afraid of him, and, above all, how to win Dracula over to good behaviour and friendship. These stories, and many of Sundari's stories too, are so saturated with knowledge of society and how it works that the social/ideological assumptions underlying the narrative discourse require a full analysis using the 'codes' Barthes describes in *S/Z*. I shall use that template to look at one of Josh's stories in the ensuing chapter. Genette is more specific about the Ideological narrating function, identifying it with genres like satire and parody which provide a special ideological slant on events. Sundari's narrator does not set out to parody or satirize any social or political issues, though she does at times mock the genre of oral storytelling itself, as the quotations given so far will have shown. One would hardly expect young children to have acquired enough knowledge to accomplish such a task, and a sense of irony is in any case thought to belong to a later stage of development. Having said that I must also add that Josh's news broadcasts and weather forecasts make steps in the direction of parody. Josh grew up in a politically oriented household where he heard radio news twice a day in addition to seeing TV news sometimes, and where there was a lot of political discussion between his parents, probably made more emphatic by the General Election which had taken place prior to his storytelling year. His mocking comments about Mrs Thatcher and President Reagan have been picked up from the adults around him, so that it would be foolish to claim for him the kind of ideological intentions that an adult might have. However, Josh is not only making jokes about well-known political figures, he is also mocking the *forms* of news broadcasts and weather forecasts, in itself an indirectly ideological activity. Satirists of the 18th century in England, for example Fielding and Swift, not only satirized current social and political situations but also the *forms* of the work of inferior writers. Fielding's *Joseph Andrews* was intended to be a satire on Richardson's novel *Pamela*. Even where satirists are not making literary forms a target for attack they often use a simple generic form as a *means* of simplifying complex political events, as Orwell did with *Animal Farm* or Swift with *Gulliver's Travels*. To mention these great works is not to imply that young children's jokes have anything in common with them, any more than to use Genette's categories of analysis implies that the five children's storytelling shared anything with Proust. These three chapters on Genette's narrative analysis are meant to show what the *beginnings* of complex narrative competences look like, and to argue that those beginnings can become apparent even before literacy in children who grow up in literate/literary environments.

In Chapter 5 I discussed the special syntactic features of Josh's news broadcasts and weather forecasts; the greatly increased use of passive constructions in newsreadings, for example, showed that he had picked up the detached and impersonal 'tune' of the genre, while his use of the future tense and collections of noun phrases to do with place and orientation gave an authentic flavour to his weather reports. These little parodies were conducted for fun and there is more and more laughter on the tapes as they get sillier, but to show that there are the beginnings of narrating in the ideological function in them I'll quote one in which Josh sets out to ridicule both the government of the day and parliamentary reporting on the radio.

[Announces:] Today in Parliament
1   Mr Whitelaw has been sitting on the roof of Big Ben (and-) (laughter) and eating some chocolate biscuits
2   (and at- and– this is true – he did do it) and when he was sitting there this little monster came and pulled the Big Ben off
    No–I'll do – that's a silly one-
3   Mr Whitelaw said that *all* the rates of Thatcher's money must be taken to Carol Fox
4   she must have the most money in the world
5   everybody in London agrees that Carol Fox must have *all* the money in London
6   and that's the end of the (ess-) Westminster News (Good-) bye-bye (*Josh story 84*)

Josh does make a clear distinction here between the slapstick 'silly one' of 1 lines and 2, and the more serious redistribution of funds suggested in 3 to 6!

In the last three chapters I have tried to show, by using the subtle categories of narrative structure defined for us by Genette, that the children, particularly the two 5-year-olds (the age for entry to school in Britain) had internalized more complex notions of story and storytelling than any simple models of story grammar or plot structure could possibly reveal. All the variations in tense and chronology in the discourse surely reflect the children's increasing awareness of the time relationships of narratives and the contribution that story-books have made to that awareness.

We need to know much more about the development of an intricate sense of temporal structure in storytelling, so that we can avoid over-simple distinctions like those made in the National Curriculum between chronological and non-chronological writing. Working with such a crude model of development may make us blind to what Genette called 'narrative possibilities' and equally to what children can achieve.

Looking at children's stories from the angle of point of view again challenges ideas about childish egocentricity and related questions of cognitive growth, for it is clear from the evidence of Josh's stories that literature is one of the places where we learn to look at things as others see them.

Observing how children's concepts of narrating interweave with their ideas of story, as Sundari's narrations allow us to do, broadens our notion of what storying is to include a special kind of role-play, the narrator who is capable of turning our attention away from the events narrated and towards herself as teller, director, communicator and witness of what she tells.

Intertextualities in Josh's and Sundari's stories, then, are not only a matter of names, plots, themes, ideas or quotations, nor a matter of coining words and re-ordering sentences to give them a literary flavour. The intertextualities are more global than that. They are deeply embedded in the whole narrative discourse itself, in the relationships of temporality, in the variations of focal length and point of view, in the ways characters utter words and thoughts, and in the presence of the narrating voice, hidden or overt. I am sure that by using limited sets of categories to investigate narrative competences, the possibilities of children's storytelling have been seriously underestimated. Studies of early development in this regard have been too obsessed with simple forms, too insistent on separating one story genre from another, and too focused on plot structure for a proper picture of what children can do to emerge.

Appendix: Sundari's story 12

Text of story 12	Tense	Mood	Voice
one day a little girl called Laura (P) couldn't find her way home so she walked along the beach looking at the cottages little ones looking so far she missed her home on the beach	*Order:* Chronological *Duration:* Summary with short pause – 'looking . . .' *Frequency:* Singulative	*Focalization:* Fixed from point of view of Laura	*Narrating:* Third person subsequent narrating *Function:* Narrative
(P) but the West wind and the North wind weren't there like they usually were (P) and the South wind (P) and the East wind none of the winds were there (P) even the calm wind that was there a tiny bit	*Order:* Chronological *Duration:* Descriptive pause *Frequency:* Singulative	*Focalization:* Fixed from point of view of Laura	*Narrating:* Third person subsequent narrating *Functions:* Narrative + testimonial (like they usually were)
(P) she liked doing things (P) playing about at the beach on sunny days (P) when cool wind was blowing making sandcastles playing with her little necklace with people on it and some little raindrops falling from the people and bags on it what the teddybears were in what the people were holding (P) and she had little teddy-bear earrings she had lots of things and she mostly played with her dolls made sandcastles for them and little beach houses and she did lots of things (P) loads of things	*Order*: Chronological *Duration*: Scene *Frequency*: Iterative: sustained use of participle: doing playing blowing making playing falling holding *Frequency:* Iterative ('mostly') *Duration:* Summary	*Focalization*: Fixed from point of view of Laura	*Narrating*: Third person subsequent narrating *Functions*: Narrative + testimonial
I can't tell you all of them like I've told on most stories	—	—	*Narrating:* First-person narrator – absent from the story Interpolated narrating *Function:* Directing
well Laura at last went back to find and she looked every cottage and as soon as she looked the second one was her house and she knocked at the door came straight in took her coat off and started playing with her dolls (P)	*Order:* Chronological *Duration:* Summary *Frequency*: Singulative	*Focalization:* Fixed from point of view of Laura	*Narrating*: Third-person subsequent narrating, except when first-person narrator surfaces 'well' *Function*: Narrative

Text of story 12	Tense	Mood	Voice
but she could hear the rough wind swaying outside like this 'swissssh swisssh swisssh' her little bells from her neck-lace-it was another necklace she was wearing-tinkled like this 'Tinkle, tinkle, tinkle (P) tinkle, tinkle, Tinkle'	*Order*: Chronological *Duration*: Scene *Frequency*: Singulative	*Focalization*: Fixed from point of view of Laura	*Narrating*: Third-person subsequent narrating with interpolated first-person ('like this') *Functions*: Narrative + testimonial
and she had never been to (P) see the wind but she had heard it blowing [makes whistling noise]	*Order*: Analepsis (pluperfect) *Duration*: Pause *Frequency*: Iterative	*Focalization*: Fixed from point of view of Laura	*Narrating*: Third-person subsequent narrating *Functions*: Narrative + testimonial
she whistled sometimes like this [whistles] but not very often	*Order*: Chronological *Duration*: Pause *Frequency*: Interative	*Focalization*: Fixed from point of view of Laura	*Narrating*: Third-person subsequent narrating *Functions*: Narrative + testimonial
now she was playing a little soft tune to her (b-)baby dolls like this [whistles a tune] like that (P)	*Order*: Chronological *Duration*: Scene *Frequency*: Singulative	*Focalization*: Fixed from point of view of Laura	*Narrating*: Third-person subsequent narrating *Functions*: Narrative, testimonial + directing ('now')
and she had loads of things she had to do at school	*Order*: Chronological *Duration*: Pause *Frequency*: Singulative	*Focalization*: Fixed from point of view of Laura	*Narrating*: Third-person subsequent narrating *Function*: Narrative
one day a girl called Meg said 'Why can't I wear that necklace? Why does Laura have to wear it all the time?' and she told the teacher	*Order*: Chronological *Duration*: Ellipsis/scene *Frequency*: Singulative	*Focalization*: Variable – Meg's point of view. *Dialogue*: Reported and narratized	*Narrating*: Third-person subsequent narrating *Function*: Narrative

Text of story 12	Tense	Mood	Voice
and the teacher said 'Laura take your necklace off'	*Order*: Chronological	*Focalization*: Variable – teacher	*Narrating*: Third-person subsequent narrating
(P) but Laura didn't know where she put it	*Duration*: Pause	*Focalization*: Variable – Laura	
	Frequency: Singulative	*Dialogue*: Narratized inner speech	*Function*: Narrative
it was her best necklace she was wearing and the teddy-bears in the bags and the people on with the raindrops	*Order*: Chronological *Duration*: Pause *Frequency*: Singulative	*Focalization*: Variable – Laura	*Narrating*: Third-person subsequent narrating *Function*: Narrative
she was crying in the playground	*Duration*: Scene (some time elided)		
but when she got in the class (P) she knew where her necklace was	*Order*: Chronological *Duration*: Summary *Frequency*: Singulative	*Focalization*: Variable – Laura (narratized inner speech)	*Narrating*: Third-person subsequent narrating *Function*: Narrative
when the teacher wasn't looking she quickly took it and put it in her pocket and as soon as it was home time when it was when she got a partner she put the necklace back on	*Order*: Chronological *Duration*: Summary *Frequency*: Singulative	Focalization: Variable – Laura	*Narrating*: Third-person subsequent narrating *Function*: Narrative
and she was very very pleased	*Order*: Chronological *Duration*: Pause *Frequency*: Singulative	*Focalization*: Fixed – Laura	*Narrating*: Third-person subsequent narrating *Function*: Narrative
she went home to play with her dollies and whistled again (P) but then she got bored went to bed next morning she ate her breakfast but didn't go to school	*Order*: Chronological *Duration*: Summary *Frequency*: Singulative	*Focalization*: Fixed – Laura	*Narrating*: Third-person subsequent narrating *Function*: Narrative

Text of story 12	Tense	Mood	Voice
she played and played in the seaside playing with her dolls making little roads and houses for them to go in little sandpies for them to eat and little cool rivers for them to wash and drink cups full of the drink from the little river for the dolls that really could drink 'cos most of them –	*Order:* Chronological *Duration:* Scene *Frequency:* Iterative	*Focalization:* Fixed – Laura	*Narrating:* Third-person subsequent narrating *Function:* Narrative
but the other dolls could really eat so could the ones who could (ea-) really drink and to dolls that could really eat and drink (what all of them- and-) (P) all little things could fit down their little (little-) mouths and when they wanted to wee (P) they went to the toilet which was really a little potty made out of paper and they got on it and a drink came out by holding their clothes	*Order:* Chronological *Duration:* Pause *Frequency:* Iterative	*Focalization:* Fixed – Laura	*Narrating:* Third-person subsequent narrating *Function:* Narrative
(P) and she clapped her hands danced about then she went to bed	*Order:* Chronological *Duration:* Summary *Frequency:* Singulative	*Focalization:* Fixed –Laura	*Narrating:* Third-person subsequent *Function:* Narrative
it's nearly nearly the end of this story now but I'll tell you the rest now	—	—	*Narrating:* First-person interpolated narrating *Functions:* Directing + communicative
and one day (P) which was when she woke up there was a dreadful sound going what the sea was making going 'Swisssh swisssh swisssh' 'Tinkle tinkle' went the bells 'Oh oh' went the dolls and her necklace rustled everything was awake	*Order:* Chronological *Duration:* Scene *Frequency:* Singulative	*Focalization:* Fixed – Laura (what she could hear)	*Narrating:* Third-person subsequent narrating *Functions:* Narrative + testimonial
they looked outside what had happened was the West wind was here it was blowing and swaying the waves 'sway sway' went the waves (whistles) went the wind	*Order:* Chronological + analepsis (pluperfect) *Duration:* Scene *Frequency:* Singulative	*Focalization:* Fixed – Laura	*Narrating:* Third-person subsequent narrating *Functions:* Narrative + testimonial

Text of story 12	Tense	Mood	Voice
(P) but soon it all stopped (P) and they all got back to sleep again	*Order*: Chronological *Duration*: Summary *Frequency*: Singulative	*Focalization*: Fixed – Laura	*Narrating*: Third-person subsequent narrating
(P) and that is the end of the story	CLOSURE		

Information supplied by Sundari's mother: Date of story: 11 June 1981. Sundari's age: 5:6. The idea of the winds came from *Words and Pictures* (schools TV). Making things for dolls at the seaside is influenced by a book read at home called *Ukelele*, about a girl who makes sandpies for dolls. The necklace comes from Joan Aitken's *A Necklace of Raindrops*, newly acquired and read at home.

Story 12 has a total of 701 words, a total of 59 T-Units, and a mean T-Unit length of 11.9 words, which is very high. Summarizing Genette's categories it uses chronological order with the beginnings of two analepses. It uses scene, summary, pause and the beginnings of ellipsis. It alternates singulative and iterative time. The focalization is nearest to Laura, but is variable in the school scene. It uses both third-person subsequent narrating and first-person interpolated narrating, and employs four out of the five narrating functions in Genette.

Chapter 11

Uncovering Many Layers of Meaning

Each system for analysing the structure of narratives has its own distinctive emphasis, usually related to the kind of text it describes. The Genette categories are ideal for revealing the children's concepts of time, point of view and narrating voice, but they have little to tell us about the ways in which a story can evoke in the reader whole networks of social conventions and cultural knowledge, networks which construct a recognizable world from the flux of words. Unless we are reading about a society which is very different from our own, we are apt to take the social world of stories for granted. We read on to find out what happens, we become involved in the fictive lives of the characters and are distracted from noticing the signifying systems which the writer has carefully put in place to elicit our tacit agreement that this or that *was*, or *must have been*, or *might have been*, so. Some stories in my data demand a multi-layered, expanded reading of the kind Barthes (1970) offers us in his reading of Balzac's short story *Sarrasine*. The distancing from the story material required by a Genette analysis has its parallel in Sundari's sceptical invented narrator, whose voice is ever urging us to take none of this too seriously. In Barthes, by contrast, the story that is told is closer to the heart of the analysis.

By working from inside Balzac's story, expanding it line by line as he uncovers the semiotic systems at work beneath the surface of the language, Barthes shows how the reader picks up several meanings at once. He reveals how the apparently 'real', socially complex world of Balzac's story is fabricated through the interplay of five hidden codes, each one a signifying system which draws on the reader's willingness to interpret all the signals set up by the text. Departing from the linguistics that had been the foundation for his earlier description (1966) of narrative structure,[1] Barthes (1970) now re-writes the text in a continuous process of interpretation and re-interpretation. His five codes rely on the reader's ability to bring to every line of the story knowledge of how societies, individuals and subjectivities establish a sense of values, traditions, ideologies and ways of behaving. In this chapter I shall apply the codes to a long story told by Josh at the age of 5: 9. The story contains a great deal of interaction between its characters in dialogue, it involves the storyteller in the creation of a world, is highly intertextual, has a clear episodic structure and plays with themes which have some symbolic force. The full text appears as an appendix to this chapter.

In *S/Z* Barthes divides Balzac's story up into units called *lexias* (defined as 'a unit of reading') but Barthes gives no guiding principles for deciding the boundaries of these units, describing the process as 'arbitrary in the extreme' and 'a matter of convenience' (p. 13). A lexia may consist of one word or a whole paragraph, and is judged by the reader to be a significant moment in the narrative where the hidden voices of the five connotative codes may be observed. Each lexia is marked (starred) by the codifications Barthes has uncovered in the text, and lexias are interspersed with numerous commentaries where Barthes pauses, as it were, to explain his theories of reading. Following the order of the text from beginning to end in slow motion, Barthes produces a new, greatly expanded text, a re-reading and re-writing which exposes the artifice of the original discourse.

The simplest way to explain this to readers who are unfamiliar with *S/Z* is to say that it is like an enormously entertaining and complex form of continuous note-taking. The one guiding principle for the division of the story is that each lexia should contain the possibility of plural meanings. The fact that lexias are so fluid in some ways makes Barthes' method a poor candidate for an analytic model. However, while lexias are ill-defined the five codes are not, and it should be possible to apply them to any story including one told by a child.

Barthes' choice of a story by Balzac was as perfectly suitable for showing up the hidden social and cultural meanings in a story as Genette's choice of Proust was for revealing the interplay of narrating and narrated. Barthes' five codes expose all the assumptions which the text needs to make to elicit our acceptance of the recognizable norms and values buried within the story. Not only is the text a network of socially constituted meanings, but so is the reader 'This "I" which approaches the text is already itself a plurality of other texts, of codes which are infinite . . .', (1970, p. 10).

For Barthes the discourses of the text and the act of reading it are inseparable, and reading and writing themselves become intertwined. Thus his analytic method for *Sarrasine* is both a re-reading and a re-writing of the text. This is helpful in considering the stories in my data, for they can be regarded as both reflections of the children's listening/reading, and as acts of speaking/writing.

In *Elements of Semiology* (1964) Barthes had shown that other elements of ordinary life are conducted according to conventions which can be codified – eating in restaurants, for example. Menus define what constitutes a course, and the relation and order of courses. The soup will precede the main course and the dessert will follow, and the ingredients of each of those courses will have been settled upon by the particular culinary values of the society in which the meal takes place. If the menu, the formal listing of all the available choices of courses is the *langue* of eating in restaurants, then the particular meal which we order is the *parole*. The Saussurean distinction between system and behaviour can be a template for the whole array of human cultural activity, be it watching television, devising a National Curriculum or holding the Olympic Games. Of course when we go to eat in a restaurant we are apt to take the *langue* of the menu for granted, to choose within the boundaries of what is on offer without regard to the web of ideologies and values that are concealed beneath the language in front of us.

Not to question the *langue* of the restaurant is in some ways to be the compliant victim of it, to accept the rules, to be manipulated by the power of the menu writer.

If this seems far-fetched, consider how rare it is, at least in an English context, to challenge the menu's laws, to order the strawberry tart for starters, the soup for dessert and to drink large gins and tonics throughout the meal. Only the very powerful or very self-confident make their own rules in this way. So how does all this relate to reading?

For Barthes reading a story is not a matter of one fixed inviolable reading, defined somehow by the author's intentions. This is to be powerless, to be manipulated by the text, as consumers are often manipulated by salesmen or advertisers. The soap opera or serial always uses cliff-hangers to urge us onwards to find out 'what happens', yet in truth we are not living in a 'natural' world as we read but are willingly participating in a discourse which is the fabrication of sets of signals, codes which, if we can decipher them, will lead us to all the social, ideological, value-laden assumptions underlying the world of the text. So for Barthes, reading is not a matter of finding some predetermined meaning, but of uncovering the possible meanings latent in the words. If we read carefully we shall discover these plural meanings by the signs of them which leak into the narrative and we shall become aware of a labyrinthine network of connections, relating the parts of the text to one another, to other discourses, to the whole cultural world beyond the text. Indeed, Barthes calls the codes 'a perspective of quotations, a mirage of structures' (1970, p. 29).

For Barthes, the pretence of the classic 19th-century realist text is that the world denoted by it is somehow an objective reality; its artifice lies in concealing the fabrication of that sense of the real that we have when we are 'involved' in the story, impatient to see what 'happens', feeling that we ourselves have become the hero or heroine and are living the story. Among the five children in my study Josh is just such a storyteller. His narratives are driven by a quality of suspense which amounts to something much more than Labov's structural category of evaluation, which suspends the action just before the climax of the story. Josh rarely stops and comments on his own storytelling as Sundari does, constantly destroying or subverting any sense of illusion she has built up. On the contrary Josh seems to be very involved in the events of his narratives as he narrates them in breathless excitement, seeming to imaginatively 'live' what he is narrating. In this sense Josh draws us *into* the story while Sundari draws us, with her interpolated comments, away from it. The kind of storying Josh does fits what Barthes calls the 'readerly' text, the kind that strives to involve the reader in its illusory world. The kind of storying Sundari does, with its violation of a sense of reality, its constant reminders that she is inventing it, Barthes would call 'writerly'. In *S/Z* Barthes explodes the illusion created by the classic, realist, readerly text, in order to expose the power relationships implicit in it between readers and writers. To 're-live' the realist text is to be at its mercy, to consume it, to be powerless before it. To become aware of the cultural codifications that constitute it, on the other hand, is to 'produce' the text, to participate in making it mean, to have an active rather than passive role in the production of multiple interpretations. As I tried to argue in Chapter 3, power, mastery and pleasure in language play are the *raison d'être* of the children's storying. Barthes claims that to become a producer of the text is to have access to 'the magic of the signifier, to the pleasure of writing' (1970, p. 4). Barthes' codes, then, are a fitting analytic system for discovering what is at work in Josh's most successful and complex story. Describing the competences revealed by the Genette analysis usually meant that I was extracting *parts* of stories from the data, though Sundari's story 12, which is her most rich and satisfying narrative, lent itself to a more complete analysis. For Josh the Barthes' codes tell us more at every structural level. The codes weave into a narrative pattern the culture of young children in the early 1980s, the literary culture of all the intertextualities, as well as the social and subjective world of the child, all of which Josh includes in a large metaphor which can be interpreted in plural ways, but which can also be generalized as himself, his life:

> A certain pleasure is derived from a way of imagining oneself as *individual*, of inventing a final rarest fiction: the fictive identity. This fiction is . . . the theatre of society in which we stage our plural.
> (Barthes, 1973, p. 62)

THE FIVE CODES

The *proairetic code* constitutes the story's actions from beginning to end. The actions in a story tell us what happened, and in some ways could be regarded as the referential aspect of the story, the aspect so often chosen by narratologists to represent the story structure. Barthes himself admits that the proaireticisms, sequentially organized as they are 'can form the favoured raw material for a certain structural analysis of narrative' (1970, p. 204). The meanings of the actions in a story take their significance from the story's closure, the way it ends, so this code drives back through the narrative rather than forward. In analysing Josh's story I have marked the proairetic code with the term ACT (following Barthes). The actions of the story are not only narrated by the story's verbs, but by the words characters choose to say things to one another. Josh's story is full of dialogues, and in conversations things are often implied rather than stated directly. It is the implication of what is done or said that the proairetic code is intended to reveal.

The *hermeneutic code* is the code of puzzles and mysteries. Whenever the text questions what will happen or leaves the reader guessing, whenever it poses a problem or enigma, the reader is propelled forward towards a solution. The hermeneutic code is a structuring device which works on the reader's desire to know the truth, to turn the page and find out what happens next. It is a particularly interesting code to identify in the narratives of young children, since it requires the storyteller to appreciate the effect of the narrating on the listener, while simultaneously composing the story, a feat which one might expect to be difficult, especially if the child's thinking is regarded as egocentric. In spite of this, all five children show considerable skill in using this code, employing quite a range of techniques to impel the listener to want to hear the rest of the story. Josh's stories, in particular, are very rich in problems and puzzles. The children's rather advanced knowledge of the hermeneutic code is not a self-conscious, thought-out strategy; the stories are too spontaneous for that. Keeping the listener in a state of suspense seems to be part of their tacit awareness of how stories work, and hermeneutic techniques are often closely associated with stories from books – *Hansel and Gretel, Burglar Bill*, and so on. The written story by Josh that I quoted at the end of Chapter 8 will show how creating an atmosphere of mystery continued to be a central attribute of his story composition, though by the age of 13 his knowledge of how to make it work was far more controlled and explicit than at the age of 5.

The *semic code* is present in what Barthes (1970) calls 'flickers of meaning' (p. 19), which, when assembled, structure the nature of a character or a setting. A character in a novel can never be 'real' however much the reader feels this to be the case; for Barthes 'the novelistic real is not operable' p. 80). What are these *semes* then? I interpret them to be the small details which give us the sense of a person or a place – anything from a hairstyle, or a particular kind of building or tree, to a character's stature or the layout of a garden. Barthes' coding of these flickers or semes reveals significances which set up relationships to other parts of the story.

The *symbolic* code structures the larger themes or ideas organized over the whole narrative. Often these themes are not relayed to the reader by the direct authorial voice, but are reflected in the myriad of happenings, descriptions, characters and so on. The reader must make the connections. Barthes suggests that in Balzac's story the central ideas emerge as antitheses, the opposition of pairs of terms. In stories told by very young children one might expect very basic and simple oppositions – goodies and baddies, for example. Other pairs emerge; the witch/mother in *Hansel and Gretel*, the male/female principles in *Burglar Bill*, and, in Josh's story, young, mortal characters who do not belong in Heaven, and older, mythical, immortal characters who do.

The *cultural* code reaches out from the text to the social world, which, it is implied by the narrative discourse, the reader will recognize and accept as real. Balzac's text structures the real by innumerable references to the world of knowledge, to the arts and sciences, to psychological 'truths', to ideologies, manners, customs. Of course, most of these references are not fictional and Barthes calls these allusions 'superlative effects of the real' (1970, p. 102). The cultural code is under much current discussion by novelists who either favour or do not the identification of recognizable brand names for clothes, furniture, cars etc. in stories about 20th-century consumerism. Using such references can make many assumptions about the reader: that s/he *knows* the brand name and its price in the world of the rich, can read the implicit messages about a character's wealth and status, even that the reader shares the desire for such things and would like to be a part of that world.[2] The children in my study do not refer to toys and possessions very often, but they do nevertheless like to put their knowledge of other things into their stories. They like to show what they know about the world, and they attempt to make their stories more real and less magical by using such references.[3] The cultural code is surprisingly strong, and is particularly useful in this context for revealing intertextualities lying below the surface of the children's storytelling.

In order to show the analysis of Josh's story 62, which he entitled *The God Fairy*, I shall use groups of T-Units as lexias. While this runs counter to Barthes' intention to use units of *meaning* rather than sentences or paragraphs, in this case it makes little difference to the process of commenting on the text. Josh's story structure cannot be compared to that of an adult 'classic' novelist, and I am dealing here with a very much shorter text than Balzac's. It is unlikely that in using T-Units as lexias I shall miss the hidden codes of Josh's text. Following Barthes, I shall extract words, phrases or sentences from the T-Units as they progress, and show which codes seem to be operating by marking them with asterisks and using the following abbreviations:

*ACT = Proairetic
*HER = Hermeneutic

*SYM = Symbolic
*SEM = Semic
*REF = Cultural

Still following Barthes, in addition to these codings with their explanatory notations, I shall comment on the text in other ways.

Josh told story 62 at 5: 9. It is an invented story, strongly influenced by several books and much 'rehearsed' in a whole series of narratives which were told during the weeks preceding the recording. At this time Josh was listening to full-length stories read aloud to him a chapter at a time every night. In this way he heard Baum's *The Wizard of Oz* and *The Land of Oz*. References to these books appear in all Josh's narratives at this time, usually as transformed material. The typical situation is that two or more boys (Josh and a friend) make a journey to another world where they encounter witches, kings and other fairy-tale characters, then return home at the end. Increasingly the stories are concerned with the boys exploring a certain type of terrain derived from the Oz stories, a terrain of mountains and valleys, rivers and clouds (see Sale, 1978). By the time he gets to story 62 Josh transforms all the 'realistic' characters into mythical ones, and makes the terrain Heaven, inhabited by God, St Peter and a crowd of 'servants'. The reader will see that this Heaven has little to do with any biblical or religious derivations, and has more in common with Baum's Oz and with the Hades of Greek mythology. Josh had been enjoying Greek myths at this time, particularly *Theseus and the Minotaur*. He was pleased with story 62 when he listened to it, and subsequently told two more chapters – stories 63 and 64. These are sustained narrations with a total of 2191 words altogether. They are unified in terms of setting and characters, and episodic in structure. At this point in my introduction of the analysis the reader may wish to read the story in its straightforward, unannotated form (Appendix B, pp. 187–8).

Assuming now that the reader will understand any references I make to the story events I shall outline the episodic structure of the story before moving on to the Barthes analysis. Story 62 is structured in a remarkably coherent, unified and satisfying form. Enclosed between the first and last T-Units is a narrative which is consistent in the following respects:

The time: Unspecified past
The setting: The palace of God
The main characters: God and St Peter
The problem: How to deal with intruders into Heaven

The Barthes-based analysis will show that God and St Peter retain consistent characteristics throughout, that the setting is always dark and labyrinthine and that the antitheses of the story (e.g. good *v* evil; living *v* dead; moral law *v* Satanic law; knowledge *v* innocence; responsibility *v* having fun) are repeated over all its episodes.

Within the overall narrative are four episodes, each with a beginning, middle and end, and each linked thematically and structurally to the others. Each episode deals with a visitor to Heaven who poses a problem, threat or potential threat:

   I   *The arrival of the puppy*
  II *The intrusion of Dracula*
 III *The interview with Frankenstein*
 IV *The arrival of the dragon*

Episode I is complete and is not referred to again, but thematically it is strongly linked to the ensuing episodes. Episode IV, in fact, is a kind of replay of Episode I; the puppy and the kind dragon are both regarded opportunistically by God as potential pets/guard-dogs; the box with a hole to look through, which is used to throw the puppy back to earth, has its parallel in the bag with a hole in it for the dragon to breathe through, which is used for him to sleep in. The dragon is linked to the puppy by his goodness, and to Dracula and Frankenstein by his magical/mythical nature.

Episodes II, III and IV are more strongly linked. With the puppy safely returned to his owners on earth, Episode II brings a new inappropriate visitor to Heaven, the legendary Dracula. Dracula is dispatched very deftly by God using the blood-sucking fangs as daggers. We know that there is to be a further visitor because God now sets St Peter on guard along with himself in case any intruders arrive in the night. Frankenstein's arrival heralds Episode III. This is essentially a linking section of the story, for it comprises a dialogue between God and Frankenstein in which Episode II is re-narrated by God as a kind of cautionary tale to Frankenstein, and Frankenstein himself introduces the next visitor to Heaven, the kind dragon of Episode IV. Though nothing happens to Frankenstein apart from his conversation with God, he is by his very nature a threat, a potential repetition of the Dracula episode. God annuls the threat by narrating the story of Dracula's death in a particularly skilful manner. There are two levels of narration in Episode III, the narrative God tells, and the effect of that narrative on Frankenstein, who wisely becomes God's ally and introduces the kind dragon as a helpful friend for God. Episode IV is linked to Episode II by the reversal of Dracula's death, which incidentally sets the schema for Josh's second chapter, story 63. Episodes I and IV are linked thematically; the puppy belongs to the living world and must be returned to his owners, leaving God and St Peter with no guard-dog. The dragon now becomes the guard-dog, compensating for the loss of the puppy, and posing no problem since as a mythical other-worldly creature there is no obligation to return him somewhere else. He can remain in Heaven both as pet and as a guard against evil intruders like Dracula. Though this is not a particularly complex plot by the standards of adults, it is agreeably neat, consistent and unified when one considers that it is the spontaneous oral creation of a 5-year-old. The plot is a matter of theme and variation, in the manner of the ancient epic bards.

Each episode is strongly hermeneutic, raising a problem or a threat which must be resolved:

    I   How to dispose of the puppy without harming him or exposing God and his servants to danger.

   II   The threat posed by the arrival of Dracula.

  III   Frankenstein's questioning of the narrative of Dracula's death, which God is concealing.

  IV   The danger which the dragon has to guard against, eventually turning out to be the reincarnated Dracula.

Thus within each section of the story is a motive for the listener to want to know what happens next, driving us forward to the end of the story.

Below the level of these four major episodes there are sub-narratives which are largely communicated in the form of the characters' talking to one another:

    I (a) St Peter's narrative of the way the puppy opened the door to the throne room. This has several functions: (i) Delaying the solution to the problem of the puppy's disposal; (ii) Showing that the puppy is clever enough to make a desirable pet; (iii) Establishing the nature of the relationship between God and St Peter.

II (a) God's narrative of what happened to Dracula. This replays the brief action of Episode II in more detail, giving us the pleasure of the gory incident again, this time as an eye-witness rather than a narrator's account.

(b) Frankenstein's introduction of the dragon, heralding Episode IV.

III (a) The narrator's report of the reincarnation of Dracula. The pluperfect tense is used to explain what Dracula had been up to during Episodes III and IV.

Below these three levels of the overall narrative, the four linked episodes and the embedded sub-narratives, are the numerous details, spread from word to word and sentence to sentence, of characters, customs and the cultural world in which the story is grounded.

ANALYSIS OF THE GOD FAIRY (JOSH STORY 62)

(Date: 8-7-81 age 5:9 mother present)

1. *Once in the palace (um) of God St Peter walked around a passageways without God*
   (**palace*/SEM: wealth/power, God the King. ***passageways* SEM: labyrinth. Difficult access to God. ***REF: literary text for children, *The Way of Danger* by Ian Serraillier, the story of Theseus in Hades.)
2. *God was sitting on his throne*
   (**throne* SEM: wealth/power. ***was sitting* ACT: to sit on throne is static, authoritative. It is St Peter who runs around on God's behalf. ***REF: literary text for children *The Wizard of Oz* by Frank L. Baum, a story heard over the previous month, retold and transformed by Josh in earlier narratives. The link to this book is in the wizard-like persona of God, and in the puppy.)
3. *once – um – St Peter went back to God*
4. *he found a clue St Peter did*
   (**went back* ACT: to return – sent by God as a scout? ***found a clue* ACT: to scout or sleuth. ****clue* HER: Enigma 1: What has he found? By mentioning clues before any problem has been identified, the narrator places this story in the mystery genre.)
5. *it was a little puppy*
   (*little puppy SYM: Antithesis: youthful/mortal *v.* ancient/immortal **HER: Enigma 1 solved, but Enigma 2 arises: What is a puppy doing in Heaven? ****puppy* REF: *The Wizard of Oz*. Toto, Dorothy's dog, is left behind when Dorothy leaves Oz by balloon at the end of the story. Dorothy has to go back and retrieve him. This motif, borrowed from a book, is the starting point of Josh's invented story. There are parallels, too, in the larger themes of Baum's and Josh's stories. Dorothy's youth and innocence is in strong contrast to the cynicism of the ageing man who turns out to be the wizard. In Josh's story God is powerful and knowing, in contrast to the youth and charm of the puppy.)
6. *'Oh no that is somebody's (from-from-from-who) who's dead who's just climbed up these mountains and just got here'* (**Oh no* ACT: to be concerned, the voice of conscience ***somebody who's dead* REF: Christian religion. Only the dead

can go to Heaven. ***mountains SEM: difficult access to Heaven. Also REF: the mountain terrain is borrowed from *The Wizard of Oz* ****just got here HER: Enigma 2 solved.)

7. *'He's alive'*
(*alive SYM: Antithesis: living *v* dead. This theme of the living and dead is replayed throughout Josh's story, which, in its second chapter especially, and at the end of this chapter, plays with the idea of Dracula's ability to come back to life whatever God and St Peter do to destroy him.)

8. *'Yes I don't know what we can do with him'*
9. *'(We'll just) – we'll just throw him back down'*
10. *'Don't throw him back down' said St Peter*
11. *'We must treat him nicely'*
12. *so they didn't throw him down*
(**I don't know* HER: Enigma 3: How to dispose of the puppy? Dorothy and Toto have the problem of leaving Oz at the end of Baum's story. Their solution is to leave by hot-air balloon. Here, Josh's characters speculate on a number of means of returning the puppy (see 37–48 below). **throw him ACT: to offer a carelessly simple solution to Enigma 3. The implication of St Peter's speech in 10 is that this is God's suggestion. Throughout this story God is pragmatic and powerful in contrast to St Peter's voice of caution and conscience. ***treat him nicely REF: code of behaviour: do not throw books, toys, rubbish, or animals. ****SEM: St Peter is the voice of conscience and polite behaviour throughout the story. ******so they didn't throw him down* HER: Enigma 3 remains: how will they dispose of the puppy?)

13. *(um) once the dog was walking along the passageways like this (and then-and then-) until he found a door*
14. *and he opened the door*
15. *and there was a throne*
(**he found . . . he opened . . . there was* HER: the succession of clauses effectively delays the solution to what lies behind the door. Suspending solutions in this way is one of Josh's most frequently used hermeneutic techniques. **throne SEM: wealth/power = God)

16. *and it had God sitting*
(*sitting ACT: to be a King. **God sitting REF: In *The Wizard of Oz* Dorothy and Toto approach the wizard in the Emerald City at the end of the story, when Toto gets left behind in 'Heaven'.)

17. *'There he is again'*
18. *'Yes I wonder how he opened the door?'*
(*I wonder HER: another puzzle ***how he opened the door* REF: laws of nature. Puppies cannot usually accomplish such feats. Barthes' codes do not focus upon point of view as Genette's do, but there is a very sharp change in focus between 13–16 and 17–18. Josh not only uses dialogue to get the story told, but also to establish the personalities of his characters.)

19. *'I know' (said) said St Peter*
20. *'I followed him*
21. *and he climbed up the door (and then) and then fell down*
22. *and as he fell down he hanged from the thingy*

23. *and then he jumped down*
24. *and then he pushed (with his) with his head until it opened*
25. *and then he came in'*
    (**followed* ACT: to scout/sleuth (for clues see 4) ***climbed . . . fell . . . hanged
    . . . jumped . . . pushed . . . came* ACT: to carry out a complex physical feat.
    Verbs are the least varied grammatical form in the stories, but here Josh
    manages a string of terms which exactly convey the process of opening the door
    without hands. '*Thingy*' is unusually inexplicit, but I think Josh meant the
    handle of the door. ****SEM: the puppy is ingenious. *****HER: St Peter's nar-
    rative is delaying the solution to the problem of the puppy's disposal.)
26. *'But where were you?'*
27. *'I came in another way*
    (**where..?* HER: Another puzzle. Why didn't St Peter simply open the door for
    the puppy? Characters in Josh's stories sometimes interrogate the text, a techni-
    que for maintaining the vraisemblance of the narrative. ***another way* SEM:
    labyrinth.)
28. *But I saw him when I went across him*
29. *he went that way*
30. *and I went like that*
31. *and then I went like that*
32. *but he went the quickest way'*
    (**saw* ACT: to witness what happens while God is sitting on his throne – St
    Peter the sleuth. ***the quickest way* ACT: to use wits – the puppy is clever.
    ****27–32* REF: the story convention of the omniscient narrator. By chance St
    Peter happened to see how the puppy opened the door to the throne room. Josh
    has difficulty making this convention work and maintaining vraisemblance, but
    he knows that story material must be credible and explicable.)
33. *'Oh he's a clever dog*
34. *I think we must have him for something'*
    (**clever dog* SYM: Antithesis: The puppy (young and mortal) has outwitted St
    Peter (old and immortal). ***we must have him* ACT: to wield power.
    ****something* SEM: God is always an opportunist in this story. The diversion
    of the story of the puppy opening the door is now seen to be justified, as the
    puppy's cleverness gives God a good reason for wanting him to stay in Heaven,
    thus returning us to the problem, which we had left, of what to do with the
    puppy.)
35. *'Oh don't*
36. *the people might want him'*
    (**Oh don't* SYM: Antithesis: St Peter is the voice of conscience and God is the
    all-powerful pragmatist. ***the people . . .* REF: moral code: we have no right
    to steal the puppy from his owners. This moral argument, on St Peter's part,
    returns us neatly to the problem of getting the puppy back to earth.)
37. *'Oh yes' said God 'But there's no way to take him down*
38. *we'll die if we (go) go down'*
    [*Josh to adult*: will they die if they go (down) down?
    Adult: Uhum.
    Josh: um-God? Will he? Will he really, Mum?

Adult: Maybe, I don't know.]
(**take him down* HER: a return to the enigma of the puppy's disposal. ***we'll die* REF: laws of Heaven and Earth. ***SEM: God's pragmatism: we can't get him home therefore we are free to 'have him for something'. At the break in the narrative Josh stops being his narrator and becomes Josh as himself checking a 'fact' of the story background with the adult. I do not know where the idea that God and St Peter will die if they go to earth comes from. It calls up Greek stories in which the dead try to leave Hades, and this story was influenced by *Theseus and the Minotaur*, where Josh's labyrinthine Heaven comes from. The whole story is about who belongs where – the living and the dead, mortality and immortality – so such details are important.)

39. *'so (so) we can't take him down*
(**can't* REF: laws of Heaven. God cannot risk the end of his universe.)

40. *the only thing we can do is send one of our servants down in an aeroplane'*
(**only thing* HER: possible solution to the puppy problem. ***send . . . down* REF: physical laws. Perhaps this will be safer for the puppy and his escort? ****servants . . . aeroplane* SEM: power/wealth. God has access to both servants and aeroplanes. REF: *The Wizard of Oz*. The aeroplane idea is parallel to the balloon in Baum's story.)

41. *'But they'll die*
(**But* HER: we are left with the problem-solution delayed again. ***they'll die* REF: moral code. This is St Peter again. We cannot send a servant to his death.)

42. *There's no way except to throw him down*
(**there's no way* SEM: God the decision-maker. We have to assume, by working out the turns in the dialogue, that God is speaking. Josh 'lives' these conversations as he tells them, and puts in minimal markers of the speaker, letting us know by intonation that there is a new turn in the conversation. **throw him down HER: what will happen? St Peter has argued earlier that this will be unkind.)

43. *I know what*
44. *Get him in a box and throw him down'*
(**in a box* ACT: to protect. REF: the box becomes the new parallel to Baum's balloon. **throw him down ACT: to compromise between the laws of nature and the moral code.)

45. *'Oh yes'*
46. *they made a box for him*
47. *(and there's your) and there was a little hole for him to look*
(**they made a box* ACT: to find a practical solution to a problem. **a little hole SYM: Antithesis: The hole seems to be provided for the puppy's comfort – another contrast between practical laws and the moral code, represented by the personalities of God and St Peter. It is interesting that this story is entirely male in its characters – as in so many of Josh's, Jimmy's and Robert's stories – a fact made more interesting in the light of Baum's choice of a girl as the central character of *The Wizard of Oz*. Nevertheless St Peter's caring attitude calls up a female principle in the partnership with God. The conversations between them often make me think of a mother and father talking together. Josh's story models for this seem to be myths rather than Baum's fairy tale.)

48. *and then they threw him down*
49. *and he landed on (on) the roof of the house that he lived in* (*threw* ACT: to resolve the problem of the puppy. **roof* REF: physical laws. The roof is nearest to Heaven. ***the house* REF: the story convention of chance. When Dorothy leaves the Emerald City she wakes up in her own bed.)
50. *then he (got-got) got (the) the box and threw it back up to Heaven and then went down the chimney and then came out* (*got . . . threw . . . went down . . . came out* ACT: complex physical feat (c.f. the puppy opening the door). **threw it back* REF: moral code – you must return things to their owners. ***went down the chimney* ACT: to go the quickest way (see 32). ****chimney* REF: story convention of folk-tales – see *The Three Little Pigs*.)
51. *and then they so pleased to see him*
(*pleased* HER: both a practical and moral solution has been found. REF: conventional happy ending.)
52. *(and then) – and then God said 'We've done it*
53. *We've done it'*
54. *and St Peter and God danced around with the servants and everybody (and then– and then) until it was bedtime*
55. *and they all went to sleep*
(*we've done it* ACT: to celebrate a difficult feat. **danced around* ACT: to have fun. REF: ending of *Hansel and Gretel*, retold in Josh's story 29. Conventional ending for comedies. ***bedtime . . . sleep* HER: this could be the start of a new mystery in the dark, rather than a form of story closure.)

Episode II

56. *in the night there wasn't anything else to do*
(*night* SYM: antithesis joy in Heaven *v* darkness/sleep **to do* HER: obviously sleep is not a closure – a new episode is implied.)
57. *somebody was creeping in*
(*somebody* HER: who could it be? **creeping* ACT: to move in a stealthy way.)
58. *it was a ghost*
(*ghost* SEM: supernatural, in a place where everything is supernatural. **REF: Josh's labyrinthine Heaven resembles Hades where the ghosts of the dead flit around.)
59. *something was creeping in*
(*something* SEM: non-human in contrast to the 'somebody' of 57. **HER: repetition continues the suspense and delays the solution.)
60. *it had sharp teeth*
(*it* SEM: non-human – continuing from 59. **sharp teeth* SEM: danger, threat. ***HER: what is it?)
61. *it was Dracula*
(*Dracula* REF: 20th-century fiction (Bram Stoker) via media of TV and comics **SEM: evil ***SYM: Antithesis: good *v* evil. The theme of Episode I now has a variation. Dracula is the second inappropriate visitor to Heaven. His evil is

represented by his creeping in at night rather than by appearing during the day as the innocent puppy did.)

62. *he came through the passageway*

63. *but when God saw him he pulled his teeth out (and)- and then he stabbed him with his teeth*

(*passageway SEM: the labyrinth in a particularly sinister context with Dracula creeping along it. Readers with a psychoanalytic bent may wish to read Freudian interpretations of the passageways in Josh's stories. There is a strong link with Josh's story 17, quoted in full at the opening of Chapter 2. In that story Josh finds his father in the middle of the night in a hole in the ground, and thinks at first that a monster is down the hole. Story 17 derives from *Burglar Bill* in which Burglar Betty conceals her baby in a brown box with little holes in it. The parallel with the puppy, and his box with a hole in it to allow him to breathe, is obvious. God in this story is paternal and the puppy is the 'baby'. Thus it can be seen that the intermeshing of intertextualities from powerful key texts is very complex in Josh's stories. ***pulled his teeth out* SEM: strength: God is a man of action. ***with his teeth SEM: quick-witted. Irony – Dracula is hoist with his own petard. ****stabbed him REF: in *Dracula* Dracula can only be killed by having a stake driven through his heart. Josh gives this a humorous twist by using Dracula's own teeth as the stake.)

64. *and then he fell down*

65. *and they buried him (with no) with no tombstone*

(*fell down ACT: defeat of evil. ***with no tombstone* REF: religious laws – mark of disgrace. Also see *Dracula*.)

66. *(and then) and then they walked around the passageways*

67. *(and there- and-and) and there's dead people (all around the pass) all around the passageways buried*

(**dead people..buried* SYM: Antithesis: Heaven described as Hades. **REF: known text, Theseus in *The Way of Danger*. ***REF: known text *How the Moon Began* (retold by James Reeves. In this story St Peter stops the dead from dancing on their graves in the night. This Grimm's tale is almost certainly Josh's source for the character of St Peter in this story.)

68. *so there's nothing to be done*

69. *every night people came in like ghosts and Dracula (and) and started to get people*

(*to be done HER: another problem presents itself. ***Dracula and ghosts* ACT: to rise from the dead. This becomes the major theme of the second chapter (story 63) in which Dracula keeps coming back to life. ***to get people REF: cultural code of children – colloquial playground term for chasing and catching in the playground.)

70. *but God said it was (alright) – alright (um-St Peter)*

71. *God said it wasn't alright*

72. *(he) he had to (um) keep an eye on as well as God in the night*

(**God said it wasn't alright* HER: danger, especially if God himself is worried by it. **as well as God SEM: God is responsible for protecting everybody at night. This links to the puppy/dragon as guard-dog theme. We can now understand why God needs a guard.)

73. *'And if the door opens you mustn't be frightened again and get down the bed when Dracula came in'*
(**and if. . . .* HER: this suggests imminent danger. ***you mustn't be frightened* SEM: God is powerfully in charge and can reprimand St Peter ****get down the bed* REF: moral code – cowardice. The direct mimetic speech here brings us back to the time of the story, and strongly suggests that St Peter has hidden down the bed in the past. Josh also reverts to direct speech because the narratized speech of 70–72 was grammatically difficult for him to sustain.)
74. *'No I will not do it'*
(**No* HER: there is a real threat if St Peter refuses God's order. What will happen? How bad will it be? A new episode is now expected.)

Episode III

75. *it was the other night then*
(**night* HER: we have been warned that something will happen at night.)
76. *(and then-and then) and then somebody else came in*
(**somebody else* HER: Josh always delays telling us who it is straight away.)
77. *(and it was) and it was Frankenstein*
(**Frankenstein* HER: the third episode is beginning. We expect Frankenstein to be as threatening as Dracula. ***REF: 19th-century literature (Mary Shelley) via media/comics ****SYM: Antithesis: good *v* evil)
78. *and then Frankenstein said 'Hey God?'*
(**Hey* REF: social code – greeting denoting familiarity. ***SEM: cheekiness)
79. *'What?'*
80. *'Dracula-where's Dracula?'*
(**where's Dracula*? ACT: to look for an acquaintance. The implication is that Frankenstein knows Dracula is to be found in God's palace, and that God and Frankenstein know one another.)
81. *'Oh he's buried'*
(**he's buried* ACT: to state a fact without explanation. ***HER: ploy: God gives a minimal response to delay telling Frankenstein what actually happened. This has the effect of a complete fait accompli.)
82. *'How?'*
(**How*? ACT: to elicit a narrative. God and the listener know what Frankenstein does not know.)
83. *'(um-er) I'm sorry to tell you but he's buried'* (**I'm sorry to tell you* SEM: cunning. God is insincere since we know he killed Dracula. ***REF: social code: politeness here is used as a ploy to conceal the truth. ****but he's buried* HER: God repeats 81, thereby gaining time. This sets up a tension in the conversation.)
84. *'Oh good I didn't like Dracula very much did you?'*
(**didn't* ACT: to put something in the past. ***like Dracula very much* SEM: insincerity. Dracula was obviously Frankenstein's buddy (see 80) but perhaps Frankenstein senses danger and now changes sides. ****did you?* ACT: to elicit agreement by tag question. Frankenstein seems to be edging closer to God's part in Dracula's death.)

85. '*No he's dead now*'
     (*No HER: agreement as a ploy. God is still avoiding the full text of the story.)
86. '*I think he's thirty-six*'
87. '*Oh he couldn't be that many*'
88. '*He could be about a hundred and one*'
89. '*Oh yes that's how many he is*'
90. '*He must be dead*'
     (**think . . . couldn't . . . could . . . must be*' ACT: to speculate about the cause
     of death. The implication is that it was old age. Josh gives us no speaker markers
     beyond intonation here, but it is clear that the turns change as I have marked
     them. In that case Frankenstein thinks Dracula was young (too young to die
     naturally?) and God, by confirming that 101 is nearer to the truth seems to be
     hinting that Dracula died of old age. ***Oh he couldn't be* . . . SEM: cunning.
     God seems to encourage these speculations about age in order to stall telling
     the truth.)
91. '*Yeah I stabbed him with one of my teeth*' said God
92. '*I pulled (one o' his) one o' his teeth out and stabbed him with it*
93. *and then he died*'
     (*I stabbed ACT: to narrate the full story after a delay of ten conversational
     turns. **I pulled HER: a cautionary tale. Frankenstein has been warned.)
94. '*Where did you stab him?*'
95. '*Right in the heart and the (teeth) tooth came right out of (his) the back of his
     heart on his back*'
     (**heart . . . back* REF: story of Dracula. The wooden stake driven through the
     heart (here the tooth is used) is the only thing which can kill him. ***back of
     his heart . . . on his back* REF: anatomy – a fatal wound.)
96. '*Oh that's good*'
97. *So now he's dead is he?*'
     (**that's good* ACT: to side with the victor. **is he? ACT: to muse to oneself
     as in 'fancy that!'. The constant repetition of the fact that Dracula is dead in
     this conversation is a preparation for the next episode in which he comes back
     to life.)
98. '*Oh oh*' said Frankenstein '*I've just got some (some) good news to tell you*'
     (**Oh oh . . . just* ACT: to remember the almost forgotten purpose of one's visit.
     **good news SEM: Frankenstein is now a goodie rather than a baddie. Has the
     cautionary tale narrated by God had its effect? HER: What could it be?)
99. '*There's a dragon (who) who's very kind*
100. *and if he comes in don't be scared of him and try to kill him*
101. *he's nice*'
     (*dragon REF: mythical creature. ***who's very kind* SYM: Antithesis: evil
     Dracula/Frankenstein *v* kind dragon/puppy. ***nice SEM: Frankenstein is
     ingratiating himself with God. The dragon will need to be nice after what hap-
     pened to Dracula. ****if he comes HER: Will he? A new episode is being sug-
     gested, and a variation on the theme of inappropriate visitors to Heaven.
     ******don't be scared* REF: moral code – good creatures must not be killed, even
     dragons.)

Episode IV

102. *one night a dragon came in*
   (**one night* HER: new episode. What will happen?)
103. *(and they said- and- and he said-and) but St Peter said to God 'Don't kill him*
104. *(remember what)-remember what he said?'*
   (**don't kill him* REF: moral code SEM: St Peter is always less violent than God.
   ***remember* SEM: trust in Frankenstein's account.)
105. *and the dragon came near him and said 'What is your command?'*
106. *and he said 'We don't have any commands*
107. *Can you be our pet?' says God*
   (**What is your command*? ACT: obeisance to King REF: code of courtly con-
   duct – formal mode of address. SEM: we have been told the dragon is 'nice'.
   ***we don't* ACT: to reject formality and make the dragon feel at home. ****pet*
   SYM: Antithesis dragon *v* pet (puppy). SEM: God the protector of pets. In the
   first episode God wanted to keep the puppy. *****Can you* SEM: politeness. God
   does not command but asks nicely.)
108. *'Of course I can'*
   (**of course* SEM: willingness. The kindness of the dragon is confirmed.)
109. *so (they kept him- in-in a- in-in-in a big) they put him to sleep in a big bag*
110. *they just left a little hole in it (for-for) for him to breathe*
   (**put him to sleep* REF: social code – hospitality. ***a big bag* SEM: security.
   ****a little hole* REF: the puppy's box in Episode I; both holes recall the brown
   box with little holes in it in *Burglar Bill*. *****for him to breathe* REF: physical
   laws.)
111. *and when it's morning they took him out for any dangers*
   (**dangers* HER: what will happen?)
112. *(and) – and one night (um) a danger happened*
   (**night* SEM: danger ***a danger happened* HER: What is it?
113. *Dracula had came alive again*
   (**had* REF: story convention of embedded narrative. ***came alive* REF: story
   convention of reversibility of death.
   ****Dracula* SYM: Antithesis: good (dragon) *v.* evil (Dracula).)
114. *and he had had his teeth in again by a special dentist underground who was*
   magic
   (**his teeth* SEM: danger ***underground* SYM: religion *v.* black magic
   ****special dentist* REF: Dracula cannot do evil without his teeth. Here the real
   world of medicine combines with magical fantasy to achieve this bit of
   vraisemblance. Josh's rule is that you can have magic and coincidences in stories
   as long as you can explain them. The pluperfect tense here implies that Dracula
   has fixed himself up under ground *during* the other events of the story.)
115. *so the dragon caught him and put fire to him*
   (**caught . . . put fire* ACT: to defeat evil by breathing fire. Neither God nor
   the puppy could have dispatched Dracula in this way. ***REF: properties of
   dragons – they always breathe fire. SYM: Antithesis: good *v.* evil. Dragon-
   fire – normally threatening to the good – is used for good purposes.)
116. *he never came alive again*

(**never* ACT: to resolve the problem of Dracula.)
117. *(and) and that's the end of the story*
      (REF: conventional closure of narrative.)

There can be no doubt that strongly hermeneutic passages in his favourite storybooks were very powerful for Josh, for they are transformed again and again throughout his narrations. Particularly important are the 'tip-tap' on the witch's door in *Hansel and Gretel*, the siren-like noise coming from the big brown box with little holes in it and the noise of an intruder climbing through the window – both in *Burglar Bill*. Describing for the listener what a character could *hear* before anything became visible is a way of creating tension in a story. Jimmy does this in story 5:

1 once upon a time I had my birthday
2 and someone gave me a magic (P) box
3 and (when I) when I put some metal things in *I heard ruckety ruck ruckety ruck*
4 *and out came real things (Jimmy story 5)*

This technique for creating suspense is an aspect of the focalization I discussed in Chapter 9. Another way to use it is to tell what characters *saw* in a way that describes what they *felt*:

5   and the baddie came near
6   and (P) he opened the door and take the key out
7   *there was some eyes*
8   and he was crawling up here
9   *and there were bats upside down*
10 *and they saw some breathing*
11 and it was a monster (*Robert story 18*)

Robert actually derived this delaying technique from a wordless picture book called *Creepy Castle* (John Goodhall), and the fact that he can turn it into a verbal structure as the central part of an invented story at the age of 3:11 convinces me that children learn how to do this from books because it is the most exciting part of the story. We have seen from Josh's story 62 that there are many ways of accomplishing this kind of suspense in a narrative: characters can question and answer one another, as God and Frankenstein do, or the narrator can raise questions of the text. Of course we do this all the time in the course of our everyday swapping of stories with others, in conversational gambits like 'Guess what?' or 'You'll never believe what happened' or 'What do you think it was?'. The difference between that and what the children do in their stories is that the children manage to sustain the suspense by withholding information over a whole series of clauses.

Barthes always stresses that it is the reader's pleasure and mastery which he is accounting for in exposing the polysemy of Balzac's text. The pleasures of reading and writing become one, for here to read the text is to re-write it. Josh, too, in story 62, shows his pleasure and mastery, both in his 'reading' of the source stories and his recreation of them into a new text. In this story we have observed how the excitement of danger and suspense gets repeated over four episodes, a structure which did not arise from a conscious plan made in advance by the storyteller, but which occurred in the course of a spontaneous impromptu oral narration whose themes had been visited and revisited in story readings and tellings over months or even years before the production of this story. The episodes are rather a design which emerges from the storyteller's desire to repeat the pleasure of excitement and suspense for himself again and again. His knowledge of other stories has taught him that pure repetition would be pointless and boring, but that theme and variation will work. Of all the Barthes' codes the hermeneutic gives more power to the storyteller and less to the listener, who is manipulated by the text. The hermeneutic code is a way of making your listener *listen* and license you to go on.

The themes of story 62, like the themes of Labov's narratives of personal experience, the verbal play forms of oral cultures around the world, and many of the stories taken from the 5 children in this study, are strong, violent and extreme. It is probably only in fantasy stories and role-play games that a young child is able to explore ideas like death, life after death, burial, re-birth, goodness and evil, mortality and immortality. You can hear the pleasure in Josh's voice as he tells story 62, and, though he is undoubtedly tackling serious ideas, burlesque is never far away. Frankenstein and Dracula, God and St Peter, are fun characters. Burlesque elements appear in the notion of sending a servant down in an aeroplane, in God and the servants dancing around, in God's warning to St Peter not to hide down the bed, in the overdone politeness of the conversation between God and Frankenstein, in the dragon's formal approach to God and in Dracula's private underground dentistry. The burlesque in this story pushes against what is conventionally expected, or acceptable, or even decent.

Storytelling, and hearing stories read aloud, expose children to linguistic and narrative conventions in the course of *the power and pleasure they experience in play*. For Josh these central affects, pleasure and power, bring him to the very borderline of his linguistic, narrative and literary competences. At the level of the word he knows that the language needs to be colourful, life-like and unusual – 'tombstone', 'stabbed', 'command', 'special dentist' are examples. In many other stories, as I pointed out in Chapter 3, he and Sundari sometimes get such words wrong; unsure of the meanings of interesting-sounding words, they take the risk of using them anyway. At the level of the sentence, narration throws up constructions which they have not quite mastered but which they are bound to try out – the narratized speech of 70–72 in story 62 for example. At the level of discourse the child's task is most complex. For instance, the rules of storytelling demand that the 'facts' (Barthes' cultural code) be credible, so between 38 and 39 Josh checks his 'facts' with his mother. Josh and Sundari tried very hard not to break their narrative flow for anything, yet this must have been important enough to justify Josh's temporarily leaving his narrator's role. All must be explained – the puppy's ability to open doors and Dracula's reincarnation complete with teeth. At the same time the story's hermeneuticisms must be set up, sustained and resolved, the dialogue must be life-like, and the protagonists must behave in character. In most story monologues the children are trying out one or another aspect of the narrative discourse, and it is not surprising that they do not often produce complex, perfectly resolved plots. But if any activity has the power to push their competences into being, the simple and universal act of telling stories must be a good candidate.

There is a sense in which story 62 is *a metaphor for Josh's own storytelling*. During this period of his life listening to stories and telling them occupied a considerable part of his free time. In his storytelling he wants to have fun, to be daring and violent, to explore forbidden areas, to go over the top. However, the conventions of narration constrain him to tell what is fictionally believable, explicable, even rational. Narrative discourse imposes an order on what is disorderly and rude, just as Abrahams (1972b) claimed the rules of 'talking broad' in St Vincent constrained the disorder of the material. God and St Peter, too, narrate, in story 62, and at the end of the next chapter, story 63, Dracula becomes a goodie and tells a new story about his life on earth (see Appendix, pp. 188–9).

If we interpret the metaphorical content of children's stories to lie in the use of similes and metaphors, we shall find, as I have, that these are rare. Barthes' codes show how narratives in their total structure use metaphoric processes to create the illusion of lived experience. Readers may well feel that I have 'over-read' some of the asterisked parts of the text, but it must be remembered that Barthes' aim was to show the readings that are possible, since we cannot ever read a text in the same way. No doubt there are other readings of Josh's narrative. My aim has been to show that his text operates at many levels of structure, that these levels are linked in surprisingly intricate ways, and that the source books of his intertextualities have shown him how to narrate in this way. Neither the crude psychological story schemas I looked at in Chapter 6, nor the more liberating story structure model described by Labov would uncover the intricacies that Genette's analysis and Barthes' codes reveal to be present in the children's narrative competences. And these systems have the advantage that they help us to see how truly embedded in literacy the children's notions of story are. They forge for us the final link with the world of books, which was initially suggested by obvious references to known texts in Chapter 2, was reinforced by the unusual uses of words and the phrase and sentence structures of Chapters 4 and 5, and which was strengthened by the overall narrative structures of story retellings in the Labov-based analyses of Chapter 7.

The greater part of this book has been devoted to analysis. It now remains in my closing chapter to turn from story structure to the educational and cognitive implications of what I have described.

NOTES

1. R. Barthes 'Introduction to the structural analysis of narratives', in *Image, Music, Text* (1977).
2. Martin Amis and Tom Wolfe are modern novelists who spring to mind in this respect.
3. I have argued elsewhere (Fox, 1989) that in storying the five children use elements of knowledge from all the curriculum areas that will later be required in school. Stories show the operation of early scientific and mathematical ideas, the beginnings of notions of history and geography, and even children's knowledge of psychology, physiology and metaphysics.

Appendix: Transcripts of Josh's stories 'God and Peter'

Story 62 (age 5: 9)

once in the palace (um-) of God St Peter walked around a passageways without
God   God was sitting on his throne   once (um-) St Peter went back to God   he found
a clue St Peter did   it was a little puppy   'Oh no that is somebody's (from-from-from-
who-) who's dead who's just climbed up these mountains and just got here'   'He's
alive'   'Yes I don't know what we can do with him'   '(We'll just-) we'll just throw him
back down'   'Don't throw him back down' said St Peter   'We must treat him nicely'
so they didn't throw him down   (um-) once the dog was walking along the
passageways like this (and then- and then-) until he found a door   and he opened the
door   and there was a throne   and it had God sitting   'There he is again'   'Yes I
wonder how he opened the door?'   'I know' (said-) said St Peter   'I followed him   and
he climbed up the door (and then-) and then fell down   and as he fell down he
hanged from the thingy   and then he jumped down   and then he pushed (with his-)
with his head until it opened   and then he came in'   'But where were you?'   'I came
in another way   but I saw him when I went across him   he went that way   and I
went like that   and then I went like that   but he went the quickest way'   'Oh he's a
clever dog   I think we must have him for something'   'Oh don't   the people might
want him'   'Oh yes' said God   'But there's no way to take him down   we'll die if (we-)
we go down'   [*Josh to adult*: Will they die if they go (down-) down? *Adult*:
Uhum.   *Josh*: um-God? Will he? Will he really, Mum? *Adult*: Maybe. I don't
know]   '(so-) so we can't take him down   the only thing we can do is send one of
our servants down in an aeroplane'   'But they'll die   there's no way except to throw
him down   I know what   get him in a box and throw him down'   'Oh yes'   they made
a box for him   (and there's your-) and there was a little hole for him to look   and then
they threw him down   and he landed (on-) on the roof of the house that he lived
in   then he (got-got-) got (the-) the box and threw it back up to Heaven and then
went down the chimney and then came out   and then they so pleased to see him
(and then-) and then God said 'We've done it   we've done it'   and St Peter and God
danced around with the servants and everybody (and then- and then-) until it was
bedtime   and they all went to sleep   in the night there wasn't anything else to
do   somebody was creeping in   it was a ghost   something was creeping in   it had
sharp teeth   it was Dracula   he came through the passageway   but when God saw
him he pulled his teeth out (and-) and then he stabbed him with his teeth   and then
he fell down   and they buried him (with no-) with no tombstone   (and then-) and then
they walked around the passageways (and there-and-and-) and there's dead people
(all around the pass-) all around the passageways buried   so there's nothing to be
done   every night people came in like ghosts and Dracula (and-) and started to get
people   but God said it was (alright-) alright (um-St Peter)   God said it wasn't
alright   (he-) he had to (um-) keep an eye on as well as God in the night 'And if the
door opens you mustn't be frightened again and get down the bed when Dracula
came in'   'No I will not do it'   it was the other night then   (and then-and then-) and
then somebody else came in   (and it was-) and it was Frankenstein   and then
Frankenstein said 'Hey God'   'What?'   'Dracula-where's Dracula?'   'Oh he's
buried'   'How?'   '(um-er-) I'm sorry to tell you but he's buried'   'Oh good I didn't like
Dracula very much did you?'   'No he's dead now'   'I think he's thirty-six'   'Oh he
couldn't be that many'   'He could be about a hundred and one'   'Oh yes that's how
many he is'   'He must be dead'   'Yeah I stabbed him with one of my teeth' said
God   'I pulled (one o' his-) one o' his teeth out and stabbed him with it   and then he
died'   'Where did you stab him?'   'Right in the heart and the (teeth-) tooth came right
out of (his-) the back of his heart on his back'   'Oh that's good   so now he's dead is
he?'   'Oh oh' said Frankenstein 'I've just got (some-) some good news to tell you

there's a dragon (who-) who's very kind and if he comes in don't be scared of him and try to kill him he's nice' one night a dragon came in (and they said-and-and he said-and-) but St Peter said to God 'Don't kill him (remember what-) remember what he said?' and the dragon came near him and said 'What is your command?' and he said 'We don't have any commands can you be our pet?' says God 'Of course I can'   so (they kept him-in-in a-in-in-in a big-) they put him to sleep in a big bag they just left a little hole in it (for-for-) for him to breathe and when it's morning they took him out for any dangers (and-) and one night (um-) a danger happened   Dracula had came alive again and he had had his teeth in again by a special dentist underground who was magic so the dragon caught him and put fire to him he never came alive again   (and-) and that's the end of the story

Story 63   (age 5: 9)

and then once St Peter was walking around *all* by hisself and looking at the pearls God had (founded-founded-when he found-) found (underneath the rocks-) underneath the clouds because there's rocks underneath the clouds (and then -and then-) and then he got (all the-all the-) all the shiny pearls and diamonds and put them on the wall and then St Peter was walking around looking at them and suddenly he got a *fright* because (God-God-) God was (was-) walking along the passageway 'Oh sorry' said God 'It's alright' said St Peter 'What you doing here?' 'I'm just looking at the diamonds and pearls on the walls' (so then-) so then he said 'Where did you get them from?' said St Peter 'Oh I got them (from some-) from some (mountains-) mountain clouds' 'Oh I thought clouds were just ordinary clouds that you could just fall through' 'Oh but sometimes I make em magic and turn into rocks and then I get all the pearls' 'Oh you greedy thing' 'Oh I'm not greedy because we need more things that's just a little one' 'It's as big as we can get it isn't it?' said St Peter (so-so-so-) so they started getting *all* the rocks to make it even bigger and getting (all the-) all the pearls to put around then they made a big big big palace (er-it could be if-if-) if the palace of Hell was built — we don't know — it'll be even higher 'n that and we touched right up to space right up to space and *then* when it was at space (um-there wasn't-) there was a tower and a window and they could see *all* the spacemen going through and one spaceman was disguising again one spaceman was disguising it was just Dracula and it came through the window and caught God (but God-) but God (um-got his hands-um-) got his *axe* [Tape ends; new cassette inserted.] and chopped his head off *then* the head came back on   Dracula was magic just like any other person St Peter said to God 'There's no way to get this evil man' 'Well the only thing we *can* do is *really* try hard to chop him up in *little tiny bits*' 'But he might come alive again' 'We'll never get him' 'We'll just have to take care of him' 'I know what-Dracula!' 'What?' 'You want to be on our side?' 'Yes I'll be pleased to' 'Right then he's our friend,' said God to St Peter 'Right then we'll take you round the palace to show you all-' 'Oh' said Dracula 'They're lovely to-[2 unclear words] Can I have one?' and God and St Peter said 'Yes you can have one or two' 'I would like two' so God whispered to St Peter ('Dracula's-) Dracula's just walking about and know what he's doing? He's looking at (the-) those lovely diamonds' 'Why shouldn't I?' [unclear word] said Dracula 'I was just talking to him to tell you what you were doing (because-because-um-I just want to tell him what you were doing-) because he wasn't looking he was just looking on the floor to see (the-) if there are any mices to chase we *should* have a cat because *I* just saw a mouse-hole' 'Oh no! We need a cat' 'Yes but I'll get him' said Dracula 'Where's my teeth?' 'Oh I don't know I think I dropped 'em when I pulled them out I dropped them Oh *I* can remember where they are' 'Where?' 'back on my throne they were under my throne' 'Oh *there* they are they're under your throne' 'Yeah thank-you (er-) I'll put them in and if I see any mouses I'll just *bite*

'em   and then they'll fall in half   'Oh great!' said God   'That's a good help   we love
you very much now'   'So do I' said Dracula   and then they made a big ring   Dracula
and St Peter and God and the servants made a big ring and danced (abou-) about
(from-from?) from six o'clock in the night-time (to-) to twelve o'clock   [*To adult*: Know
six o'clock when I come in?   *Adult*: Uhum.] well (then) then to six o'clock (to-) to
twelve o'clock they danced in a big circle   (and-and then-) and then it was bedtime
but they didn't go to bed [brief conversation with adult about tape recorder] but they
didn't go to bed because (they-) all the servants h-had a chatter to St Peter and
God   and God and St Peter had a chatter   and all the servants had a chat to
Dracula   and Dracula had a chat to St Peter (and-) and God and all the
servants   (and then-and then they-) and then (they-God-) God got the big bed out
which he had never done before   and they all slept in it   in the night they went right
(u-) under the blankets for if there was any danger   for the big dragon *he* (was-) was
(in-) in the bed somewhere   but God forgotten where he was   he was right down the
bed   God c-could f-feel his little ear with his toe   (and then-) and then God said
'Dragon! *Where's* the dragon?'   (said-) I'm getting out of here' said one of the
servants   [*Adult laughs*]   (and then-) and then they said '*Don't* get out of here   (it's a
good-it's a good-) it's a good one'   (so-so then they-) so then it crept out and said (to
the servant-) to the servant who was frightened   'I'm not a bad one   I'm a good
one'   'Oh I'm not running away   one's already run away   and all the rest has not
running away   Hey! Come back!'   so the other servant came back and said 'It's all
right   he's a good one'   and (God-) God said 'Look here servants (this one was-)
Frankenstein gave (th-) this one to us for any dangers   (and-) and Dracula wanted to
be on our side for dangers so there's two people (who will-) who will save *all* our
lives'   'Yes well once I'll tell you the life I had on earth once   once somebody *tried* to
get me   they couldn't get me   I didn't suck anybody's blood   I'm a good (Dracula-)
Dracula'   '(um-um-) we were sorry to chop your head off and all the rest of the
things'   'Oh it's alright for that'   (um-) so then he said 'Why don't we have a climb
up the mountains?   why don't we make a house in the mountains?'   'Yes'   so they
all made a house in the mountains   the mountains' rocks   and then they slept in it
with all their things   (and then-) and then they lived happily ever after   and that's
the end

Chapter 12

Closing Thoughts on Story and Education

In this chapter I want to draw together some of the threads which can potentially link children's thinking and language to the affects associated with imaginative play. For although my analyses, with their technicalities, may appear to be remote from the situation which generated the stories, yet the competences I have described emerged from casual, spontaneous play. I often wish we had another word for play, one indicating something of the intensity and effort that co-exists with the inconsequential, ephemeral nature of it. Perhaps we could talk about 'serious play' or 'play for real'. In any case we need a term that encourages us to look harder at play, especially at its verbal forms, and to value certain kinds of play as central to the curriculum in the early years. I am not suggesting that when children come to school they should just do what they like all day, as though school were another more social version of home. That would disappoint many children, who expect to be given 'work' to do, just as they know older children and adults 'work'. What I have in mind is that we ought to find ways to build into the work we do in school in the early years those properties of imaginative play described by Vygotsky – desire and self-discipline tightly bound together.

The kind of imaginative play I am describing reflects learning which has already taken place, makes visible learning which is in the process of being grappled with and generates new learning – new operations which, perhaps with the help of a teacher, will be mastered in the future. Not only does it reflect all this, but it can show us what children are like inside, how they make sense of their experience, how they make things meaningful.

Past, present and future learning can be demonstrated quite easily in the different kinds of sound (aural) play in the children's stories. I choose sound from the array of other features I could pick out simply because current research (e.g. Bradley and Bryant, 1983) tells us that phonological awareness is an important predictor of reading ability. In a climate where debates about learning to read seem to settle around 'phonics' versus 'real books', the recent work on phonological awareness could show us that the terms of this debate are wrong. To return to the stories, Sundari, for example, has already learned, from Edward Lear, how to manipulate phonemes and rhymes to create upside-down worlds and characters. Her 'nonsense' story, quoted in Chapter 4 (p. 45), is an example of Chukovsky's 'topsy-turvies'. Chukovsky (1925) tells us that it is only when children have mastered the referential conventions of language that they can feel confident enough to play about with them as Sundari does. Her nonsense story is not only a child having fun (though from her point of view that's probably all it is). It is also a reflection of what she has already learned: the rhymes, rhythms, consonant clusters, separability of phonemes and syllables from words, as well as the syntactic and semantic structures of the language she speaks. Since she sings some of her stories we can be fairly sure that Sundari's phonological awareness has come from other 'play' activities – songs, nursery rhymes, jokes and stories. If we look at her long lyrical passages in story 12 (see Chapter 10, pp. 163–7) we can see that she is in the active process of trying out new forms and patterns, for she doesn't quite manage the linguistic structures she needs to describe how her heroine manages to get the dolls to eat and drink. The articulation of new ideas brings about a struggle with linguistic form. And future developments are predicted too. Sundari's mother sent me another tape, made when Sundari was 6½ and without her being aware of it. In this monologue Sundari is apparently playing with two friends, though in reality all the very convincing voices are her own. During this solitary play, in which she sings 'Baa baa Black Sheep' and 'Sur le pont d'Avignon' Sundari produces a spontaneous poem:

> I love to see the waves where the horses go galloping they love to go in water where the ships are sailing and the boats are sailing always I'm going down to the sea where the sand is bright quickly quickly I hurry into the waving sea . . .

A few minutes later she has another try, during the same play session:

> I love to hear the wind when it makes the sea brighten going swoosh and going swoosh and going swoosh I love to hear the wind where it' s so quiet in my house I love to hear the wind going swoosh and swooshing the waves wind wind rust rustle wind wind rustles rustles on the house of the wind it messes up the things of the gardens of the gardens of the gardens it messes up the wind of the garden and that is the end of my song

Readers will recall the wind 'rustling' in story 12, told a whole year before this. Sundari's images of galloping horses, rustling and swooshing, quiet houses and the brightening sea are vivid both visually and *aurally*. In her case I do not regard the strong lyrical themes of her stories with their musical phonological patterns to be instances of the 'verse stories' that Sutton-Smith considered were the first stages of narration in young children. On the contrary, the narrative competences I have described in Sundari's texts seem several years ahead in development – exactly as Vygotsky described the potential of imaginative play. Sundari is developing styles of narration that are moving in the direction of poetry. A concern with plotting in story structure can divert us from other rich and complex forms, more experimental and subversive ones, of the kind Sundari employs. For education to build fully on Sundari's competences, her teachers would need to know what she can do, to discover her feeling for poetic and lyrical forms, to develop her talent for role-play, to sustain her interest in the creative uses of language, perhaps to encourage her to retell stories with plots, and to harness it all to her literacy. Her teacher would do this not because all these things are merely *useful* for learning to read and write, but because literacy itself is what Sundari is already doing, and developing it will take her much further in her search for narrative voices and forms which are such important metaphors for her inner and outer experience.

On the same tape, when she was 6½, though on a different occasion, Sundari does some 'pretend' reading. She has no book. Her voice, her intonation, her sentences all change dramatically. Each word is stabbed out separately and her expressive skills disappear (unless one regards this as expressive in a deliberate ironic sense). Sundari is showing how she perceives 'reading' is done through the stiff, unyielding texts of the reading scheme. It is clear that the notion of story, imaginative play, phonological patterns, rhythms and rhymes and topsy-turvies have to be abandoned in the forms of language used in the scheme Sundari is pretending to read from. It is also clear that there is a huge mismatch between the content of Sundari's stories and the way she is required to 'read' in education, for her lonely heroines on windswept beaches are replaced by bland, uninteresting children who speak in ways none of us has ever heard either in narratives or in life. If this little piece of play reading seems too anecdotal, I have a tape of Josh, made during his first year at school (when he was also telling the stories in this book), reading two books. One is a picture story-book he had heard two or three times before. There is no doubt as one listens to the tape that he is seriously looking at the words and attempting to read them. On the whole the story is read with fluency and gusto, and his miscues make sense and do not disturb the flow of the narrative. Immediately afterwards he reads a page of the scheme reader he is currently 'learning to read' with in school. We now hear a different reader, one who can't do it, who stumbles, becomes silent, shows distress and, like Sundari in her pretend reading, stabs out the words in meaningless single units. Sundari and Josh learned to read anyway, so did the other children in this book.[1] Nevertheless for many children the consequences of not starting with forms and contents that are already deeply embedded in their imaginative play must be quite serious. Reading and learning to read become a dull exercise, a useful skill required for future life rather than a vital, present pleasure and need. For some children these arduous encounters with lifeless texts will be their *only* experiences of literacy, for I am well aware that not all children come to school from the kinds of literacy practices at home that I have written about in this book.

What of these children? I am constantly asked why I did not record stories from children with no literacy in their homes before school, so that I could compare two kinds of social context for storytelling. There are several reasons why I didn't do that. When I began this study there was virtually no evidence that children were capable of using book language in their talk to the extent that these children do. Scollon and Scollon's account (1981) of their 2-year-old daughter's storytelling proposed that literacy is internalized very early indeed for some children; Gordon Wells (1981a and b), in his long-term study of 129 children in Bristol had discovered that experience of books and stories before age 5 was the only significant factor to correlate with success in school and reading at age 7; Margaret Clark (1976) had shown us that 32 children in Scotland had learned to read completely fluently before school in a context of strong parental interest in books and regular library visiting; Margaret Meek (1983) was suggesting that storybooks themselves give readers more powerful reading lessons in how literacy works than the controlled texts of many schematic approaches ever can. What I aimed to do was amplify these different kinds of evidence by supplying case studies which I hoped would show how the transformation of language from the page to the child's competences worked. I merely wished to show that it was possible to talk a written language and thereby to fill a gap in our language acquisition study.

But there were other reasons why I did not look at the stories of children from non-literate backgrounds. First of all I would have needed proper evidence of a lack of literacy in the children's homes, and I doubted that there were any convincing sources of such evidence. Professionals can make assumptions about children's home backgrounds which are not supported by real, first-hand knowledge. When ethnographic researchers looked at the narrative competences of children from families whose experiences of literacy were different from these five children's, they made some interesting discoveries. Shirley Brice Heath (1983), for example, found that the shared literacy practices of Trackton often centred on oral/ literate presentations of biblical texts, and that young children in Trackton 'come up as talkers' through the storytelling and verbal play modelled by older children, rather than through the 'motherese' of the BT studies. Mary Waterson, the author of *Gypsy Family*, collected stories from traveller children. She passed on to me some transcripts from a 6-year-old traveller child called Leila, whose stories were outstandingly communicative and well told. When I saw these and other transcripts I found that the strong oral storytelling tradition in the background of some of these children had generated competences similar in some respects to those I found in the five children of the present study. If stories are powerful, fundamental forms for the mental organization of experience, arising in development with the onset of language, memory and mental imaging, and if they are also the original forms of literature at the inception of our history, then the stories of these communities, however 'oral' their cultures, can be harnessed to literacy development, indeed, as Shirley Brice Heath argues, they make an ideal basis for it. Trackton children, or traveller children, or any others from rich oral cultures should have no problem with the literacy of good children's authors, since these authors know how to write down the oral tradition in the forms of the stories they tell, and to lead children into literacy through what they already know and can recognize. This does not mean that other factors may not play their part in the literacy learning of groups who have often been marginalized in Western societies. Teacher and school expectations, racial prejudice, ignorance of non-'mainstream' cultures, the monocultural nature of many book collections, and so on, can all get in the way of children's success in reading, not to mention all the disadvantages experienced by children who have to live in poverty. But if teachers are to be able to build on the oral cultures I have referred to then they will need to be aware of them and of the competences the children bring to school.

More worrying, perhaps, are the children who do not have rich story backgrounds, either oral or literate. Most children in countries like the UK have frequent access to TV even if there are few books available to them. TV, often scorned as the enemy of children's literacy, uses dozens of stories, especially in its presentation of soaps, cartoons, films. children's programmes and the news. We need to know more about the similarities and differences between narrative as TV/film and narrative in books; and, I believe, between shared and solitary viewing.[2] Teachers sometimes reject the stories pupils bring to school from TV or films, but, as Meek argues, TV actually helps children to 'keep the story going' and find out how narratives work (Meek, 1991, pp. 216–22). If this is the major shared story culture for many children – possibly for *all* of them, even the readers – then we ought to find ways to legitimize that culture, and let children retell, act out and write down these stories too, however 'unsuitable' or predictable some of us might think they are. After all, the stories I have presented here are hardly anodyne, and compare well to fairy-tales in terms of their powerful themes. What I am saying is that it is a complicated business to know what kinds of story culture children belong to if one is to start comparing one group to another. However, it is surely the business of school to offer rich and plentiful literature to all children; those who have little experience of books or the language of writing will soon learn it if they receive enough demonstrations from those who are the experts at engaging their interest – the authors of really well-told, meaningful stories. Most teachers are not in a position to carry out in-depth ethnographic research on the young children in their classes, even if it were desirable that they should do so. But by developing a storytelling-reading-writing-changing-acting-drawing-sharing culture at the centre of classroom activities in the early years, they will find that children themselves, through their responses to stories and their story inventions, reflect what they know and love most. Such a story-centred classroom would be an action-based ethnography in itself. I'd better be clear here, too, that I'm not saying that children will automatically become literate by being surrounded by good stories and left somehow to 'pick up' reading from them. My colleague Henrietta Dombey (1991) has argued most powerfully that reading stories requires the orchestration of several quite complex strategies; learning to read by means of well-written narratives demands as much structure in the teaching as other kinds of reading programme. What my study indicates for me, however, is that along with the other sensible strategies teachers use, stories ought to be regarded as the central resource.

I have written elsewhere (Fox, 1989a) about the kinds of knowledge that are borne along on the backs of the stories in my data. The evidence from these five children is that stories carry with them children's classificatory systems, their forms of reasoning and argument, their observations of natural and physical laws, their concepts of number, size, shape and so on, even their awareness of moral and metaphysical possibilities. The narrative literacy I have been describing could be seen as a narrow one, belonging to the world of literature with a capital L. On the contrary, I think all kinds of storying, non-literary as well as literary, involves the storyteller in the organization of knowledge structures. We need to remember James Moffett's suggestion (Moffett, 1968) that before children have the conventions of different discourses mediated to them through school subjects, narrative must 'do for all'. Until the non-narrative genres have been learned, children use story to sort out their own knowledge and ideas, for this is implicit in the effort to create storyworlds which are credible if not 'real' in the sense that we can actually see them around us.

In one of my earlier articles I argued that children use comparisons and metaphors to take the place of scientific and mathematical terminology of the sort they will encounter later. For example, when Josh wants to convey the height of a wall he says

'a very high bit of a big wall that a castle would have' (*Josh story 10 5:0*).

This is as near as one can get without mathematical terminology to a verbal picture of a height, and it draws forth complex language – the collection of noun phrases and the modal verb. Having to think through the idea of height in words is surely a good conceptual preparation for future mathematics, which will also be concerned with making comparisons of a more exact kind.

Jimmy makes another comparison when he is comparing teddies, which are small, to 'chooydas', which are medium-sized monsters, and to children, who are large:

'and the chooyda came but it was very small for us [*children*] but big for them [*teddies*]' (*Jimmy story 9 4:9*)

Here Jimmy, at under 5, shows that he is capable of judging what size might look like from somebody else's point of view. Juxtaposing children, chooydas and teddies in his story involves him in sorting out these relationships and seeing a larger perspective than his own. This surely represents a move away from the egocentric operations associated with infancy by Piaget, and is similar to the kind of thing Donaldson (1978) discovered when she recast Piaget's conservation experiments as play. She found that the fantasy context helped children to perform mental operations which had been difficult and confusing without the props of play.

I have also argued previously that children's stories, which so often contain problems and difficulties for characters to overcome, can show us the early forms of reason and argument. I proposed then that narrative might initially contain the discourses of argument until the stage when children are able to tackle problems and issues outside the narrative framework. It was suggested in response to what I wrote that argument might match narrative as a fundamental mental organizing device (Wilkinson, 1990). I certainly agree that children have, and hear, arguments and discussions from the time they first use language, yet I still feel that narrative has the primacy that Barbara Hardy claimed for it. Arguments require us to *imagine* something, another viewpoint, an alternative way of looking at things, even if only to counter that view with our own. And that is exactly what stories make us do. It isn't so much that argument is a more mature discourse which young children can know little of, as that it is something that initially needs the support of real external contexts or circumstances, or of the story structure. It is abstraction outside these sorts of context that young children, at least most of them, find so difficult. Josh has to look at things from several sides in his God and St Peter stories, and he articulates that looking in the text he utters. Narrative is deeply tied into the way we experience memory, as Suzanne Langer (1953, pp. 264–5) and Margaret Meek (1991) have pointed out. And memory in its turn means organizing things in a mental sequence so that we can hold them in our minds. Otherwise it would be impossible to impose any order on the chaotic flux of events. Organizing experience as narrative memory can mean putting things in a chronological order ('and then . . .'), or in a pattern of cause and effect, just as children start to operate with numbers by counting them forward in sequence, and later learn to turn them backwards, regroup them and find new relationships. Even the little semi-scientific explanations the children fill their stories with have this temporal sequence:

'and he tells the knight to come and catch the witch
but the knight says 'No 'cos I'm on your side and I'm on the witch's side'
'Oh so if you're on the witch's side I have to be on the witch's side 'cos I'm
on your side' (*Josh story 46 5:5*)

This may have the form of a syllogism in reasoned argument, but for Josh it is the narration of a dialogue in a sequence of turns. His enjoyment of the characters in his story helps him to place himself in this rather complicated kind of thinking. When Jimmy says

> 'once in Highbury fields we dug a hole right to the core of the earth and we saw the rocks moving' (*Jimmy story 16 4:9*)

his conception of a melted core at the centre of the earth is tied to a sequence of events in which he (metaphorically) plays a part.

Narrative does not seem to me to be opposed to scientific reasoning or argument at all. Both require mental operations which are abstract, complex and 'autonomous' or independent of an immediate context. Scientific discourses can become part of narratives of events which have little to do with the operations of reason – think of Primo Levi's use, in *The Periodic Table* (1986), of his specialist chemist's knowledge to give metaphorical representations of the experience of the holocaust. And arguments, whether in the discourses of laboratories or law courts, often have narratives embedded within them. Margaret Rader (1982) points out that it is the *functions* of these discourses which are different. (She also asks us to reconsider just how 'autonomous' non-narrative or 'essayist' discourse can ever really be.)[3] In their stories the children do not set out with the explicit intention of working on problems and finding solutions for them, as they may later be required to do in school. I think they rather want to entertain themselves by imagining this or that situation and trying out 'what if . . .' kinds of experiences, especially those that are forbidden, dangerous, excessive or impossible in everyday life. Saying things doesn't make them happen, and we can on the whole emerge unscathed from our verbal fantasies. The stories act as play because there are no consequences. And, as I argued earlier, this kind of verbal play gives us linguistic mastery, the power of the voice, the authority of the spell-binder, the freedom to be and become whatever we choose without restraint. This is the pleasure/desire axis of play that Vygotsky thought should not be intellectualized. Perhaps if we could find ways to include these very beneficial aspects of play into school work we would be less inclined to regard narrative and argument as so different from one another. Literature often includes representations that teachers might recognize as 'work' though children reading it probably start from the involvement and emotional engagement associated with hearing and telling stories. For example, a book like Michael Foreman's *War Boy* gives children an enormous amount of interesting factual information about World War II, but it includes the reader in that new knowledge by engaging him or her in a personal and communicative account of how it was acquired. In thinking about literacy and narrative, we need to look hard at our reasons for wanting knowledge systems to be so 'disembedded' from the personal experiences of the knower, and at why we should need to detach knowledge from meaningful communicative contexts or even from the aesthetic preferences of the learner. Children quickly lose the special kinds of learning that come through play when they go to school – at least the less fortunate ones do – because too often we forget to make a place for children themselves in the new knowledge systems we want them to acquire.

I was surprised to find how strongly the children's interests at age 4 or 5 persisted as they grew older. Josh's written story quoted in Chapter 8 continues some of the themes of the God and St Peter stories: is there anything beyond our material world? Can God go down to earth in an aeroplane and survive? Are there really spirits or 'presences' for the conman to exorcise? In most primary schools in the UK children pass on to new teachers every year, and it must be difficult to learn afresh what these deep interests for each child are, especially with large classes. The kind of record-keeping described in the CLPE Primary Language Record (Barrs *et al.*, 1990) creates the space for teachers to make finely-grained observations of children's language and literacy development, and promotes the detailed kind of watching that is needed if teachers are to be able to tap into children's affective and cognitive centres. The PLR also makes the space for parents to participate in that process. It shows us a way to develop learning which is not divorced from the spontaneous, enjoyable and personal aspects of children's earlier playing. It also creates a continuous 'zone of proximal development'.

There has been much discussion in recent years (e.g. Andrews, 1989) of children's acquisition of genre knowledge. Narrative has sometimes been entangled in this debate, as though it were a tightly definable genre with clear rules, like business letters or reports of laboratory experiments. Narrative suffers in the discussion by being what Rosen calls 'common coin', so universal and primary that it is apt to be regarded as something we grow out of when more powerful discourses have been mastered. But to see narrative as a genre in this sense is a mistake, for it seems more to be a generator of genres. It can certainly include almost any other genre that one cares to name. The Ahlbergs have demonstrated this for children in their picture story-book *The Jolly Postman*. Some highly academic adult genres operate very well within a narrative framework too. History, for example, another form of remembering, can encompass the most complex kinds of evidence and argument within a basic story structure, as Simon Schama showed in *Citizens*, his account of the French Revolution.[4] My analyses of the children's stories do show that within the context of free storytelling and listening they are sensitive to some quite advanced generic features of texts. This seems to imply that if we want children to learn a range of generic features in their writing they will need to have many powerful models of texts with those features, just as these five children had before they went to school. Unfortunately there are still too few information books and textbooks that are so well written that we would want to read them aloud, savour their language and notice the features of their construction. We need to continue to demand better-written factual books from the publishers. Or we could, with the help of our Junior pupils, write them ourselves to serve the purposes of our own teaching and learning.

In children's imaginative writing, however, it should be possible to make some of the techniques employed by good storytellers more explicit as children grow older. This does not mean giving lessons on analysing literary texts. On the contrary, we can accomplish it both pleasurably and rigorously through role-play, storytelling, retelling and changing stories, and by including considerations of form in the way we teach writing. Wanting children to write from their own concerns, to choose their own topics, purposes and audiences, does not mean that we ought to leave them empty of any formal knowledge. The authors of books for young children are showing us the way. We now have no end of fairy-tales written from the (feminist) princess's point of view, or from the wolf's. Children can try out being the sort of detached narrator that Sundari is, or telling their story in the first person, or in the present tense, or letting the reader know how the story ends in the first few lines, as Toni Morrison does in *Jazz*. The compilers of the National Curriculum for England and Wales

(DES/Welsh office, 1990) seem to have been singularly unimaginative in this respect, focusing on chronological sequences and logical resolutions as though there were only one way to tell a story. We really don't need to worry too much if children close their stories by going to sleep or revealing that everything was only a dream. Sundari closes her story about Cletcher at the fair with bedtime, but has learnt from a book how to make such a banal closure a narrative event in itself by *the way it is told*. Logical resolutions to stories are a late development in the history of literacy. For children, there is plenty of scope in the rest of the telling to explore the huge variety of ways of narrating fictional events. To encourage children to experiment with these ways would be to give them metanarrative knowledge. Writing a story in the first person, for example, brings a host of technical problems with it. The omniscient third-person narrator can no longer see inside the head of every character. Children can work together to solve these problems, which are as much to do with the telling as with the told. They would learn in the process that writing is crafted in terms of its form as well as in terms of its meaning – indeed that the two are indivisible.

In earlier chapters I've stressed that using the tape-recorder led the five children to imagine a distant audience, and that this in turn led to a high level of explicitness in their narrations. Since that imagined audience is required for literacy its educational significance must be considerable. Recently much importance has been given to children learning to write for 'real' audiences and 'real' purposes. It is probably very helpful for children to write 'for real', to achieve actual outcomes for their writing, and to communicate with real readers other than their teachers. But that does not mean that what these five children were doing was *un*real. Their distant, imagined audience – who could have been any fictional, unknown 'public' – is no less valid than the real infant class who will read the stories written for them by Year 6 children, or the parent who will read the carefully written letter home. Indeed, any writing involves the author to some degree in imagining the audience. We need to remember that the kind of unknown audience the five children were beginning to conceptualize is a liberating one. As an *imagined* other it licenses the children to invent it as well as themselves. Of course children need real audiences and pragmatic purposes for some writing, but they will need the imagined audience for all of it. Because they listened to themselves on the tapes after each recording these children became their own audience. I'm sure this was very valuable, and teachers could experiment with tape-recorded readings as ways of presenting children's writing both for the authors themselves and for other pupils. It is curious how difficult many children find it to put enough distance between themselves and their own texts to edit or proof-read without a lot of help. The tape-recorder can support this distancing, for it is easier to listen than to read, especially if handwriting is still in the early stages of formation.

I hope I do not sound too certain in these closing thoughts. There is still far too much we don't know about the processes I have been touching upon, and we need a lot more detailed research. We need to know more about both storytelling and role-play. We need ethnographic research that will tell us about the variety of literacy practices stories emerge from; we need linguistic research that will tell us more about what children's knowledge of different discourses actually looks like; we need more studies of play, especially imaginative and verbal play, as this is still a neglected area; also neglected has been research into children's aesthetic awareness and preferences; above all we need research by teachers to show us how children's imaginative development can best be nurtured in classrooms.

I would like to close this book as I opened it – with a story. This one was told by Justine. By now she was just over 5 and attending her reception class. She heard this story in school and it had obviously made quite an impression on her. In her story Justine shows a very clear understanding of the role of thought and intentionality in narrative, and that she knows stories really happen in our minds.

> I'll tell you a story I've been told at my school once upon a time (there were-) it was a little boy's birthday (P) (another-) a little girl went to buy his birthday present – Mummy bought him a helicopter (and then- and then-) and there was loads of toys (P) in that toyshop and she picked a helicopter then they went to the sweet-shop (and she-and-and the-) and the little girl that was three got some chocolate kittens and in the night she couldn't go to sleep because of the chocolate kittens then she just said to herself in a whisper like this (P) 'I wonder if Timothy would mind if I just got one kitten?' then she ate it all up and then there was four kittens and she could not go to sleep because she's still thinking of them 'I wonder if (Timmy-) Timothy would let me have just one more?' so she ate another one so there was two and then she could not go to sleep because there was only two left then she went to the cupboard where she had hid them (she-) and she just said 'I wonder if Timothy would just mind if I had just one more?' and there was none more left and the next day it was Timothy's birthday Mummy gave him her present Nanny gave him her present and then the little girl Suzie gave (a-the-if-) her present there was none chocolate kittens and Nanny said 'I think I know where they are in Zoe's tummy' so they all went to see and then Daddy went out of the room they saw that the (kit-) Mummy had got new-born babies (P) baby kittens they were just a furry ball (gasps) and then daddy said to the others when he had gone back in 'I've got a surprise for you my little dear and my little brother' and it was that that made them all happy and bright (*Justine story 26 5:0*)

NOTES

1. I sent a questionnaire to each of the five children's schools when they were age 7. I was actually interested in discovering whether the children's storytelling ability had been noticed in school, but I embedded those questions in others which were to do with their progress in reading and writing. In fact all five children at age 7 were judged by their teachers to be well ahead of their chronological age in reading.
2. Muriel Robinson at the University of Brighton is currently writing a doctoral thesis on this topic. See Robinson (1992).
3. *Rader M* (1982) Ibid See pp. 194–7 where Rader suggests that all language, including scientific prose, contains 'nuances' and 'signs of personal involvement'.
4. See also Schama's article 'A Room with a view', (Guardian, review section, 26 September 1991), in which he urges educationalists not to forget the power of narrative to draw pupils into historical discourses.

Appendix A

Transcripts of Josh's Retellings of *Hansel and Gretel*

Story 29   Based on Walt Disney recording with Humperdink's music
Date: 9-11-80   Age: 5:1

once upon a time there were two fireworks boxes who had faces   they lived in a big
big tree among branches   and there was (a-) some children in the forest by the name
of Hansel and Gretel   and this little cottage was the house of Hansel and Gretel   now
they weren't (a-) of a very rich family   (Da-) Dad gets up early in the morning and
starts his long walk to the village where he sells brooms   the mother does some of
the chores around the house   and Hansel and Gretel have their jobs to- but children
would much rather like to play   but they make brooms (P) and do the chores   (till
they were) and they were playing   and when the mother saw them playing (um-um-)
and laughing she was furious   (till-) till she accidentally knocked over the kitcher of
milk and- [*Adult*: The pitcher of milk? Pitcher?] mmm   (and she-and sh-) and then she
sent the children out in the forest till they had picked two baskets of
strawberries   when their Dad learnt (u-um-what-) they were deep in the forest he
scolded his wife   (a-) and he said that they in danger of the wicked old witch in the
forest   (er-) their parents ran from the house in search of their children   (and she-
um-) they were deep in the forest   (and-) and it was getting dark   'I can't find a
path'   'What about the bread er-crumbs you dropped to mark the path?'   'Well that
wasn't very clever'   'Why?'   '(Be) Because the birds ate them all'   'Then we are lost'
(P)   [Referring to the gramophone record] um- that's the other side   now I'm going to
do this side   as morning approached the little dewer man spread his dewdrops to
meet the day   'I'd better find a path home' said Hansel   'Oh look Gretel a house
made of sweets'   'Shall we go near?'   'I don't think so we'd never-[unclear
word]'   'Come on here's some sweets for you'   'Ahahaha   nibble nibble little
mousey   who's eating my little housey? [spoken in cackley voice]   'Who is that?'   'I
don't know'   'We'd better go'   'Oh why- [unclear word] — who has made this for
us?'   'I don't know'   'Ahahaha (little -er-) Nibble nibble little (er-) mousey   who is
eating my little housey?'   she quietly slipped around Hansel and tied the rope
around   'Ahahaha'   'Get off me'   'Who are you?'   'You leave my brother alone'   'Now
now is that any way to talk to a friend?'   'A friend doesn't tie someone up with a
rope'   'I'm just getting you ready for (a-) a big supper Ahahaha'   '(the-) a step and
you'll become a tree'   'Izzard gizzard – a step and you won't feel so well'   'I'll put
her in and she'll be done for tea' (P)   just then she quietly slipped around Hansel and
put him in a cage   'Let me out of here'   'You leave my brother alone'   'Who are you

you stupid crow?' 'Just put your head in like this' 'Push her' 'We see we see [or 'we're free we're free—not clear] the wicked witch is dead' 'Think this we must be gingerbread children' (um-) soon their Dad has come to collect them (and they-) when they saw Hansel and Gretel safe they danced a circle round them and they got all the sweets from the old witch's house and they walked down the forest and that's the end

Story 32   Based on Amabel Williams-Ellis version
Date: 11-11-80 (only 2 days after Version 1)   Age: 5:1

once upon a time there was a man who cut down trees (P) (and-and he-and-) and he had (P) two children but the boy was called Hansel and (the-) the girl was called Gretel and their stepmother would go out to the forest (and they each-and they each-) and they each ate their little breads when dinner-time came and then they went to sleep (and-) and he slipped out -a-side and he saw newly coined silver money in the house and he put (any-) lots into his pocket as it could hold and then he put his coat on and holded his sister's hand (and they-and they-) and they got some breadcrumbs by the way (and-and they dropped-) and they dropped them and when they came out there was no breadcrumbs thousands of birds lived in the forest and they picked them up and eat them and then (and we-and-) they *were* lost indeed till they saw the prettiest bird they have never seen and it had [unclear word] (on the-) on the roof of the cottage well a cottage what a cottage windows chimneys walls are made of bread (or br-) or cake (a-) and the windows were made of sheets (of-) of dry clean sugar the roof was made of cake and they each broke their li- as they ate they heard a 'tip-tap tip-tap who raps my door?' and (the-) the door suddenly opened and a old lady came out walking with two sticks they were so frightened that they turned round at what they had in their hands 'Come in [unclear word] dear children' and they came in (and-and-) and the witch grumbled 'they need fattening' when they were asleep they had pancakes and sugar and (e-) eggs and wine on the table and they ate it when they could eat no more they slept on a little bed and then (and-) when it was the night the witch carried Hansel out of his bed and put it into a cage (Han-) poor Hansel shouted but it was no use and (she picked the sis-) she shaked Gretel till she woke and she said in a loud in a grumbling voice 'I'm going to get that boy (to-when he-) till he's fat and when he's fat I'm gonna eat him' (so-) so she had to (coo-) kill cook her and eat them 'And first we will bake' the witch cried (They need-) 'They need fattening' and she called in a grumbling voice 'Gretel let me feel that your hands are getting fat' (and-) and then she did she pulled out a bone (and she-) and in dismay she thought it was his finger [*Adult*: In dismay?] so then 'First we can bake however' what she really meant was push (Han-) Hansel and Gretel in the oven as well as Hansel (but-) but 'Put your head in just like me I can even get in myself' so she got in Gretel pushed—gave a big push and she pushed the door (on-) on the witch and (she-) she bolted the door and the witch was locked the witch grumbled but she took no notice and she ran to the cage 'The witch is in the oven' (so-) so they saw some stones and precious jewels and they took them home (but they-) but of their stepmother she had died but (the-) for a hour they came to a river there was no bridge or boat or stile a (b-) beautiful duck came by (and she- and sh-) Gretel said 'There's no stile or bridge Hansel and Gretel here we stand kindly take us on your back to land' so the good little duck did and they saw something that they really knew and it was their father's cottage so they ran and bursted (in-) into the house they fell on their father's neck and that's the end

Story 34   Based on both Walt Disney and Williams-Ellis
Date; 15-11-80 (four days after story 32)   Age: 5:1

once upon a time (um-um) Hansel and Gretel were safe at their cottage   but they
knew that there was a little house covered with sweets in the wood that had a big
pine trees with wooden faces   now they knew that that was the house of a very bad
woman   she was the wicked old witch   (now-) now Hansel and Gretel were not of a
very rich family   and it's (and-) very hard for them to have four meals a day   like
everybody must do their chores   father gets up early in the morning and starts his
stupid walk to the village where he sells poohs   (and-and Hans-) and the mother
does all the (ch-) poohs around the house   and Hansel and Gretel have to do their
poohs   (now Han-now Hansel-) [*Adult*: Could you tell it properly please?] and now
Hansel and Gretel were in the woods   (but their-) but their stepmother had died   but
do you know wh-   (so they passed the-) till they passed a wicked witch cottage
(and they-) and they knocked on the door   and they've ran behind to hide (till-) till
they heard a tip-tap coming round the corner   and in [unclear word] the wicked witch
had got them into her power   she had to kill cook and eat them   [*Adult*: Kill what
and eat them?] (kill-kill-) Oh I've already done it [*Adult*: Sorry, kill, cook and eat them.
Yes, sorry.] (and- and now-) and now (um-sh-) she said 'creep inside'   'How can
I?'   'You silly fool I can get in myself' [witch's voice]   and so she got in herself   (but
-er-and-) Gretel matched a light   she put (i-) the light in the oven   (and she locked-)
and she pushed the door (open-um-) shut   and she bolted it   and how horrible the
witch grumbled   but she didn't wait to listen   she just went to the cage and
said 'Hansel we are saved   the wicked witch (is on-) is in the oven'   (so-) so when
his cage opened he spread his arms out like a bird   and they walked home till (they-)
after fifteen minutes they came to a large piece of river   'How can we both get over?'
Hansel said till (a beau-) a beautiful duck (um) came what they have never
seen   (and- and Hansel and Gretel) and Gretel said 'Good little duck little
duck (Hans-) Gretel and Hansel here we stand   there is no stile nor bridge   take us
to land on your back'   Hansel got on her back and told his sister to come on the
back   (and-) and (no-) Gretel said 'It's too many for the good little duck'   (so they-) so
they're safely on the other side   and then there's something that they really
knew   (and-) and they saw it was a big house   and it was their father's cottage   so
they ran and ran and burst (into-) into his arms   they fell on their father's neck   now
can I hear it?

Story 44   Based on the Williams-Ellis version
Date: 19-2-81 (3 months after story 34)   Age: 5:5

Hansel and Gretel lived with a woodcutter   and they were very (P) very poor   one
day (the-um-he—the-) the woodcutter was riding out on a horse with Hansel and
Gretel   (and-and suddenly-) and suddenly (they-um-) their wife died   and they had to
get a new one and married her   but as she became her wife she got much more
wicked and didn't like the woodcutter (and-) for being her wife   now one day (they-)
Hansel and Gretel walked out in the forest (with-) with some bread   (and-) and as
they went Hansel picked up (some-) some white pebbles which (it-) they
remembered   then (the-) they left them there   (and- and-) and then they went   no-
and now they were left all alone   but Hansel said 'I can get back with these stones'
he dropped each one   (and they-) and it glittered in-the moonlight   and then they
found their way home   and their father was so delighted   this time they left him
there   and the children walked on (until -first-) until they saw a house (made-) made of
gingerbread   and they started to eat some of it (and suddenly-) until they heard a tip-
tap tip-tap 'Who's that knocking on my door?'   and then the door of the cottage
opened   (a-) and (it's-) Hansel and Gretel were very frightened   (er-) they had to drop

their pieces of cake before the witch came out   and (er-er-) then the witch said 'What has brought you here my dear children?   Come in and rest yourselfs down'   (and the-) and then who was very pretending in being very kind (who was-) who put Hansel off to bed   (she was-) she cackled to herself   (she was no mo-) she was no mother but (a wicked-) a wickedest witch in the forest   this witch was the worst   (and-) and do you know what?   she said ('Crawl into the-) 'Put your head into the oven (so-) so we can put the bread in'   and (but Han-) Gretel said 'It's too big'   so 'You silly thing I can even put my head in myself'   so she put her own head in   and Gretel gave her a hard push   and in the witch went head-long   and then they got some jewels from the witch's house and some money   (a-) and they went home   (a-) about halfway through the forest they found a lake   but there was no bridge or boat so they had to-   (they-) there was a little goose there   and then she sailed them across   (and-) and they came back   (a-and their-) and the old stepmother had died   and their father was so delighted and (um-) gave them some more money ('cos-) 'cos they gave him some   and then they were richest people (in-) in England   and that's the end   and there's no wicked witch in the forest again

Appendix B

Robert's Retelling of *The Three Little Pigs* (Galdone version)

Adult: Once upon a time . . . Off you go then.
Child: once upon a time there was three little pigs and they hadn't had any money
to go (but-but the-) [to adult] What's that?   *Adult*: That's a bundle really, isn't it?]
Child: (it had) the children had some money (but-) but (um-) they had some
sandwiches as well (and-) and (today-um-) yesterday (he-um-) the blue one (well-um)
to make the house with straw and the wolf came knock knock 'Please can I come
in?' 'No no you can't (for-) for my little chin chin chin'
[*Adult*: What else did he say?]
Child: (um-) 'I'll huff and I'll blow your house in' so he ate (the pig up- the sec-) the
first pig up
[*Adult*: That's the first pig with the house of?]
Child: Straw.
[*Adult*: Straw, yes.]
Child: (um-um-um) the coloured blue one the dark one build the house with sticks
and the wolf came 'Please can I come in?' 'No no you can't come in hair of my
chin chin chin' 'I'll huff and I'll puff and I'll blow your house in' and he huffed and
he puffed and he blowed the house in and he ate the second pig up and then
(um-um-the-) the green one met a (li-) man and was a packet of bricks and he
maked (the-) the house very good and 'Please can I come in?'   'No no you can't
cos my hair of my chin chin chin' 'I'll huff and I'll puff and I'll *blow* your house
in' and he huffed and he (puffed-) puffed he couldn't blow him (um-) he didn't
blow any more he stopped blowing (and 'do you-) 'and do you want to come home
with the farm?' 'When you going to get me?'   'at half past s-seven' he came at half
past two and (he-he-he-) he went with 'Are you ready pig?' 'No I'm not' (um-um-
um-) 'and I'll throw one down there (throw the apple-)
[*Adult*: What's happening?]
Child: he threwed the apple down to him   (and-) and (um-) in the little field there's a
little (P) fair and 'Do you want to come to it?' 'Yes I do' and he rolled down into a
barrel 'I brought a barrel' and it's a round thing and then he was just going to fall
down the chimney and he falled down the chimney (and-) and he ate him up for
supper then he (was-) was a big boy now and now then that's the end of the
story can-can we hear it?
Robert story 20 4:0

Appendix C

Josh's Pre-sleep Monologue

there were castles a long time ago   (er − th'were − th'were-) there were all sorts of castles   (er-er-er-) (P) and the soldiers (P) came on big boats and pulled London Bridge down   (and-) and the soldiers shot arrows from London (Bridge-) Bridge   and (er-) some of them got shot (P)   some fell into the water   some (er-we-) were falling over (P)   they could fall into the water   but they were all right (P)   so they went (er-) back across [unclear words here] (PP)   once upon a time there were two men   they were walking in the street behind the police station   and (they-) they were (I-) looking through the window if they saw anyone   but they still didn't   they had a look   but look   all that was there were three police cars standing in a row   there were robbers in a house   and the robbers [unclear word] (P)   they let them out for [unclear word]   (and they got-) Bill was a bakery   and Betty sold her house for [b] enevolent fund for the police (PP)   and he went   when it was over they had a look   and it was a very nice sunny day   first they waited cos it was a little bit rainy   but it came stormier and stormier   and the boat got flooded (P)   and (all the-) all the houses were flooded   nothing was left   but the three dwarfs were arriving home   when they came home their darling Snow White was lying on the ground   well she was lying on the ground   she couldn't move once (PP)   (but then-) [sings] de-de-dee-de-da-de-de-de-dee   (it looks-) dwarfs (don't bur-) don't bury her here in that horrible ground   I don't like that   so they buried her in a little safe   (they-they-put-) they made a little glass cone   and they put her in there   and they set her there   when Prince Charming came to have a look he said 'Oh they've carried it   Can I have it?   and they said 'Yes'   (and he saw-) and they saw her name wrote in golden letters   (and-) and Snow White was (lying-er-) going to sleep   when she awoke (they took-) they were married   (and-) and they went back   and they loved it   but till they loved it   and they loved it   and that's the end
Josh story 26 5:0

Appendix D

Josh's Poem and Verses

N.B: 'Poems' was Josh's term.

i

what does the custard and the moon look like? red stars   what does cake and
custard look like? (l-l-) it looks like (er-) a sunshine rising too early in the
morning (what is-) what is the moon like and the stars? they are like lovely king's
hair and lovely green custard what is (the-the cake -I mean-) the stars like? lovely
cake mixed up with lovely cream and that's the end
Story 41 5:5

ii

the rocks and shore scatter upon the lighthouses some days storm breaks up
ships and buildings get shipwreck under the water (sh-) pirate shipwreck has
become the treasure under the sea   unless the lighthouses could be falling
over and that's the end
Story 42 5:5

iii

the sharks catch the fish and the white things in the sea get harder and spikey and
the little fish have no hiding places from the sharks cos the sharks can easily get
through under the rocks because with their terrible claws (a-and-) and their terrible
tusks they can push the stone away with their forehead and the fishes can be saved
somehow but I don't know and the sharks still can get and the lighthouses can
blow up easily even if it's a stormy day now if it rains another day it will be good for
the sharks and the fishes cos they'll have lots of water and that's the end
Adult: Was it a poem or a story?
Child: A poem.
Story 43 5:5

iv

the snowdrifts come and (it-) the snowdrifts (come off-) come up   they are really
winter flies you know (P) at the daytime (P) (they-) they open their pebbles
wide (and when it's-) and when it's night (and-and-) and rains (th-) they close their
pebbles very tight
Adult: Petals?

Child: Yes but (those) they are snowflakes that drift up like that are there any in (y-) this country?
Adult: Is that the end of it?
Child: Yes. Can I listen?
Story 45 5:5

N.B: Between 43 and 45 comes story 44, a long retelling of *Hansel and Gretel* (for transcript see pp. 202–3).

v

the shores and the lighthouses could been blown away rescue helicopters are up in the sky every night the seasick comes   (and the sea-and the sea-) and the boats get wrecked and that's the end
Adult: Was that a poem or a story?
Child: A poem.
Story 51 5:5

vi

rainbow rainbow in the cloud nearly lovely to climb above   rainbow rainbow in the sky nearly lovely to sit above   rainbow rainbow in the sky it's very lovely looking to me   rainbow (ra-) rainbow in the sky lovely better to put a house on the rainbow I love you I love you I love you I love you and God
Child: Do you like that?
Adult: Is it the end?
Child: Yes.
Adult: Thank you.
Story 74 6:1

vii

sea rocks sea rocks on the shore (P) light ones dark ones on the shore   when the waves came (up-) up to spray (P) those little shells ran a-way [laughs]
Adult: Any more?
Child: Yes, another one.
lighthouse lighthouse flashing there   when the waves came out to share [laughs] by the little (light-) lighthouse swings away
Story 76 6:1

viii

Adult: Is this a nonsense poem?
Child: Yeah. They're nonsense poems. Can I do another one 'cos I like them.
Adult: Go on then.
Child: All about sea.

dolphin dolphin went to colph when he had colphed he called a dolph [laughs] and when he had called that ugly dolph [laughs] he went to Bingo and did a pump
N.B: 'Pump' is a dialect term in northeast England for breaking wind.
Story 77 6:1

ix

mummy mummy did a dummy [laughs] when she had done that ugly dummy mummy did a canny pummy when (he-) she had done that canny mummy mummy went to the shops and then when she was at the shops she got herself (for the- the tonight-)

for the tonight's meal
oh no it was a poem
mummy mummy coming out mummy mummy mummy
Story 79 6:1

x

> *Child*: I'll do a seashore one.
> *Adult*: Maybe not a silly one?
> *Child*: A seashore one and it will be silly.
>
> wave wave go away   go back to your girl-friend   wavey wavey stop at the
> seashore   say hello to the waving lighthouse   waves waves wave good-bye   waves
> waves pull mummy's skirt up   waves waves they are crazy   waves waves never go
> near them
> *Story 79 6:1*

This session was becoming more and more hilarious and Josh becoming more rude and daring.
I did protest and could have stopped the session, but Josh was enjoying himself enormously.
Had I switched off the tape-recorder, I should have missed the news and weather imitations
that immediately followed these nonsense verses.

xi

> peckish peckish [laughs]   mummy did a deckish   when she did this awful
> deckish   mummy did a lovely sneckish [laughs]   after she'd done this lovely
> sneckish   she ate the whole of Manor Park up   after she had ate this Manor Park up
> she was fat as Newcastle General Hospital   when she had ate this Newcastle
> General she was *fat* as the (P) Palace Pier [laughs]   she went back home   she did a
> pome   after she did that horrible pome she pumped her knickers out [laughs]
> *Story 80 6:1*

xii

> [laughter] I'll do another two.
> (seashore seash-) seashells seashells on the seashore   kissed the waves and waved
> good-bye   after they had had a marry at St General's Church they ran away and say
> good-bye   when they had done that (they-) the lighthouse pumped   it pumped
> all over mummy's skirt   mummy's skirt was full of pooh   she did a pooh herself
> [laughs]
> *Story 81 6:1*

xiii

> *Child*: I'll do another one.
> *Adult*: No, it's too rude. It's getting too rude.
> *Child*: No, no, a different one. This'll be *really* rude but it's the last one.
> *Adult*: Do you think we ought to tape it if it's going to be really rude?
> *Child*: Yeah.
> *Adult*: No one will want to listen to one that's as rude as that.
> *Child*: Can I listen to it when I do it?
> peckish peckish peckish [laughs] mummy does a deckish   when she does this awful
> deckish (mummy-) daddy does a awful wee-wee [laughs]
> *Adult*: Oh, no, they're getting very silly now.

Child: Please, please, can I do one?
and when daddy did that awful wee-wee [laughs] mummy did a pee-pee
[laughs]   when they went to the be-e-each   all the seashells and all the te-e-ach
[laughs] all of them were full of pee and peckish and peckish and yuk and puk and
yuk   and when that lighthouse bent over to smell one   it burst its kell one   and fell
one down
Adult: Very nonsense, very rude, and very crazy. Have you 'finished now?
Child: peckish peckish   mummy did a deckish   when she'd done this awful
deckish   she pumped up her knickers   and did a pickers up her nose
Story 82 6:1

Verses vi to xiii were immediately followed in the same recording session by stories
83 to 86 – the news broadcasts/and weather forecasts given in Appendix F.

Appendix E

Josh : News Broadcasts and Weather Forecasts

i

Josh starts by singing some introductory music for BBC TV News.
Child: You do the introduction.
Adult: The introduction? er — This is the six o'clock news for Tuesday March 10th, 1981. Here is Josh, your newsreader.
Child: there's been a crash [sighs] at Newcastle Polytechnic two people were (in-) injured in the crash (and-) and some more people were injured (it was a-) it was some people driving in a car (and they were-and the-and the-) on a snowy day and the car (was-) had all snow on the window thing (a-and-er-) and the wipers were broken down and then they crashed (a-and-and-) and they were injured the Prime Minister says (er-) Mr Michael Foot has presented Mrs Thatcher (er-er-) to go to Ireland for her produce [pronounced as in 'producer'] (and-) and here we go back to Carol Fox
Adult: Thank you, Josh.
Child: there'll be some snow on (er-) dry things (across the Ir-) across the North of Scotland (P) and there'll be some more rain and cloud in the West of Greenland [laughs] and it'll be some more (s-) sun and rain in the West of Scotland and that's the end
Story 49 5:5

The following 'broadcasts' come after a gap of eight months.

ii

on the news last night (one of-) at Belfast a big pooh-pooh was dropped from nonsenseland to conscienceland at that conscienceland Mr Reagan came out (with some-with some-) with a chimney for a nose and some daggers for a toes and really peculiar pet dragon nose
Adult: All right. Are you going to do the news properly?
Child: Yeah. [sings snatches of BBC TV News introductory music]
[spoken in a twangy nasal voice, as if Mr Punch or a ventriloquist's doll] this is the one o'clock news at Belfast there's a bomb dropped one of the men (P) were half injured one of the men were half kunjeoned
Adult: No, not nonsense.
this is the one o'clock news this morning again there's a bomb dropped at Belfast twenty-five people were killed and this week police are searching for Bobby

Sands he-e-e's the one that did it [Mr Punch voice]
Adult: I — don't — it's a silly voice.
and Bobby Sands they're looking for him because he-e-e's the one who did it [Mr
Punch voice] right then and then another killer happened here right then it's the
news time sports news [sings snatches of sports news tune] Fulham won Newcastle
yesterday and the other day (Ful-) Newcastle won Newcastle and then after that
Fulham (gave-) gave really big cheer and jumped out of their seats and ran to the
policeman and killed them all around him and that's the end [sings snatches of news
tune] back to the one o'clock news [sighs]   (at Belfast-) [Josh now resumes his
normal voice] oh no at Finchale Hall there's been a break-in the person who did it is
Mr Kiddit Mr Kiddit is a really crazy man he lives on number two Benton Road I
knocked on his door once and there he was right there   and he came to a old
lady's house and she was found dead in the bath because that little (P) person who
smashed into Finchale Hall got her and that's the end of the evening news back to
the sports news and the racing with the horse of course one of the races won the
course
Adult: How about the weather forecast?
it'll be sunny (at-) on the mouth of Newcastle it'll be *very* rainy on the nose of
Newcastle [laughs] and it'll be *very* nice and silly on the head of Newcastle and it'll
be very (P) wet on the tinkle of Newcastle [laughs] and it will be *lovely* and *warm* in
the *South* of the *ear* [laughs] and it will be very nice and smudgey and soft and
warm [laughs] (in the-) in the West bum [laughs] it will be very nice and warm (at-)
(P) in the mouth of Newcastle now it's the weathical forecast of London at London
it was raining and poor old Joshua was walking down the street surrounded with
rain and after that we go back to the one o'clock news [Josh now uses a 'posh'
plummy voice] [sings snatches of news tune] somewhere in Australia a hundred
bargains has been cut off by Thatcher Mr Whitelaw required in the Commons today
and said 'I beg this [*very* plummy voice here] we have lost hundreds of pounds and
I don't like this' [laughs] and that's the end of the one o'clock news goodbye [sings
snatches of news theme]
Story 83 6:1

iii

today in parliament Mr Whitelaw has been sitting on the roof of Big Ben (and-)
[laughs] and eating some chocolate biscuits (and at-and this is true — he did do it-)
and when he was sitting there this little monster came and pulled the Big Ben
off (no-I'll do-that's a silly one-) Mr Whitelaw said that all the rates of Thatcher's
money must be taken to Carol Fox she must have the most money in the
world everybody in London agrees that Carol Fox must have *all* the money in
London and that's the end of the (ess-)
Westminster news   (good-) bye-bye
Story 84 6:1

iv

in Australia there has been a failure in Australia it's been very rainy on the nose of
Australia it's been very nice and warm and people have been chattering all over
things at (th-Ea-) the South and West ear of (P) Australia there's been lots of
rain [nasal voice again] and (on-) on the nose of Australia there's been lots of snots
dripping down rain and on the tinkle of Australia it's (b-) been very nice and
warm (on the bum of Australia-) on the West bum of Australia it has been *very* rainy
and cloudy at London it was (l-) lovely and warm at Newcastle incidentally the (trem-
the trem-tremp -temp-) temperature has gone up to (sixty-) sixty degrees *now* in
Greece it's really hot so mind out that's the end of the weather forecast   [sings
snatch of tune]
Story 85 6:1

vi   (*train guard's announcement*)

the buffet car will be open at two o'clock in the morning   (and-) and *all* the ladies on this train (must- must be-do-) must beware because they are going to do a pooh any minute
Adult: [in protest] Oh!
Child: So are you in a minute.
Adult: That's silly.
Child: I'll do another one.
Adult: No, you've had enough now.
Child: I'll do a one.
Adult: No, really.
well we'll be arriving at Newcastle in a minute   up there passengers can change for Durham Newcastle London *and* (P) South Pole and North Pole [laughs]   and that's the end that we are arriving at Newcastle-upon-Tyne   and don't leave your passenger stuff whatever it is
Story 86 6:1

I have included the train guard's announcement with Josh's newsreadings because it seems closer to that kind of formal discourse than to any other kind in the story monologues.

Bibliography 1

Children's Books

The following list contains books referred to or transformed in the children's stories, or referred to in this text.

Jean and Gareth Adamson (1977) *Topsy and Tim Go Camping*. London: Blackie.

Jean and Gareth Adamson (1982) *Topsy and Tim Go Hospital*. London: Blackie.

Allan and Janet Ahlberg (1977) *Burglar Bill*. London: Heinemann.

Allan and Janet Ahlberg (1986) *The Jolly Postman*. London: Heinemann.

Joan Aitken (1975) *A Necklace of Raindrops*. Harmondsworth: Penguin.

Hans Christian Andersen (1979) *The Snow Queen*, trans. by Naomi Lewis. London: Kestrel.

Edward Ardizzone (1956) *Tim All Alone*. Oxford: Oxford University Press.

Kathleen Arnott (1962) *Ferreyal and Debbo-Engal the witch*. In K. Arnott (ed.), *African Myths and Legends*. Oxford: Oxford University Press.

L. Frank Baum (1900) *The Wizard of Oz*. Chicago: Rand McNally.

L. Frank Baum (1904) *The Land of Oz*. Chicago: Rand McNally.

J. Becker and B. Cooney (1975) *Seven Little Rabbits*. London: Abelard.

John Burningham (1979) *Mr Gumpy's Outing*. London: Jonathan Cape.

John Burningham (1977) *Come Away from the Water Shirley*. London: Jonathan Cape.

Eric Carle (1970) *The Very Hungry Caterpillar*. London: Hamish Hamilton.

P. Donnison (1977) *More Stories of William the Dragon*. London: Piccolo/Pan.

Z. Edwards (1977) *Jack and the Beanstalk*. New York: Prestige Books.

Michal Foreman (1989) *War Boy*. London: Pavilion Books.

Paul Galdone (1971) *The Three Little Pigs*. London: Pan.

John Goodhall (1975) *Creepy Castle*. London: Macmillan.

John Goodhall (1977) *The Surprise Picnic*. London: Macmillan.

Kathleen Hale (1972) *Orlando Buys a Farm*. London: Jonathan Cape.

Gail Haley (1979) *The Green Man*. London: Bodley Head.

Dr H. Hoffman (1903) *Strewelpeter*. London: Blackie (Piccolo/Pan, 1972).

Randall Jarrell (1972) *Snow White and the Seven Dwarfs*. London: Kestrel.

T.B. Jensen (1975) *What Tina Can Do*. London: Dent.

P. Krasilovsky (1958) *The Cow who Fell into the Canal*. London: World's Work.

P. Krasilovsky (1971) *The Shy Little Girl*. London: World's Work.

Walter Kreye (1973) *The Poor Farmer and the Robber Knights*. Harmondsworth: Penguin.

Edward Lear (1969 ed.) *The Quangle-Wangle's Hat*. London: Heinemann.

Edward Lear (1973 ed.) *The Owl and the Pussycat*. London: Collins.

C.S. Lewis (1950) *The Lion, the Witch and the Wardrobe*. London: Geoffrey Bles (Fontana, 1980).

Robert Lopshire (1966) *Put Me in the Zoo*. London: Collins.

Colin McNaughton (1980) *The Rat Race*. Harmondsworth: Penguin.

Spike Milligan (1973) *Bad Jelly the Witch*. London: Michael Joseph.

Helen Nicholl (1975) *Meg's Eggs*. Harmondsworth: Penguin.

S. Oram (1972) *Castles*. London: MacDonald.

S. Oram (1972) *Vikings*. London: MacDonald.

A.I. Perkins (1970) *King Midas and the Golden Touch*. London: Collins.

Beatrix Potter (1902) *The Tale of Peter Rabbit*. London: Frederick Warne.

Eve Rice (1977) *Sam Who Never Forgets*. Harmondsworth: Penguin.

Gerald Rose (1977) *Ironhead*. London: Faber & Faber.

Maurice Sendak (1970) *Where the Wild Things Are*. Harmondsworth: Penguin.

Maurice Sendak (1971) *In the Night Kitchen*. London: Bodley Head.

Ian Serraillier (1965) *The Way of Danger, The Gorgon's Head*. London: Heinemann.

M. Thaler (1976) *How Far Does a Rubber Band Stretch?* London: Collins.

Alison Uttley (1929) *The Story of Fuzzypeg the Hedgehog*. London: Heinemann.

Amabel Williams-Ellis (ed.) (1959) *Grimm's Fairy Tales*. London: Blackie.

K. Wright and E. Browne (1978) *Arthur's Uncle*. London: Methuen.

References

Abrahams, R. D. (1972a) The training of the man of words in talking sweet. *Language in Society* **1** (1), 15–30.

Abrahams, R. D. (1972b) Joking: the training of the man of words in talking broad. In T. Kochman (ed.), *Rappin' and Stylin' Out*. Chicago: University of Illinois Press.

Abrams, D. M. and Sutton-Smith, B. (1977) The development of the trickster in children's narratives. *Journal of American Folklore* **355**,

Albert, E. M. (1972) Culture patterning of speech behaviour in Burundi. In D. Hymes and J. J. Gumperz (eds), *Directions in Sociolinguistics: The Ethnography of Communication*. New York: Holt, Rinehart & Winston.

Ames, L. B. (1966) Children's stories. *Genetic Psychology Monographs* **7**, 337–96.

Applebee, A. (1978) *The Child's Concept of Story*. Chicago: University of Chicago Press.

Applebee, A. (1980) Children's narratives: new directions. *The Reading Teacher* **34** (2), 137–42.

Barrs, M. *et al.* (eds) (1990) *Primary Language Record Handbook* and *Patterns of Learning: The Primary Language Record And The National Curriculum*. London: Centre for Language in Primary Education (CLPE).

Barthes, R. (1957, trans. 1973) *Mythologies*. New York: Hill & Wang.

Barthes, R. (1964, trans. 1967) *Elements of Semiology*. London: Jonathan Cape.

Barthes, R. (1966, trans. 1977) *Image, Music, Text*. London: Fontana/Collins.

Barthes, R. (1970, trans. 1974) *S/Z: An Essay*. New York: Hill & Wang.

Barthes, R. (1971) Style and its image. In S. Chatman (ed.), *Literary Style: A Symposium*. New York: Oxford University Press.

Barthes, R. (1973, trans. 1976) *The Pleasure of the Text*. London: Jonathan Cape.

Barthes, R. (1979) *A Lover's Discourse*. London: Jonathan Cape.

Bartlett, F. C. (1932) *Remembering*. London: Cambridge University Press.

Bennett, R. (1980) Proficiency in storytelling. In *Proceedings of the Sixth Annual Meeting of the Berkeley Linguistics Society*, pp 120–32. Berkeley, CA: Berkeley Linguistics Society.

Bettelheim, B. (1976) *The Uses of Enchantment*. London: Thames & Hudson.

Bettelheim, B. and Zelan, K. (1982) *On Learning To Read*. London: Thames & Hudson.

Beveridge, M. (ed.) (1982) *Children Thinking through Language*. London: Edward Arnold.

Black, J. B. and Bower, G. H. (1980) Story Understanding as problem solving. *Poetics* **9** (1), 223–50.

Bower, G. H. (1976) Experiments on story understanding and recall. *Quarterly Journal Of Experimental Psychology* **28**, 511–34.

Bowles, P. (1955) *The Spider's House*. London: Abacus.

Bradley, L. and Bryant, P. (1983) Categorizing sounds and learning to read: a causal connection. *Nature* **301**, 419–21.

Bradley, L. and Bryant, P. (1984) Awareness of sounds and reading. In *Children's Reading Problems*. Oxford: Basil Blackwell.

Bricker, V.R. (1976) Some Zinacanteco joking strategies. In B. Kirschenblatt-Gimblett (ed.), *Speech Play*. Philadelphia: University of Pennsylvania Press.

Brown, H. Rap (1972) Street talk. In T. Kochman (ed.), *Rappin' and Stylin' Out*. Chicago: University of Illinois Press.

Brown, R. (1977) The place of baby talk in the world of language. In C.E. Snow and C.A. Ferguson (eds), *Talking to Children: Language Input and Acquisition*. Cambridge: Cambridge University Press.

Chomsky, N. (1957) *Syntactic Structures*. Cambridge, Mass.: MIT Press.

Chomsky, N. (1965) *Aspects of the Theory of Syntax*. Cambridge, Mass.: MIT Press.

Chomsky, N. (1968) *Language and Mind*. New York: Harcourt, Brace & World.

Clark, M. (1976) *Young Fluent Readers: What Can They Teach Us?* London: Heinemann.

Chukovsky, K. (1925, trans. 1963) *From Two to Five*. Berkeley and Los Angeles: University of California Press.

Clark, E.V. (1982) The young word maker: a case study of innovation in the child's lexicon. In E. Wanner and L.R. Gleitman (eds), *Language Acquisition: The State of the Art*. Cambridge: Cambridge University Press.

Conklin, H.C. (1964) Linguistic play in its cultural context. In D. Hymes (ed.), *Language in Culture and Society*. New York: Harper & Row.

Cormier, R. (1988) *Fade*. London: Victor Gollancz.

Coward, R. and Ellis, J. (1977) *Language and Materialism; Developments in Semiology and the Theory of the Subject*. London: Routledge & Kegan Paul.

Culler, J. (1975) *Structuralist Poetics*. London: Routledge & Kegan Paul.

Culler, J. (1981) *The Pursuit Of Signs: Semiotics, Literature, Deconstruction*. London: Routledge & Kegan Paul.

DES/Welsh Office *English in the National Curriculum*. London: HMSO.

De Villiers, J. and De Villiers, P. (1978) *Language Acquisition*. Cambridge, Mass.: Harvard University Press.

De Villiers, J. and De Villiers, P. (1978) *Early Language*. London: Fontana/Collins.

Dombey, H. (1983) Learning the language of books. In M. Meek (ed.), *Opening Moves*, Bedford Way Papers 17. London: University of London, Institute of Education.

Dombey, H. (1991) The lessons children need to learn in learning to read. In *On the Teaching of Reading*. Falmer: University of Brighton, Literacy Centre.

Donaldson, M. (1978) *Children's Minds*. London: Fontana/Collins.

Dundes, A., Leach, J.W. and Ozkok, B. (1972) The strategy of Turkish boys' verbal duelling rhymes. In D. Hymes and J.J. Gumperz (eds), *Directions in Sociolinguistics: The Ethnography of Communication*. New York: Holt, Rinehart & Winston.

Favat, F.A. (1970) *Child and Tale: The Origins of Interest*. NCTE Committee on Research. Report 19. National Council for the Teaching of English (USA and Canada).

Ferguson, C.A. (1977) Baby talk as a simplified register. In C. Snow and C. Ferguson (eds), *Talking To Children: Language Input and Acquisition*. Cambridge: Cambridge University Press.

Fox, C. (1979) *Early Reading: A View of Children, Parents and the Reading Process*. MA dissertation, Institute of Education, London University.

Fox, C. (1983) Talking like a book. In M. Meek (ed.), *Opening Moves*, Bedford Way Papers 17. London: University of London, Institute of Education.

Fox, C. (1987) *The Origin and Development of Narrative Competence in Young Pre-literate Children*. Ph D thesis, Polytechnic of Newcastle-upon-Tyne.

Fox, C. (1989a) Divine dialogues. In R. Andrews (ed.), *Narrative And Argument*, pp. 33–42. Milton Keynes: Open University Press.

Fox, C. (1989b) Children thinking through story. *English in Education* 23 (2), 25–36.

Fox, C. (1990) The genesis of argument in narrative discourse. *English in Education* 24 (1), 23–31.

Fox, C. (1992) The language of pre-school children's oral stories. In H. Dombey and M. Robinson (eds), *Literacy for the Twenty-first Century*. University of Brighton, Literacy Centre.

Fox, C. (1992) The literacy environment of the classroom. In M. Coles and C. Harrison (eds), *The Reading for Real Handbook*. London: Routledge & Kegan Paul.

Fox, C. (1993) Children's stories: the implications for literacy in school. *Reading*, special issue: *Children's Literature and Literacy*.

Frake, C.O. (1964) How to ask for a drink in Subanan. *American Anthropologist* **66** (6), Part 2.

Freud, S. (1900) *The Interpretation of Dreams*. London: Hogarth Press (standard ed.), 1955. Harmondsworth: Penguin, 1976.

Freud, S. (1905) *Jokes and Their Relation to the Unconscious*. London: Hogarth Press (standard ed.), 1960. Harmondsworth: Penguin, 1976.

Freud, S. (1914) *On Narcissism: An Introduction*. London: Hogarth Press (standard ed.), 1955. Harmondsworth: Penguin, 1984.

Freud, S. (1920) *Beyond the Pleasure Principle*. London: Hogarth Press (standard ed.), 1955. Harmondsworth: Penguin, 1984.

Gardner, H. (1973) *The Arts and Human Development*. New York: John Wiley.

Gardner, H. (1983) *Frames of Mind: The Theory of Multiple Intelligence*. London: Heinemann.

Gardner, H. and Gardner, J. (1971) Children's literary skills. *Journal of Experimental Education* **39** (4), 42–6.

Gardner, H., Kircher, M., Winner, E. and Perkins, D. (1975) Children's metaphoric productions and preferences. *Journal of Child Language* **2**, 125–41.

Gardner, H., Winner, E., Bechofer, R. and Wolf, D. (1978) The development of figurative language. In K. Nelson (ed.), *Children's Language* **1**. New York: Gardner Press.

Gardner, H., Shotwell, J. and Wolf, D. (1979) Exploring early symbolization: styles of achievement. In B. Sutton-Smith (ed.), *Play and Learning*. New York: Gardner Press.

Garnica, O.K. (1977) Some Prosodic and paralinguistic features of speech to young children. In C. Snow and C. Ferguson (eds) *Talking to Children*. Cambridge: Cambridge University Press.

Garnica, O.K. (1978) Non-verbal concomitants of language input to children. In N. Waterson and C. Snow (eds), *The Development of Communication*. New York: John Wiley.

Garvey, C. (1977) Play with language and speech. In S. Ervin-Tripp and C. Mitchell-Kernan (eds), *Child Discourse*. New York: Academic Press.

Genette, G. (1972, trans. 1980) *Narrative Discourse*. Oxford: Basil Blackwell.

Glenn, C.G. (1978) The role of episodic structure and of story length in children's recall of simple stories. *Journal of Verbal Learning and Verbal Behaviour* **17**, 229–47.

Glenn, C.G. (1980) Relationship between story content and structure. *Journal of Educational Psychology* **72** (4), 550–60.

Gossen, G.H. (1976) Verbal duelling in chamula. In B. Kirschenblatt-Gimblett (ed.), *Speech Play*. Philadelphia: University of Pennsylvania Press.

Green, G.M. (1982) Competence for implicit text analysis: literary style discrimination in 5-year-olds. In D. Tannen (ed.), *Analyzing Discourse: Talk and Text*. Washington, DC: Georgetown University Press.

Halliday, M.A.K. (1975) *Learning How to Mean*. London: Edward Arnold.

Halliday, M.A.K. (1978) *Language as Social Semiotic*. London: Edward Arnold.

Hardy, B. (1975) *Tellers and Listeners*. Athlone Press.

Heath, S. Brice (1982a) What no bedtime story means: narrative skills at home and at school. *Language in Society* **2** (1), 49–76.

Heath, S. Brice (1982b) Protean shapes in literacy events: ever-shifting oral and literate traditions. In D. Tannen (ed.), *Spoken and Written Language*, volume IX of *Advances in Discourse Processes*. Norwood, NJ: Ablex.

Heath, S. Brice (1983) *Ways with Words*. Cambridge: Cambridge University Press.

Henriques, J., Hollway, W., Urwin, C., Venn, C. and Walkerdine, V. (1984) *Changing the Subject*. London: Methuen.

Holt, G.S. (1972) Stylin' outa the black pulpit. In T. Kochman (ed.), *Rappin' and Stylin' Out*. Urbana, IL: University of Illinois Press.

Hudson, J. and Nelson, K. (1984) Play with language; over-extensions as analogies. *Journal of Child Language* **11**, 337–46.

218   *At the Very Edge of the Forest*

5Hunt, K. (1965) *Grammatical Structures Written at Three Grade Levels*. NCTE Research Report no. 3. Champaign, IL: NCTE.
Hunt, K. (1970) How little sentences grow into big ones. In M. Lester (ed.), *Readings in Applied Transformational Grammar*. New York: Holt, Rinehart & Winston.
Hymes, D. H. (1973) On communicative competence. In J. B. Pride and J. Holmes (eds), *Sociolinguistics*. Harmondsworth: Penguin.
Jacob, E. (1984) Learning literacy through play: Puerto Rican kindergarten children. In H. Goelman, A. Oberg and G. Smith. (eds), *Awakening to Literacy*. London: Heinemann.
Jakobson, R. (1960) Linguistics and poetics. In T. Sebeok (ed.), *Style in Language*. Cambridge, Mass.: MIT Press.
Kernan, K. T. (1977) Semantic and expressive elaboration in children's narratives. In J. Ervin-Tripp and C. Mitchell-Kernan (eds), *Child Discourse*. New York: Academic Press.
Kintsch, W. and Greene, E. (1978) The role of culture-specific schemata in the comprehension and recall of stories. *Discourse Processes* 1, 1–13.
Kirschenblatt-Gimblett, B. (ed.) (1976) *Speech Play*. Philadelphia: University of Pennsylvania Press.
Kirschenblatt-Gimblett, B. (1979) Speech play and verbal art. In B. Sutton-Smith (ed.), *Play and Learning*. New York: Gardner Press.
Kirschenblatt-Gimblett, B. and Sanches, M. (1976) Children's traditional speech play. In B. Kirschenblatt-Gimblett (ed.), *Speech Play*. Philadelphia: University of Pennsylvania Press.
Klein, M. (1921) *Love, Guilt and Reparation. The Writing of Melanie Klein*, Vol. 1. London: Hogarth Press.
Kochman, T. (1972) Toward an ethnography of Black American speech behaviour. In T. Kochman (ed.) *Rappin' and stylin' out: Communication in Urban Black America*. Urbana, IL: University of Illinois Press.
Labov, W. and Weletsky, J. (1967) Narrative analysis. In J. Helm (ed.), *Essays on the Verbal and Visual Arts*. Univ. of Washington Press, Seattle.
Labov, W. (1972a) The transformation of experience in narrative syntax. In W. Labov, *Language in the Inner City*. Oxford: Basil Blackwell.
Labov, W. (1972b) Rules for ritual insults. In W. Labov, *Language in the Inner City*. Oxford: Basil Blackwell.
Labov, W. (1982) Speech actions and reactions in personal narrative. In D. Tannen (ed.), *Analysing Discourse: Text and Talk*. Washington, DC: Georgetown University Press.
Lacan, J. (1977) *Ecrits: A Selection*. London: Tavistock.
Langer, S. (1953) *Feeling and Form*. London: Routledge & Kegan Paul.
Leach, E. (1964) Anthropological aspects of language: animal categories and verbal abuse. In E. H. Lenneburg (ed.), *New Directions in the Study of Language*. Cambridge, Mass.: MIT Press.
Levi, Primo (1986) *The Periodic Table*. London: Abacus.
Levi-Strauss, C. (1955) The structural study of myth. *Journal of American Folklore* **128** (270), 428–44.
Loban, W. (1963) *The Language of Elementary School Children*. NCTE Research Report no. 1.
Loban, W. (1976) *Language Development: Kindergarten through Grade 12*. NCTE Research Report no. 18.
Lord, A. B. (1960) The singer of tales. In *Harvard Studies in Contemporary Literature*, no. 24. Cambridge, MA: Harvard University Press.
Mahoney, D. H. (1977) The society and geography of the story world. In P. Stevens, Jr (ed.), *Studies in the Anthropology of Play*. New York: Leisure Press.
Mair, M. M. (1976) *Metaphors for Living*. Nebraska Symposium on Motivation.
Mandler, J. M. and Johnson, N. S. (1977) Remembrance of things parsed: story structure and recall. *Cognitive Psychology* **9**, 111–51.
Maranda, E. K. and Maranda, P. (1971) *Structural Models in Folklore and Transformational Essays*. The Hague: Mouton.
Meek, M. (1982) *Learning to Read*. London: Bodley Head.
Meek, M. (1983) (ed.) *Opening Moves*. Bedford Way Papers 17. London: University of London, Institute of Education.

Meek, M. (1984) Speaking of shifters. In M. Meek and J. Miller (eds), *Changing English*. London: University of London, Institute of Education.

Meek, M. (1988) *How Texts Teach What Readers Learn*. Stroud, Glos.: Thimble Press.

Meek, M. (1991) *On Being Literate*. London: Bodley Head.

Meijsing, M. (1980) Expectations in understanding complex stories. *Poetics* 9, 213-21.

Menig-Peterson, C. L. and McCabe, A. (1978) Children's orientation of a listener to the context of their narratives. *Developmental Psychology* 14 (6), 582-92.

Mitchell-Kernan, C. (1972) Signifying, loud talking, and marking. In T. Kochman (ed.), *Rappin' and Styling Out: Communication in Urban Black America*. Chicago: University of Illinois Press.

Moffett, J. (1968) *Teaching the Universe of Discourse*. Boston: Houghton Mifflin.

Morrison, T. (1992) *Jazz*. London: Chatto & Windus.

O'Donnell, R. C. (1974) Syntactic differences between speech and writing. *American Speech* 49, 102-10.

O'Donnell, R. C., Griffin, W. J. and Norris, R. C. (1967) *Syntax of Kindergarten and Elementary School Children: A Transformational Analysis*. NCTE Research Report no. 8.

Olson, D. R. (1977) From utterance to text: the bias of language in speech and writing. *Harvard Educational Review* 47 (3), 257-81.

Ong, W. (1983) *Orality and Literacy*. London: Methuen.

Ortony, A. (1985a) *Metaphor and Thought*. Cambridge: Cambridge University Press.

Ortony, A. (1985b) Theoretical and methodological issues in the empirical study of metaphor. In C. R. Cooper (ed.), *Researching Response to Literature and the Teaching of Literature*. Norwood, NJ: Ablex.

Paley, V. G. (1981) *Wally's Stories*. Cambridge, Mass.: Harvard University Press.

Perera, K. (1984) *Children's Writing and Reading*. Oxford: Basil Blackwell.

Piaget, J. (1926, 3rd ed. 1959) *The Language and Thought of the Child*. London: Routledge & Kegan Paul.

Piaget, J. (1951) *Play Dreams and Imitation in Childhood*. London: Routledge & Kegan Paul.

Pitcher, E. G. and Prelinger, E. (1963) *Children Tell Stories*. New York: International Universities Press.

Pradl, G. M. (1979) Learning how to begin and end a story. *Language Arts* 56 (1).

Pratt, M. L. (1977) *Toward a Speech Act Theory of Literary Discourse*. Bloomington, IN: Indiana University Press.

Propp, V. (1928, trans. 1958) *The Morphology of the Folktale*. Austin: University of Texas Press.

Rader, M. (1982) Context in written language: the case of imaginative fiction. In D. Tannen (ed.), *Spoken and Written Language*, volume IX of *Advances in Discourse Processes*. Norwood, NJ: Ablex.

Ricoeur, P. (1970) *Freud and Philosophy: An Essay on Interpretation*. New Haven: Yale University Press.

Ricoeur, P. (1978a) *The Rule of Metaphor*. London: Routledge & Kegan Paul.

Ricoeur, P. (1978b) The metaphorical process as cognition, imagination and feeling. In *Critical Inquiry*. Chicago: University of Chicago Press.

Robinson, M. (1992) Making sense of Television: children and genre. In H. Dombey and M. Robinson (eds), *Literacy for the Twenty-first Century*. Falmer: University of Brighton, Literacy Centre.

Rogers, D. (1976) Information about word meanings in the speech of parents to young children. In R. Campbell and P. Smith (eds), *Recent Advances in the Psychology of Language*. London: Plenum Press.

Rosen, H. (1969) *An investigation of the effects of differentiated writing assignments on the performance in English composition of a selected group of 15/16-year-old pupils*. Unpublished PhD thesis. University of London, Institute of Education.

Rosen, H. (1984) *Stories and Meanings*. Sheffield: National Association for the Teaching of English (NATE).

Rosen, H. (1986) The importance of story. *Language Arts* 63 (3).

Rumelhart, D.E. (1975) Notes on a schema for stories. In D.G. Bobrow and A. Collins (eds), *Representation and Understanding*. New York: Academic Press.

Rumelhart, D.E. (1977) Understanding and summarizing brief stories. In D. La Berget (ed.), *Basic Processes in Reading*. Hillsdale, NJ: Laurence Erlbaum.

Rumelhart, D.E. (1979) Some problems with the notion of literal meaning. In A. Ortony (ed.), *Metaphor and Thought*. Cambridge: Cambridge University Press.

Sacks, H. (1972) On the analyzability of stories by children. In D. Hymes and J.J. Gumperz (eds), *Directions in Sociolinguistics*. New York: Holt, Rinehart & Winston.

Sale, R. (1978) *Fairy Tales and After*. Cambridge, Mass.: Harvard University Press.

Saussure, F. de (1916) *Course in General Linguistics*. London: Peter Owen.

Schama, S. (1990) *Citizens*. Harmondsworth: Penguin Books.

Schama, S. (1991) A room with a view. *Guardian*, review section, 26.9.1991.

Scollon, R. and Scollon, S. (1981) The literate 2-year-old: the fictionalization of self. In *Narrative, Literacy and Face in Inter-Ethnic Communication*, Volume VII of *Advances in Discourse Processes*. Norwood, NJ: Ablex.

Scollon, R. (1982) The rhythmic integration of ordinary talk. In D. Tannen (ed.), *Analysing Discourse and Talk*, pp. 335–49. Washington, DC: Georgetown University Press.

Sebeok, T.A. (1960) (ed.) *Style in Language*. Cambridge, Mass.: MIT Press.

Serraillier, I. (1965) *The Way of Danger* and *The Gorgon's Head*. London: Heinemann.

Sherzer, J. (1976) Play languages: implications for sociolinguistics. In B. Kirschenblatt-Gimblett (ed.), *Speech Play*. Philadelphia: University of Pennsylvania Press.

Singer, J.L. (1977) Imagination and make-believe play in early childhood. *Journal of Mental Imagery* **1**, 127–44.

Snow, C.E. (1977) Mothers' speech research: from input to interaction. In C. Snow and C. Ferguson (eds), *Talking to Children: Language Input and Acquisition*, pp. 31–49. Cambridge: Cambridge University Press.

Snow, C. and Ferguson, C. (1977) *Talking to Children: Language Input and Acquisition*. Cambridge: Cambridge University Press.

Steedman, C., Urwin, C. and Walkerdine, V. (1985) *Language, Gender and Childhood*. London: Routledge & Kegan Paul.

Stein, N.L. and Glenn, C.G. (1979) An analysis of story comprehension in elementary school children. In R.O. Freedle (ed.), *New Directions in Discourse Processing*, pp. 53–120, volume II of *Advances in Discourse Processes*. Norwood, NJ: Ablex.

Street, B. (1992) Cross-cultural perspectives on literacy. In H. Dombey and M. Robinson (eds), *Literacy for the Twenty-first Century*. Falmer: The Literacy Centre, University of Brighton.

Sutton-Smith, B., Abrams, B., Botvin, G., Caring, M. and Stevens, T. (1975) The importance of the storytaker: an investigation of the imaginative life. *Urban Review* **8**, 82–95.

Sutton-Smith, B., Botvin, G. and Mahoney, D. (1976) Developmental structures in fantasy narratives. *Human Development* **19**, 1–13.

Sutton-Smith, B. and Botvin, G. (1977) The development of structural complexity in children's fantasy narratives. *Developmental Psychology* **3** (4), 377–88.

Sutton-Smith, B. (1977) Towards an anthropology of play. In P. Stevens, Jr (ed.), *Studies in the Anthropology of Play*. New York: Leisure Press.

Sutton-Smith, B. (1979) Presentation and representation in children's fictional narratives. *New Directions for Child Development* **6**, 53–65.

Sutton-Smith, B. (1981) *The Folk Stories of Children*. Philadelphia: University of Pennsylvania Press.

Swift, G. (1983) *Waterland*. London: Heinemann.

Tannen, D. (1980) Spoken/written language and the oral/literate continuum. In *Proceedings of the Sixth Annual Meeting of the Berkeley Linguistics Society*, pp. 207–18. Berkeley, CA: Berkeley Linguistics Society.

Tannen, D. (ed.) (1982) *Spoken and Written Language: Exploring Orality and Literacy*. *Advances in Discourse Processes*, Vol. IX. Norwood, NJ: Ablex.

Thaler, M. (1976) *How Far Does a Rubber Band Stretch?* London: Collins.

Thorndyke, P.W. and Yekovitch, F.R. (1980) A critique of schemata as a theory of human story memory. *Poetics* **9**, 23–49.

Todorov, T. (1971, trans. 1977) *The Poetics of Prose*. Oxford: Basil Blackwell.
Umiker-Sebeok, D.J. (1979) Pre-school children's intraconversational narratives. *Journal of Child Language* **6**, 91–109.
Urwin, C. (1984) Power relations and the emergence of language. In J. Henriques *et al., Changing the Subject*. London: Methuen.
Vargos Llosa, M. (1975, trans. 1986) *The Perpetual Orgy*. London: Faber & Faber.
Vygotsky, L. (1962) *Thought and Language*. Cambridge, MA.: MIT Press.
Vygotsky, L. (1978) *Mind in Society*. Cambridge, MA.: Harvard University Press.
Walkerdine, V. (1982) A psychosemiotic approach to abstract thought. In M. Beveridge (Ed.), *Children Thinking Through Language*. London: Edward Arnold.
Walkerdine, V. (1984) Developmental psychology and the child-centred pedagogy. In J. Henriques *et al., Changing the Subject*. London: Methuen.
Walkerdine, V. (1991) *Schoolgirl Fictions*. London: Verso.
Waterson, M. *Gypsy Family*. London: A. & C. Black.
Watson-Gegeo, K.O. and Boggs, S.T. (1977) From verbal play to talk story: the role of routines in speech events among Hawaiian children. In S. Ervin-Tripp and C. Mitchell-Kernan (eds), *Child Discourse*. New York: Academic Press.
Weir, R. (1962) *Language in the Crib*. The Hague: Mouton.
Wells, G. (1979) Describing children's linguistic development at home and at school. In *British Journal of Educational Research* **5** (1), 75–89.
Wells, G. (1981a) Some antecedents of early educational attainment. *British Journal of Educational Sociology* **2** (2), 180–200.
Wells, G. (1981b) *Learning through Interaction*. Cambridge: Cambridge University Press.
Wilkinson, A. (1990) Argument as a primary act of mind. *English in Education* **24** (1), 10–22.
Winnicott, D.W. (1971) *Playing and Reality*. Harmondsworth: Penguin Books.
Wright, E. (1984) *Psychoanalytic Criticism: Theory in Practice*. London: Methuen.
Zipes, J. (1983) *Fairy Tales and the Art of Subversion*. London: Heinemann.

Index 1

The Children's Stories

Index 2

Authors and Book Titles

Index 3

Subject Index